The Future of Children

PRINCETON · BROOKINGS

D1217974

VOLUME 15   NUMBER 2   FALL 2005

Marriage and Child Wellbeing

Introducing the Issue

Sara McLanahan, Elisabeth Donahue, and Ron Haskins

Marriage has become a hot topic on the American domestic policy scene. The Bush administration is proposing to spend $1.5 billion over the next five years to increase "healthy" marriages.[1] Gays and lesbians are demanding the right to marry.[2] A few states are reconsidering no-fault divorce laws and experimenting with new types of "covenant marriage."[3] And legislators are scrutinizing tax and transfer policies for "marriage penalties."[4] These initiatives have been spurred by changes in marriage and childbearing during the latter part of the twentieth century and by mounting social science evidence that these changes are not in the best interests of children.

The goal of this volume is to lay out the major issues in the debate over marriage and to provide readers with some facts and a context to help them understand the debate. Most people find it difficult to talk about marriage, because many of the issues reflect deeply felt values. Thoughtful people are torn about what to make of all the changes in marriage and family life over the past half-century and what

to do about them. Moreover, the social science evidence is not as conclusive as we might like it to be. Of necessity we lack the gold standard of evaluation research: people cannot be randomly assigned to different family structures and then compared with respect to their outcomes. Instead we must rely on theory and empirical evidence drawn from non-experimental data. Nevertheless, given the importance of marriage and family life and given the government's growing involvement in funding marriage programs, we believe the topic merits the attention of a journal devoted to improving policies for children.

Background

From roughly 1900 until 1960, the ages of both men and women at marriage declined steadily, and the share of adults who ever married grew. After 1960, both trends reversed. Couples began postponing marriage, and cohabiting unions became more common. Divorce rates, which had been rising throughout the century, accelerated after 1960, and the share of children born to unmarried parents increased sharply.[5] Together these trends led to a dramatic increase in

www.futureofchildren.org

Sara McLanahan is editor-in-chief of *The Future of Children* and director of the Center for Research on Child Wellbeing at Princeton University. Elisabeth Donahue is associate editor of *The Future of Children* and a lecturer at the Woodrow Wilson School of Public and International Affairs at Princeton. Ron Haskins is a senior editor of *The Future of Children* and a senior fellow in the Economic Studies program at the Brookings Institution.

single-mother families. Whereas in 1970 only 12 percent of families with children were headed by a single mother, by 2003 that share had more than doubled, to 26 percent.[6] More than half of all children born today are expected to live apart from a parent before they

> *Whereas in 1970 only 12 percent of families with children were headed by a single mother, by 2003 that share had more than doubled, to 26 percent.*

reach age eighteen; the shares are even higher among African American and Hispanic children.[7]

The decline in two-parent families after 1960 was closely linked with a rise in child poverty. Poverty rates have always been higher in single-mother families than in two-parent families. Indeed, government programs such as Mothers' Pensions, Survivors Insurance, and Aid to Families with Dependent Children were created in the first half of the twentieth century to help alleviate the poverty of single mothers, most of whom were widows.[8] The rapid growth in single-mother families after 1960, together with the declining share of widowed mothers and the rising share of divorced and never-married mothers, however, led to renewed interest in the economic plight of single mothers and their children. The term "feminization of poverty" was coined by Diana Pearce to emphasize the increasing concentration of poverty in the United States in families headed by single mothers.[9] To dramatize her point, Pearce ar-

gued that if then-current trends were to continue, all of the nation's poor would be living in female-headed families by the turn of the millennium. Although that prediction turned out to be an overstatement, the link between single motherhood and poverty continues. In 2003, the U.S. poverty rate for children living in married households was 8.4 percent. For children living in single-mother households, it was 38.4 percent.[10]

Social science research on children in divorced families also contributed to the growing concern over the long-term consequences of changes in marriage and family formation. In the early 1970s the prevailing view among scholars was that, aside from the problem of low income, single motherhood was an acceptable alternative to marriage. But the empirical evidence compiled during the 1980s and 1990s suggested otherwise.[11] In her 1999 presidential address to the Population Association of America, Linda Waite argued that marriage had multiple benefits for adults and children over and above its effects on child poverty, including better health and greater socioeconomic attainment.[12] Nobel prize–winning economist George Akerlof made a similar case for fatherhood being beneficial to men and society.[13]

Questions and Controversies

Although most people today would probably agree that a "good" or "healthy" marriage is the ideal setting for raising children, substantial disagreement exists about what it takes to achieve such a union. Some people argue that a good or healthy marriage is one in which both parents have a strong commitment to stay together "for the sake of the children." Others contend that it is a low-conflict relationship or a relationship in which parents resolve their disagreements amicably. Still others maintain that it is a union that provides economic and social security to the family.

Observers also disagree about the role of government in promoting one family form over another. Some people believe that intimate relationships, including marriage, are private and should not be the province of the government. This "zone of privacy" is cited in a long line of Supreme Court cases governing the rights of individuals to make their own choices regarding private matters such as reproductive and sexual conduct.[14] All these cases confirm that constitutional protection must be afforded personal decisions about marriage, procreation, contraception, and family relationships.

Others believe that government should do more to strengthen two-parent families but disagree about exactly what should be done. Some argue that the decline in marriage is rooted in cultural problems and that the best way to increase marriage rates is to change attitudes, lifestyles, and interpersonal skills. As noted above, the Bush administration, for example, is proposing to spend $1.5 billion over the next five years on programs to educate people about the benefits of marriage and to improve relationship and communication skills among low-income couples.[15] Critics of this proposal argue that marriage programs may encourage some single mothers to remain in violent relationships.[16] They also worry that money for low-income single mothers will be diverted to marriage education programs.

Others argue that the decline in marriage rates is rooted in structural problems that have reduced the economic advantages of marriage.[17] If so, policies that increase the income of disadvantaged two-parent families by reducing marriage penalties in the nation's tax and transfer systems may be more effective than those that aim to change attitudes and lifestyles. Even among those who believe that economic barriers are more important than cultural barriers, there is disagreement about the importance of marriage penalties in discouraging marriage. Underlying this debate is a fear that federal and state policymakers might try to eliminate marriage penalties in social programs by reducing benefits to single-parent families rather than increasing benefits to married couples.[18]

Finally, disagreement about whether extending marriage to gay and lesbian parents would help or harm children is widespread. Conservatives argue that allowing gays and lesbians to marry would harm children and, more important, weaken the institution of marriage.[19] Liberals, in contrast, argue that all couples should have the right to marry regardless of their sexual orientation.[20] Values are much more important than social science evidence in this debate.

What Does This Volume Do?

To provide our readers with a context for understanding the debate over marriage, we selected several central topics and invited some of the country's leading scholars to share their expertise. Two authors were asked to examine recent economic, demographic, and social developments that have affected marriage and to comment on the causes and consequences of these trends.

A second group of authors was asked to review the social science research on the economic, social, emotional, and cognitive benefits of marriage for adults and children. They also were asked whether these benefits extend to children raised by same-sex parents. The literature on the benefits of heterosexual marriage is vast, so the authors were asked to give their assessments of the very best research in these areas. In contrast, data on the benefits to children of same-sex marriage are quite limited. Here, we asked the authors to draw on theory as well as empirical evidence to make their case.

One notable feature of the many demographic changes over the past half-century is the increasing concentration of single motherhood, in particular never-married motherhood, among low-income women. Thus we asked a third pair of authors to focus explicitly on low-income single mothers and to examine the barriers to marriage facing this group. Finally, we asked two groups of authors to examine two marriage proposals now being discussed by state and federal policymakers: the Bush marriage-promotion initiative and efforts to reduce the marriage penalties in the tax and transfer system.

What Do We Learn from the Articles?

The articles in this volume provide the latest information and findings on marriage. Full summaries are provided at the beginning of each article. In this section, we focus on the findings we think are most important.

Marriage as a Public Issue

Steven Nock observes that there is an emerging political, cultural, and scientific consensus that children do best in families with two loving parents. He sees the contemporary marriage debate as the nation's recognition of the cultural nature of the problem. In this view, the debate is a crucial national conversation among Americans struggling to interpret and make sense of the role that marriage and the family play in today's society. He also points out that although large cultural and social forces are driving the decline in marriage, most of the new U.S. programs attempting to restore or strengthen marriage focus on changing individuals, not their culture or society. He argues that the problem cannot be addressed solely at the individual level and cautions that given how little researchers and professionals know about helping couples get or stay married, expectations of policies in these areas should be modest.

Trends

Andrew Cherlin notes that sentiment in favor of marriage appears to be stronger in the United States than it is in other developed countries. The share of U.S. adults who are likely to marry is larger, but so is the share likely to divorce. U.S. children are also more likely to live in single-parent families. Given these patterns, American policymakers are unlikely to be able to raise U.S. family stability to levels typical of other developed countries.[21] Consequently, a family policy that relies too heavily on marriage will not help the many children destined to live in single-parent and cohabiting-parent families—many of them poor—during their formative years. Cherlin argues that assistance must be directed to needy families regardless of their household structure. Policymakers must craft a careful balance of marriage-based and marriage-neutral programs to provide adequate support to American children.

Financial Consequences

Adam Thomas and Isabel Sawhill show that across all races and for a variety of income measures, children in single-parent families have less family income and are more likely to be poor than children in married-parent families. Cohabiting families are generally better off economically than single-parent families, but considerably worse off than married-parent families. The authors acknowledge that although "selection" (the fact that more-educated couples are more likely to marry than less-educated couples) may explain part of the link between family structure and family economic resources, their evidence indicates that family structure *does* affect family resources; single parenthood reduces children's economic prospects and marriage improves them. Like Cherlin, they argue that policymakers may not be able to do much to reverse the trends in family structure. They also point out that marriage is not an economic cure-all for the complex problem of child poverty. Instead, Thomas and Sawhill suggest that declines in single parenthood may offer the greatest promise for improving the economic welfare of children in the United States.

Cognitive, Social, and Emotional Consequences

Paul Amato shows that children growing up with two continuously married parents are less likely than other children to experience a wide range of cognitive, emotional, and social problems, not only during childhood but also in adulthood. He attributes the advantages associated with two-parent families to a higher standard of living, more effective parenting, more cooperative co-parenting, better quality relationships between parents and children, and fewer stressful events and circumstances. Despite these advantages, Amato argues that interventions that increase the share of children who grow up with both parents would produce only modest improvements in the overall well-being of U.S. children, because children's social or emotional problems have many causes. Nevertheless, interventions that lower only modestly the overall *share* of U.S. children who experience various problems could lower substantially the *number* of children facing these problems. Even a small decline in percentages, when multiplied by the many children in the population, is a substantial social benefit.

Gay Marriage

William Meezan and Jonathan Rauch argue that marriage confers three types of benefits on children of heterosexual parents—material benefits, stability, and social acceptance—and that these benefits would be likely to carry over to children of married same-sex

---

A family policy that relies too heavily on marriage will not help the many children destined to live in single-parent and cohabiting-parent families—many of them poor—during their formative years.

---

parents. They also note that the empirical research carried out to date suggests that children being raised by gay parents are doing about as well as children normally do. The existing research, however, is based on rather special samples, and thus we do not know whether the children in these studies are typical of the general population of children raised by gay and lesbian couples. We also have little sense of how changing marriage laws for gay and lesbian couples might affect children in heterosexual families. The authors note that the best way to ascertain the costs and benefits of same-sex marriage on children is to compare it with the alternatives. And they suggest that such a comparison is now possible because the United States is already running a limited, localized experiment: Massachusetts is marrying same-sex couples; Vermont and Connecticut are offering civil unions; and several states are offering partner-benefit programs.

Marriage in Low-Income Communities

Kathryn Edin and Joanna Reed review recent research on social and economic barriers to marriage among the poor and discuss the efficacy of efforts by federal and state policymakers to promote marriage among poor unmarried couples. They note that disadvantaged men and women place a high value on marriage but are reluctant to make a formal commitment because they are unable to meet the high standards of relationship quality and financial stability they believe are necessary to sustain a marriage and avoid divorce. In view of these findings, Edin and Reed argue that public campaigns to convince poor Americans of the value of marriage are preaching to the choir. Because disadvantaged men and women view some degree of financial stability as a prerequisite for marriage, policymakers must address the instability and low pay of the jobs lower-income people typically hold as well as devise ways to promote homeownership and other asset development to encourage marriage. Encouraging more low-income couples to marry without giving them the tools to maintain a stable union may simply increase divorce rates.

Marriage Programs

Robin Dion examines some of the programs that have inspired the Bush administration's marriage initiative and asks whether they are likely to be effective. She notes that they were designed for and evaluated using middle-class couples rather than the disadvantaged couples whom the Bush initiative will target. For the initiative to succeed, program curriculums will need to be responsive to and respectful of the interests and circumstances of low-income families. Although efforts to adapt these programs to disadvantaged populations are now under way, it is not yet known whether they will be successful. Dion notes that the Administration for Children and

Families is planning to test several of the most important of the new marriage programs scientifically and on a large scale to learn whether they will work and whether the effects on couple relationships will translate into benefits for children.

Marriage and the Tax and Transfer Systems

Adam Carasso and Eugene Steuerle argue that marriage penalties are a result of policymakers' efforts to achieve the goal of progressivity—giving greater tax and welfare benefits to those with lower income—while trying to keep down program costs. Under the current tax and transfer system, tax obligations rise and transfer program benefits fall, sometimes steeply, as households earn more income. As a result, many low- to moderate-income families face high effective marginal tax rates. These high rates produce large marriage penalties: additional income brought into a household by marriage causes other benefits to be reduced or lost altogether. In extreme cases, households can lose a dollar or more for every dollar earned. The authors offer several options for reducing or eliminating the marriage penalty, and recommend two in particular. The first is to set a maximum marginal tax rate for lower-income individuals, similar to the maximum rate set for highest-income individuals. The second is to provide individual wage subsidies to lower-income earners, so that such workers who marry can combine their income with that of their spouses without incurring penalties.

Implications: What Should Be Done?

The articles in this volume confirm that children benefit from growing up with two married biological parents. The articles also support a more active government role in encouraging the formation and maintenance of stable, low-conflict, two-parent families. We use the words "stable" and "low-conflict" because the evidence is clear that unstable marriages and high-conflict relationships are harmful to children. The articles also suggest that two specific public policies, one to improve the economic conditions of low-income two-parent families and the other to enhance relationship quality among low-income couples, may well lead to higher marriage rates and more stable unions.

The first policy would reduce the marriage penalty. That a low-income single mother faces a larger financial penalty than a middle-income mother if she decides to marry is a serious problem that appears to run counter to the values of most Americans. As the volume points out, marriage penalties are not the result of deliberate government action; they are an accident of history. When the welfare system was created in the mid-1930s, most single mothers were widows, and policymakers did not worry about the negative incentives implicit in any income-tested program. Today widows account for only a small share of single mothers, and marriage penalties in the transfer system are likely to affect many more poor single mothers.

The problem, we realize, is complicated. The competing interests of providing a safety net for low-income families and taxing higher-income families at higher rates sometimes conflict with a policy to encourage parents to combine incomes and marry. That said, we believe that the decision to marry should not result in a loss of tax or transfer benefits for lower-income families. Such losses, as the articles in this volume point out, have serious negative repercussions for children. Economic security is essential to the development of healthy children; indeed, it is one of the main arguments for increasing marriage

rates. Because most of the penalties for low-income couples come from transfer programs rather than the tax system, reform efforts should be focused there.[22] Although extending benefits to low-income married couples will increase public costs, such a step is not without precedent: Congress reduced the tax

That a low-income single mother faces a larger financial penalty than a middle-income mother if she decides to marry is a serious problem that appears to run counter to the values of most Americans.

penalties for low-income families in the 2001 tax legislation by making the child tax credit partially refundable for low-income working families.

A second promising policy is marriage programs. Although several articles note that the scientific basis for programs that promote and strengthen marriage is weak, that only a few model programs have been evaluated using scientific methods, and that no program has been tested on low-income couples, there is some evidence to suggest that middle-class couples have benefited from such programs. This finding has several implications for the new marriage programs. First, it suggests the need to proceed slowly and cautiously. Second, it suggests that the Bush administration's plan to make funds available to design and implement innovative programs and to conduct demonstrations and evaluations is good policy, particularly if the evaluations are based on random-assignment and long-term experimental designs. Finally, it implies that the Department of Health and Human Services should make all findings of the evaluations available to all states and should provide technical assistance to states or other groups that are starting marriage programs. Programs that receive federal or state funding should also be required to show that the curriculums they chose are effective for the population being served.

Marriage programs must also be tailored to meet the needs of low-income parents. We say this not because we think that government involvement is appropriate only for poor people, but because marriage is in the most trouble in low-income families. Wealthier families are able to purchase private marriage counseling, and over the past two decades divorce rates for well-to-do families have been falling. To be effective, marriage programs aimed at low-income couples need to address the serious financial issues these couples face, as well as the problems created by multiple-partner fertility, domestic violence, and the culture of distrust explored by Edin and Reed in this volume. Such programs would teach relationship skills, help couples reach their economic goals by bolstering their earnings, and address substance abuse as it imperils a marriage. Researchers who understand low-income communities should help plan these programs.

Finally, the volume tells us that marriage is not a cure-all for poverty, and that single-parent households will always be a part of the American family scene. Although we wholly support the funding and evaluation of marriage programs aimed at low-income families, we believe it would be a mistake for policymakers to focus on marriage to the exclusion of other strategies for helping single-parent families. Among such strategies, alleviating poverty, improving parent-child bonds, and reducing teenage childbearing and unintended pregnancies are especially promising. Although examining such strategies is outside the scope of this volume, we want to make clear that we see efforts to reduce out-of-wedlock births, teen pregnancy in particular, as an essential part of a marriage-promotion strategy. Similarly, the public safety net for single-parent families must remain intact. Promoting marriage should not be a proxy for cutting programs for single parents. Finally, even if parents do not marry, it is still important for children to have relationships with both their mothers and their fathers. Programs to encourage fathers' involvement—both monetary and emotional—must continue. A strong child support system that holds both parents financially responsible for their children and a fair court system that encourages joint involvement must be supported and improved. All these programs are crucial to the overall mission to increase the number of healthy marriages.

Although marriage has undergone profound changes in the past forty years, it continues to be the most effective family structure in which to raise children. Low-income children, in particular, stand to reap large gains in terms of family stability if marriage can be restored as the norm for parents. Despite our many caveats, we support government efforts to increase the numbers of children raised in healthy, married households. Because the subject of marriage is deeply personal and fraught with emotion for most people, discussing government involvement in marriage can be difficult. We hope that this volume can bring both evidence and balance to the debate.

Endnotes

1. The Bush administration proposal on building healthy marriages would create two programs. One would provide $100 million a year in grants to states to design and implement marriage-promotion activities. The second, also of $100 million a year, would be retained by the secretary of the Department of Health and Human Services to fund research on healthy marriage and demonstration programs. In the former program, states must match the federal grant on a dollar-for-dollar basis, thus bringing total funding for the state program to $200 million a year if states match all the federal dollars. The funding for both programs together would be $300 million a year for five years, or $1.5 billion. Both the House and Senate bills would terminate an existing program that provides $100 million a year in bonuses to states for reducing rates of nonmarital births, thereby offsetting part of the cost of the marriage initiative. See Mary Parke, *Marriage-Related Provisions in Welfare Reauthorization Proposals: A Summary* (Washington: Center for Law and Social Policy, March 1, 2004).

2. Kate Zernike, "Groups Vow Not to Let Losses Dash Gay Rights," *New York Times*, November 14, 2004.

3. Theodora Ooms, Stacey Bouchet, and Mary Parke, "Beyond Marriage Licenses: Efforts in States to Strengthen Marriage and Two-Parent Families" (Washington: Center for Law and Social Policy, 2004); Steven L. Nock and others, "Covenant Marriage Turns Five Years Old," *Michigan Journal of Gender and Law* 10, no. 1 (2003).

4. Gregory Acs and Elaine Maag, "Irreconcilable Differences? The Conflict between Marriage Promotion Initiatives for Cohabiting Couples with Children and Marriage Penalties in Tax and Transfer Programs," *New Federalism: National Survey of American Families* (Washington: Urban Institute, April 26, 2005); Adam Carasso and C. Eugene Steuerle, "Saying 'I Do' after the 2001 Tax Cuts," *Tax Policy Issues and Options* (Washington: Urban Institute, August 27, 2002).

5. Sara McLanahan and Lynne Casper, "Growing Diversity and Inequality in the American Family," in *State of the Union: America in the 1990s*, vol. 2, *Social Trends*, edited by Reynolds Farley (New York: Russell Sage Foundation, 1995), pp. 1–45.

6. U.S. Census Bureau, "America's Families and Living Arrangements: 2003," Current Population Reports (November 2004), p. 8. Although the vast majority of single parents are women, the number of single fathers is also rising rapidly in the United States. From 1970 to 2003, single-father families grew from 1 percent to 6 percent of all families with children. Ibid. Although the incidence of poverty in single-father families is about half that of those headed by single mothers, children living with single fathers are a little more than two times as poor as those living with married parents. U.S. Census Bureau, *Current Population Survey, 2003, Annual Social and Economic Supplement*, table C3.

7. Larry L. Bumpass and Hsien-Hen Lu, "Trends in Cohabitation and Implications for Children's Family Contexts in the United States," *Population Studies* 54 (2000): 29–41.

8. Walter I. Trattner, *From Poor Law to Welfare State: A History of Social Welfare in America*, 6th ed. (New York: Free Press, 1999).

9. Diana M. Pearce, "The Feminization of Poverty: Women, Work and Welfare," *Urban and Social Change Review* 11, nos. 1–2 (February 1978): 28–36.

10. U.S. Census Bureau, *Current Population Survey, 2003, Annual Social and Economic Supplement*, table C3.

11. Sara McLanahan and Gary Sandefur, *Growing Up with a Single Parent: What Hurts, What Helps* (Harvard University Press, 1994).

12. Linda Waite, "Does Marriage Matter?" *Demography* 32, no. 4 (1995): 483–507.

13. George Akerlof, "Men without Children," *Economic Journal* 108 (1998): 287–309.

14. See *Griswold* v. *Connecticut*, 381 U.S. 479 (1965); *Eistenstadt* v. *Baird*, 404 U.S. 438 (1972); *Roe* v. *Wade*, 410 U.S. 113 (1973); *Lawrence* v. *Texas*, 539 U.S. 558 (2003).

15. www.acf.hhs.gov/programs/opre/project/projectIndex.jsp?topicId=7; see Wade Horn, "Closing the Marriage Gap," *Crisis Magazine* 21, no. 2 (June 2003).

16. Andrew J. Cherlin and others, "The Influence of Physical and Sexual Abuse on Marriage and Cohabitation," *American Sociological Review* 69, no.6 (2004): 768–89.

17. William Julius Wilson, *The Truly Disadvantaged* (University of Chicago Press, 1987).

18. Some liberals such as Wendell Primus, an economist who works for Nancy Pelosi, the minority leader of the U.S. House of Representatives, argue that marriage penalties are much lower than usually portrayed. Wendell E. Primus and Jennifer Beeson, "Safety Net Programs, Marriage, and Cohabitation," in *Just Living Together: Implications of Cohabitation on Families, Children, and Social Policy*, edited by Alan Booth and Ann C. Crouter (Mahwah, N.J.: Erlbaum, 2002). A recent analysis of nationally representative data by Gregory Acs and Elaine Maag of the Urban Institute shows that most low-income cohabiting couples (those below 200 percent of poverty) would receive a bonus of around $2,400 from tax provisions if they got married (in 2008, when tax changes enacted in 2001 had been fully phased in). However, if the cohabiting couple had been on cash welfare from the Temporary Assistance for Needy Families program, marriage would result in a loss of nearly $2,000 in TANF benefits, thereby greatly reducing their total marriage bonus. Acs and Maag, "Irreconcilable Differences?" (see note 4).

19. Maggie Gallagher, "Why Marriage Matters: The Case for Normal Marriage," Testimony before the U.S. Senate Subcommittee on the Constitution, Civil Rights and Property Hearing: "What Is Needed to Defend the Bipartisan Defense of Marriage Act of 1996?" September 4, 2003.

20. Charlotte J. Patterson, Megan Fulcher, and Jennifer Wainright, "Children of Lesbian and Gay Parents: Research, Law and Policy," in *Children and the Law: Social Science and Policy*, edited by Bette L. Bottoms, Margaret B. Kovera, and Bradley D. McAuliff (Cambridge University Press, 2002), pp. 176–202; Judith Stacey and Timothy J. Biblarz, "(How) Does the Sexual Orientation of Parents Matter?" *American Sociological Review* 66, no. 2 (April 2001): 159–83.

21. Gunnar Andersson, "Children's Experience of Family Disruption and Family Formation: Evidence from 16 FFS Countries," MPIDR Working Paper 2001-028 (Rostock, Germany: Max Planck Institute for Demographic Research, September 2001).

22. See Acs and Maag, "Irreconcilable Differences?" (see note 4), and the article by Adam Carasso and C. Eugene Steuerle in this volume. Generally, Acs and Maag find far fewer penalties than do Carasso and Steuerle. Much of the difference stems from the transfer programs on which the analyses are based: Acs and Maag include only TANF, while Carasso and Steuerle incorporate a host of means-tested social programs. Both sets of authors find that if one looks just at the tax system, most low-income families receive subsidies rather than penalties; only when the transfer programs are considered do their conclusions diverge.

Marriage as a Public Issue

Steven L. Nock

Summary

Over the past fifty years, powerful cultural and social forces have made marriage less central to Americans' family lives. In reaction, the United States is now engaged in a wide-ranging debate about the place of marriage in contemporary society.

In this article, Steven Nock examines the national marriage debate. He begins by reviewing the social and demographic trends that have changed the role of marriage and the family: the weakening link between marriage and parenthood caused by the contraceptive revolution, the declining significance of marriage as an organizing principle of adult life, and the increasingly accepted view that marriage and parenthood are private matters, relevant only to the individuals directly involved. He then considers the abundant scientific evidence on the positive consequences of marriage for both the economic well-being and the health of American adults. He notes that based partly on the evidence that marriage is good for adults and children, numerous public and private groups, including religious activists, therapeutic professionals, family practitioners, educators, and federal and state government officials, have initiated programs to strengthen marriage, lower divorce rates, reduce out-of-wedlock births, and encourage responsible fatherhood. He then reviews some of those programs.

Nock observes that although large cultural and social forces are driving the decline in marriage, most of the new programs attempting to restore or strengthen marriage in the United States focus on changing individuals, not their culture or society. He argues that the problem cannot be addressed solely at the individual level and cautions that given how little researchers and professionals know about how to help couples get or stay married, expectations of policies in these areas should be modest. But despite the shortage of effective strategies to promote marriage, he notes, a political, cultural, and scientific consensus appears to be emerging that the best arrangement for children is to live in a family with two loving parents. He believes that the contemporary marriage debate is an acknowledgment of the cultural nature of the problem, and views it as a crucial national conversation among Americans struggling to interpret and make sense of the place of marriage and family in today's society.

www.futureofchildren.org

Steven L. Nock is a professor of sociology and director of the Marriage Matters project at the University of Virginia.

Steven L. Nock

Following several decades of sweeping demographic, social, and legal changes that have minimized the importance of marriage in U.S. society, a wide-ranging assortment of Americans—religious activists, family practitioners, therapeutic professionals, educators, and state and federal officials—is now conspicuously promoting marriage. Public discussions of family formation often support the goal of having all children raised in healthy, married families. Social science research offers evidence that marriage, unlike other family structures, confers special benefits on both adults and children. Public policymakers promote stable marriages and discourage unmarried births. Congress has declared out-of-wedlock births, reliance on welfare assistance for raising children, and single-mother families contrary to the national interest. This article reviews this renewed national interest in marriage, focusing first on the demographic trends behind the debate and then on the scientific evidence about the consequences of marriage for the economic well-being and health of Americans. It next identifies the primary actors and activities involved in the marriage-promotion effort, and concludes by considering the significance of this renewed national focus on marriage.

Marriage as a Public Issue

Marriage is no stranger to national debate in the United States. It has been at the center of a variety of American social, religious, and political movements over the nation's history. Past political activists, most at the state level, have worked to deny access to marriage to certain groups—slaves, people of certain races, certain categories of immigrants, or homosexuals—or to grant married women greater legal rights or to liberalize divorce laws.[1] Social and religious activists have typically focused on such matters as reducing divorce. What is new—and remarkable—about the current marriage movement is that its purpose is to promote matrimony.

In certain respects, today's marriage movement may seem surprising. After all, most Americans value marriage highly, and the overwhelming majority marry at some point in their lives.[2] Indeed, by international standards they marry at high rates and divorce at lower rates than they did two decades ago. But the institution of marriage has recently undergone dramatic transformation. Rapid demographic and social changes in the United States over the past four or five decades have fundamentally disrupted traditional marriage and family patterns. What once forcefully organized American life no longer does so. In many respects, the current debate about marriage represents the nation's attempt to interpret and make sense of these wrenching social changes.

Demographic Trends

The chief demographic and cultural trends driving the marriage debate have been the weakening link between marriage and parenthood, the declining significance of marriage as an organizing principle of adult life, and the increasingly accepted view that marriage and parenthood are private matters, relevant only to the individuals directly involved.

In his article in this volume, Andrew Cherlin provides a full discussion of the demographic shifts over the past half-century in the way Americans organize their households and families. The most significant for my discussion are the following. First, people now postpone marriage to later ages. They often live in their parents' homes, with friends, or with unmarried partners, thus increasing the time adults spend unmarried. Second, more couples now live together without getting married, either as a precursor or an alternative to marriage or as an alternative to living alone. The availability of such alternatives naturally makes marriage less central to domestic life. Third, high divorce rates and births to unmarried mothers leave more households headed by single parents, increasing the time both adults and children spend outside married-couple families. Fourth, because more women, especially more married women, are in the labor force, the prevalence of one-wage-earner, two-parent families—what has been called the "traditional" family—has declined. Finally, delayed and declining fertility and increasing longevity result in fewer children, smaller families, and longer lives, adding to the time parents spend "post-children" and to the number of married couples without children.[3]

These five demographic trends reflect other important social and economic changes, including increasing equality between the sexes, the legalization of abortion, increasing tolerance for diverse lifestyles, and liberalized laws governing divorce. Perhaps the most important change, however, has been the development of effective birth control.

Gaining Control of Fertility

The centrality of marriage in American culture and law during the nineteenth and twentieth centuries can be understood, in part, as a consequence of poorly controlled fertility.[4] As long as sexual intercourse naturally resulted in births, marriage (or engagement) was the only permissible venue for sex. Marriage was an institutional and societal arrangement that allocated responsibility for children. No alternative civil or religious arrangement could accomplish that task, except in extraordinary circumstances. By restricting sex to marriage, communities were

able to reduce births of children for whom no male kin were obviously and legitimately responsible.

Children born outside marriage were denied certain legal rights, such as inheritance and claims on paternal assets. These children—and their mothers—were also stigmatized in the eyes of the community. By such means, communities effectively limited the number of births outside marriage. But once effective

---

By restricting sex to marriage, communities were able to reduce births of children for whom no male kin were obviously and legitimately responsible.

---

contraception uncoupled sex from fertility, this social justification for marriage became irrelevant. The convention of "shotgun" weddings, for example, gradually disappeared.[5] Before the advent of effective contraception and legal abortion, a wedding to avoid the stigma of an illegitimate birth typically followed a premarital pregnancy. That it no longer does so illustrates the changing understanding of the importance of marriage for births.

The birth control pill was introduced in 1960. Within a decade, more than a third of all married women in America were using oral contraception. There was also a noteworthy increase in voluntary sterilization among women older than age thirty. Indeed, by 1970, six in ten American married women were using medical, effective, non-coitus-related methods of birth control. Ten years earlier, wives had extremely limited access to contraception, and much of what existed was ineffective.[6] These technological innovations in birth control have been described as a "contraceptive revolution" or a "reproductive technology shock" because of their profound implications for social customs and norms.

Sex Becomes a Private Matter

The contraceptive revolution made sex a private matter legally and essentially removed it from state control. A series of U.S. Supreme Court decisions during the 1960s had major implications for the legal and cultural meaning of sex and childbearing. In the most important case, *Griswold* v. *Connecticut* (1965), the Court declared unconstitutional a state law forbidding the use of contraceptive devices, even by married couples. Writing for the Court majority, Justice William O. Douglas explained that various guarantees of the Bill of Rights "create zones of privacy," making "the very idea of prohibiting the practice of birth control . . . repulsive to the notions of privacy surrounding the marriage relationship." *Griswold* and subsequent Court decisions established a constitutional right to privacy in matters of sexual behavior among consenting adults, married or single, and, most recently, heterosexual or homosexual. [7]

Before *Griswold*, sexual matters had never been completely private because of their potential public consequences. Communities prohibited sexual freedoms because adultery and illegitimacy disrupted family lines, sometimes creating collective obligations for the care of offspring. Premarital and extramarital sexual intercourse were illegal. The ability to separate intercourse from reproduction removed the rationale for such regulations.

Sexual intercourse was long the legal symbolic core of marriage; consummation defined its de facto creation. Sexual exclusivity was the basis for a range of legal restrictions surrounding marriage. Adultery, for example, provided grounds for lawsuits by the aggrieved spouse. A married person's *consortium*, the legally protected emotional stakes a spouse has in his or her marriage, was protected in family law. Those who damaged a marriage by adultery or by luring a married partner into an extramarital relationship (enticement) were subject to tortuous legal actions for damages to consortium.

Such "heart balm" claims are now more a curiosity than a conspicuous feature of domestic relations law, except when physical injury is involved. Most jurisdictions have abolished or limited such suits. That such actions are now pursued so infrequently (in the few remaining states where they are still permitted) attests to the declining legal significance of sexual exclusivity in marriage.[8] Similarly, the rapid spread of no-fault divorce laws since 1970 has effectively eliminated adultery as a condition for divorce. Culturally, once sexual relations came to be viewed as private decisions unrelated to marriage, so did reproduction choices. In other words, once sex and procreation could be separated, so could sex and marriage. But so, too, of course, could reproduction and marriage, as they increasingly have been.

Both the social stigma and the legal consequences of having an "illegitimate" child have virtually vanished in recent years. In a series of decisions between 1968 and 1978, the U.S. Supreme Court declared unconstitutional the legal distinctions associated with the marital status of a child's parents.[9] In this as in most areas of domestic relations, American family law has shifted its primary focus from the married couple to the individual.[10] The marital status of parents is legally irrelevant from the perspective of either generation.

In short, now that fertility can be controlled, parenthood and marriage are less institutionalized and much less predictably connected. A once near-universal insistence on an adult social script governing marriage has given way to an expanding range of acceptable, though less traditional, life course options, such as cohabitation. Living together in a sexual relationship, once taboo, is now so acceptable that a majority of Americans cohabit before they marry.[11] And yet the practice is still so novel that it lacks a vernacular name. Nor, importantly, is it yet governed by norms or explicit laws. Like many social changes fostered by sexual freedom, cohabitation is not yet institutionalized, not yet integrated fully into the nation's culture or law.[12]

The old rules have changed, but new standards have yet to emerge. The new living arrangements are often incompatible with old customs and conventions. Even more vexing, the new arrangements offer fewer traditional solutions when problems arise, because many of the problems themselves are the result of nontraditional arrangements. Cohabiting couples, for example, have little tradition to follow when dealing with the informal equivalent of their "in-laws." Relations with the older generation are strained as a result.[13]

Predictably, when a stable system of social conventions is so quickly altered, some will react by seeking to restore it.[14] Today's marriage movement is one such reaction.

Scientific Evidence about the Consequences of Marriage

Participants in the marriage movement draw heavily on the research findings of social scientists. One key line of research, which finds consistent correlation between various health and economic outcomes and marriage (or divorce), suggests that children and adults benefit from satisfying and stable marriages. Another line of research, especially the province of psychologists, has spurred the development of strategies to improve problematic relationships through marriage or family therapy and, more recently, to prevent such problems through marriage or couples education. Robin Dion reviews the latter strategy in her article in this volume. Here, I consider the research on health and economic outcomes, focusing on how marriage affects adults. The articles by Paul Amato and by Adam Thomas and Isabel Sawhill in this volume survey the effects of marriage and divorce on children.

The Consequences of Marriage

For well over a century, researchers have known that married people are generally better off than their unmarried counterparts. As early as 1897, sociologist Emile Durkheim was theorizing about why married adults have lower suicide rates than unmarried adults. In a recent survey David Ribar notes that links between marriage and better health in children and adults "have been documented in hundreds of quantitative studies covering different time periods and different countries."[15]

The accumulated research shows that married people are typically healthier, live longer, earn more, have better mental health, have better sex lives, and are happier than their unmarried counterparts. They have lower rates of suicide, fatal accidents, acute and chronic illness, alcoholism, and depression. In 1995 Linda Waite reviewed and highlighted the entire range of such benefits in her presidential address to the Population Association of

America, "Does Marriage Matter?" And she, together with coauthor Maggie Gallagher, answered her own question emphatically in their subsequent book, *The Case for Marriage: Why Married People Are Happier, Healthier, and Better Off Financially.*[16]

Despite abundant evidence documenting such correlation, however, a question recurs: is marriage the cause of the health and happiness enjoyed by married people, or are

Is marriage the cause of the health and happiness enjoyed by married people, or are healthier and happier people the ones most likely to marry?

healthier and happier people the ones most likely to marry? If people who are less healthy, happy, or successful are also less attractive as potential spouses, then they will be less likely to be selected into marriage. The ranks of the unmarried will thus contain a disproportionate number of such people. On the other hand, if marriage actually causes people to have better health, happiness, or success, then the unmarried would, again, be less happy, healthy, or successful. Because both the "selection" and the "causal" arguments lead to the same empirical results, debate has continued for many years.

It is impossible to settle the issue definitively through a rigorous scientific experiment: people cannot be randomly assigned to marry or remain single, divorce or remain together. Before the 1970s, researchers relied on cross-sectional data (either a single survey or

one point in a long-term data series) that simply compared the married with the unmarried on various outcomes.[17] But cross-sectional associations do not make a convincing case that marriage has beneficial effects. They may be confounded by omitted variables that influence both the likelihood of being married and of enjoying better outcomes, or by reverse causation (for example, better health leading to marriage rather than vice versa).

Since the 1970s marriage researchers have been using long-term data that follow the same group of people as they move into and out of marriage. If changes in marital status (marrying, divorcing, remarrying) are consistently correlated with comparable changes in health or economic well-being, this is strong evidence for the plausibility of a causal connection. Such a long-term data design is as close to a true experiment as researchers can hope to get. These studies have provided evidence for both causal and selection arguments, with the causal argument sometimes seeming stronger and sometimes weaker in its effects.[18]

Theoretical Underpinnings

Before I review the research findings, it is worth considering why married adults might differ (especially in beneficial ways) from their unmarried counterparts. What theory would predict or explain such differences? A variety of such explanations exist and can be grouped under three broad themes: marriage as a social institution, specialization, and the domesticating role of marriage.

The institutional perspective argues that marriage changes individuals in positive ways, both to the extent that others treat them differently and to the extent that they come to view themselves differently.[19] The marital relationship carries with it legal, moral, and conventional assumptions about what is right and proper. It is, in other words, institutionalized and defined by social norms. It is culturally patterned and integrated into other basic social institutions like education, the economy, and politics. In this sense, married individuals have a tradition of solutions to rely on when they confront problems. For many matters in domestic life, marriage supplies a template.

Moreover, the institutional nature of marriage implies that others will treat married people differently because of the cultural assumptions made about husbands and wives. Employers may prefer married to unmarried workers, for example, or may reward married employees with greater opportunities and benefits. Insurers may discount policies for married people. And the law gives married partners legal rights vis-à-vis each other that are not granted to unmarried people.[20] Economists refer to this aspect of marriage as its "signaling" function. Economic signals are activities or attributes of a person that convey information to others. The most effective economic signals are those that involve significant cost to the sender. A classic example is a college degree, which transmits, for example to an employer, valuable information about the sender. Because marriage, like a college degree, has significant costs attached, it serves as an economic signal of those things culturally associated with marriage: commitment, stability, and maturity, among other things. Friends, relatives, and employers will be inclined to assume such things about married people. To the extent they do, married people will benefit.[21] Because cohabitation is relatively costless (in signaling theory, cohabitation is "cheap talk"), it does not convey the same positive signal marriage does. Thus, for example, it is not surprising that cohabiting

men earn less than married men, even when other aspects of their relationships are similar.[22] Regardless of what marriage may mean to an individual in a relationship, it has broader implications in what it means to others. This is a core assumption of the institutional argument about marriage.

The institution of marriage also involves what Andrew Cherlin calls "enforceable trust." "Marriage still requires a public commitment to a long-term, possibly lifelong relationship. . . . Cohabitation, in contrast, requires only a private commitment which is easier to break. Therefore, marriage, more so than cohabitation, lowers the risk that one's partner will renege on agreements that have been made." Many observers now believe that this aspect of marriage has become less central as the private, individualized view of marriage has become increasingly dominant.[23]

The second theory about why married people might differ from unmarried people is specialization. When two people marry and merge households, they not only gain obvious economies of scale but also tend to develop an efficient division of labor. To the extent that spouses have different skills, preferences, or abilities, marriage allows each to concentrate on those in which he or she has a relative advantage. Such efficiencies have traditionally implied that wives would focus on nonmarket labor, such as child care and homemaking, because women's wages were so much lower than men's. But even in contemporary marriages, efficiencies from a division of labor still arise. For example, married parents with young children sometimes stagger their work hours to permit one to deliver the children to school and the other to be home when school is out. This simple strategy reduces the demand for expensive day care.[24] As couples refine their division of tasks, the household benefits to the extent that each partner's productivity increases. Such specialization produces greater interdependencies and lowers divorce rates.[25] The interdependencies also have economic value ("marriage-specific capital") and have been protected in tort law as consortium.[26] Such specialization diminishes the wife's earning potential in the market to the extent that her skills or credentials, or both, decay. Still, even in contemporary marriages, in which the

---

Researchers found that married men had higher performance ratings than unmarried men and that their higher productivity was largely responsible for their higher earnings.

---

large majority of wives are employed, couples continue to divide household tasks. Cohabiting couples are less likely to do so.

The third theory about differences between married and unmarried people involves marriage's domesticating role. Men are thought to change more when they marry than women do because unmarried men live less healthy lives than unmarried women do and therefore have more room in their lives for positive change. Specifically, once men are married, they are much less likely to engage in risky behaviors such as drinking heavily, drivingly dangerously, or using drugs. They are also more likely to work regularly, help others more, volunteer more, and attend religious services more frequently. Durkheim argued that such changes occur because mar-

riage integrates men into social groups of like-minded others and, by doing so, establishes acceptable boundaries around their behaviors. Others have made similar arguments about how marriage "domesticates" men by fostering a sense of responsibility for their families, orienting them toward the future and making them sensitive to the long-term consequences of their actions, and providing someone to offer advice, schedule medical appointments, or encourage pro-social behaviors (the so-called nagging factor). And both partners' mental health appears to benefit from the support and understanding they share (more in marriage than in cohabiting relationships).[27]

Economic Changes Associated with Marriage

As noted, the correlation between marriage and economic outcomes involves both selection and causal factors. Men with favorable expected earnings are more likely to marry and less prone to divorce. But research has found that marriage also improves earnings, at least for men. The so-called marriage premium is the additional income that men generate once they marry. Men's earnings, not only in America but in other developed countries, increase once they marry (over and above any change associated with age or experience), and their earnings increase faster than those of comparable unmarried men. And the marriage premium is lost when men divorce. The generally accepted explanation is that men's productivity increases after marriage, largely because of specialization.[28]

After replicating, and thus validating, earlier findings of a marriage premium for men, especially in the first years of marriage, economists Sanders Korenman and David Neumark examined employment records that included performance evaluations and other indicators of productivity. They found that married men had higher performance ratings than unmarried men and that their higher productivity was largely responsible for their higher earnings.

Women's earnings consistently fail to increase as a result of marriage. But they do not consistently drop, either. Rather, marriage-linked changes in women's earnings are probably due more to fertility. Both married and unmarried women who have children earn less, as a result.[29]

Research that controls for selectivity typically finds somewhat smaller marriage earnings premiums for men, but it nevertheless finds a premium. (For women, the situation is less clear.) Such findings, as well as new evidence that marriage is increasingly viewed as something to postpone until one is already financially stable (that is, reverse causality), mean that it is probably true that both causal and selection effects operate for both sexes in matters of marriage and economic well-being.[30]

Health Changes Associated with Marriage

People who are involved with others typically enjoy better health than those who are socially isolated.[31] Because marriage is a form of social integration, it is not surprising that married people are healthier. Almost without exception, long-term studies of health find that marriage (especially when it is satisfying or long term, or both) is associated with better health and increased longevity. With respect to physical health and mortality, most people adopt a healthier lifestyle once married, thereby avoiding illness or death caused by harmful behavior such as excessive drinking.[32] A spouse is likely to encourage healthier behaviors in his or her partner, such as smoking or drinking less, going to the doctor

when ill, having regular checkups, and visiting the dentist. And marital interactions typically reduce stress, thereby contributing to better health.[33]

There is some, albeit limited, evidence of selectivity with respect to health. For example, good health appears to make unemployed women—but not working women—more likely to get married. Research in the Netherlands found that poor health increased the chances of divorce, though it did not affect entry into marriage. Such a line of research offers minimal support for the "selection" argument.[34]

Overall, both causal and selection arguments are probably true in matters of health. Healthier people are more likely both to marry and to avoid divorce. At the same time, marriage promotes healthier lifestyles and reduces the chances of death. Research indicates that the positive effects of marriage seem stronger for men than for women. The most likely explanation for such findings is that unmarried men lead more unhealthy lives and take greater risks than unmarried women do.

The Marriage Movement: E Pluribus Unum

Based in part on research showing that marriage is good for adults and children, strengthening marriage has become a goal of both public and private initiatives in recent years.

Proponents of strengthening marriage form a diverse group. Many are in religious communities, especially conservative Protestant denominations. Their aim is to rebuild a traditional model of lifelong monogamous marriage. Others—practitioners and professionals in various fields—are motivated by concerns about rising divorce rates or about the welfare of couples, individual adults, and children. Many are therapy-oriented and seek to educate or counsel people about strategies and skills to build healthy relationships, whether through marriage or otherwise. Others belong to fatherhood groups concerned about absent fathers. Still others are state government officials concerned about the problems of the poor (see the article by Robin Dion in this volume). Most of these latter are affiliated with programs targeting unmarried parents, many growing out of changes in welfare law in the late 1990s.

Religious Mobilization

The dramatic transformation of American households and families from the late 1960s through the late 1980s came on the heels of one of the most homogeneous cultural periods of U.S. history in matters of marriage and living arrangements. The postwar era of the 1950s featured historically high fertility rates, low divorce rates, and youthful ages at marriage. The postwar economy and veterans' programs significantly expanded the middle class. Attendance at religious services was high. Culturally, it was the most "familistic" decade of the century: the family was understood as *the* crucial social institution, both for the individual and for society as a whole. Familism, an ideology that emerged during the seventeenth and eighteenth centuries, associated the prevailing family principles of marriage, childbearing, motherhood, commitment, and sacrifice for family with a sense of sacredness. It stressed sexual fidelity in marriage, chastity before marriage, intensive child-rearing, a commitment to a lifelong marriage, and high levels of expressive interaction among family members.[35]

Against this backdrop, the demographic and cultural trends of the 1960s and 1970s raised grave concern among conservative religious communities, who saw most of these trends as signs of decay. Feminism, the sexual revolution, legalized abortion, divorce, cohabitation, homosexuality, and open challenges to authority energized the rise of a religiously affiliated movement to restore the basic features of 1950s familism. The new Christian Right, which included such groups as Jerry Falwell's Moral Majority, Beverly LaHaye's Concerned Women for America, and James Dobson's Focus on the Family (later the Family Research Council), became a powerful political force, mobilizing millions of voters and establishing lobbying groups with close ties to Republican leaders and conservative members of Congress. More generally, conservative Protestantism has been, and remains, an important force in matters of the family because its adherents are very active, devoting more time and money to their churches and affiliated organizations than any other major religious group in America.[36]

With increased sexual freedom driving many of the liberalizing trends of the later twentieth century, it is not surprising that sexual matters were the focus of much of the reaction. As Karen Armstrong notes in her historical review of conservative religious movements, the fundamentalists of the 1970s and 1980s "associated the integrity and even the survival of their society with the traditional position of women." Feminism, homosexuality, and abortion were central themes in a religious movement to restore family values.[37]

Professional Mobilization

Others involved in the marriage debate include professionals, practitioners, and social scientists with an interest in divorce and marital stability. Psychologists have analyzed interpersonal behaviors and strategies associated with various outcomes of relationships and have identified styles of conflict resolution, coping, and communication as critical elements in marriage. Demographers and sociologists have identified background traits such as cohabitation, parental divorce, young age at marriage, and low levels of religiousness as strong predictors of divorce.

About twenty-five years ago, a field now known as couples education or marriage education began integrating such research into therapeutic approaches to helping couples prepare for or prevent problems in relationships. Couples education, offered in class-like settings, teaches both individuals and couples strategies to avoid the known risks to marriage.

Yet another group of professionals launched programs to promote and help fathers. Fatherhood programs, many in state government, focus on pregnancy prevention (most target young men), child support enforcement and the establishment of paternity, visitation issues, and services for poor fathers, especially those unable to comply with child support orders. Many national organizations support fatherhood. The National Fatherhood Initiative, founded in 1994, seeks to increase the involvement of fathers with their children through a range of educational and training programs. The National Center for Fathering, founded in 1990, sponsors seminars for corporations and schools to encourage greater family involvement by fathers. The Families and Work Institute's Fatherhood Project works with corporations, government agencies, and local fatherhood groups to develop father-friendly programs and policies, such as paternity leave. Other groups supporting fatherhood include the National Partnership for Community Leadership and the National Practitioners Network for Fathers and Families.

Several independent professionals, national professional organizations, and educational and research institutions have also launched efforts on behalf of marriage. Diane Solee, a marriage and family therapist who coined the term "marriage education," founded the Coalition for Marriage, Family, and Couples Education in 1995. She sponsors a national clearinghouse for marriage information, organizes an annual national conference called "Smart Marriages," and maintains web sites and listservs to provide additional information. The Center for Law and Social Policy, which maintains a section on families and couples, publishes policy-related materials and maintains a web site with links to such information. The Institute for American Values maintains a Council on Families that sponsors conferences, publishes original research, and reviews public policy relating to marriage. Academic centers at universities and at well-respected think tanks such as the Brookings Institution, the Urban Institute, and the Heritage Foundation produce analyses of and take positions on issues related to marriage.[38] And marriage therapists, religious leaders, and think tank intellectuals have launched community marriage initiatives, typically in couple-to-couple formats that target entire communities. In the mid-1980s, journalist Michael McManus began promoting a faith-based project called "Marriage Savers" that involved couple-to-couple mentoring organized through religious congregations.

Political Mobilization

Policy analyst Theodora Ooms and her colleagues trace the origins of public policy efforts to promote marriage to the late 1980s, as evidence accumulated to document the adverse effects on children of growing up in a single-parent home. State efforts focused initially on making divorce more difficult, through means such as covenant marriage,

Federal and State Marriage Programs

With the election of President George W. Bush in 2000, federal funding to support marriage-promotion programs grew. The Healthy Marriage Initiative within the Administration for Children and Families supports many such projects.[1] (See the article by Robin Dion in this volume for more details on these projects.) One project develops ways to approach unwed parents to emphasize the importance of healthy marriages for their children, as well as to promote the establishment of paternity and strengthen marital and co-parenting relationships with nonresident fathers. Another develops and tests curriculums and training to help welfare staff address issues of marriage and family formation. Large research and evaluation grants are helping develop coalitions and strategies to promote healthy marriage and responsible fatherhood in communities. Building Strong Families is a nine-year random-assignment experiment to assess programs to strengthen relationships and support the marital aspirations of unmarried couples around the time of the birth of a child. Supporting Healthy Marriages, likewise, is a random-assignment experimental evaluation of interventions to support marriage among low-income couples in their child-rearing years. Community Healthy Marriage Initiatives: An Evaluation will assess communitywide initiatives to promote and support marriages. Awards for these and similar programs have significantly increased federal support for research and programs targeting marriage.

The major source of marriage activities in states is federal welfare grants. As detailed by Theodora Ooms, Stacey Bouchet, and Mary Parke in *Beyond Marriage Licenses*, the range of state marriage efforts is impressive by any standard.[2] Every state has done something to try to promote marriage, reduce divorce, or strengthen two-parent families. The origins of these efforts are diverse. Some began as grassroots community programs, some were organized through religious congregations, and some were borrowed from other states. All are relatively new, dating back no more than ten years or so. So far, importantly, few of the efforts have been scientifically evaluated for safety or effectiveness, though, as noted, the Administration for Children and Families is now supporting such evaluations.

In the past decade ten states have undertaken policy initiatives such as high-level commissions, media campaigns, proclamations, or conferences, or implemented laws and policies to establish and fund programs to promote marriage and reduce divorce.

Many states have also made changes in their marriage and divorce laws, including incentives for couples to prepare for marriage with counseling or education. Five states offer reduced fees for marriage licenses to couples who receive such services. Three states have enacted covenant marriage laws, and another twenty state legislatures have debated such legislation. In Louisiana, Arkansas, and Arizona, couples voluntarily select between the existing marriage laws or a covenant marriage regime, which includes premarital education or counseling, a legally binding affidavit accepting the terms of the covenant marriage, and required counseling before divorce. Divorce is granted only for the traditional faults (adultery, abuse, abandonment) or after a two-year waiting period. Couples who are already married may convert their marriages to covenant marriages.

Many states offer fatherhood promotion and marriage education programs. Some encourage an unmarried father to marry the mother of his child. At least eleven states now fund fatherhood programs that promote co-parenting. The programs stress greater involvement by nonresident fathers, offer mediation services and co-parenting classes to help estranged parents resolve problems, and encourage marriage.[3] Not all fatherhood programs, however, promote marriage. Indeed, leading analysts suggest that the question of whether to emphasize marriage is contentious and may threaten the entire fatherhood effort.[4]

The most conspicuous state marriage-related programs are those called couples and marriage education. Thirty-two states have at least one such program, as do all branches of the U.S. military. Many cooperative extension county educators (once known as county extension agents) are trained family life educators. Six states have launched new marriage-related activities that are being conducted by these agents through land grant universities. Public schools also offer marriage education. Six states offer such programs through high schools as electives. Many more individual school districts do so as well. Florida requires four hours of relationship and marriage education for high school graduation.

Multisector programs, often begun by religious leaders, unite public officials, community leaders, clergy, and interested citizens. Chattanooga's First Things First began in 1997; Families Northwest started in 1996 as a statewide project in Washington state and since has been extended to Oregon; Healthy Marriages Grand Rapids began in 1997. These and similar programs sponsor marriage and couples education, support like-minded grassroots efforts by others, offer mentoring programs to couples, and generally raise awareness about the importance of marriage. All include informal agreements signed by local clergy and other officials who agree to abide by locally developed minimum guidelines, such as requiring premarital counseling and relying on premarital inventories to identify strengths and weaknesses, to prepare couples planning to marry.[5]

States have also made big changes in their welfare regulations. The 1996 welfare reform law gave states considerable latitude in establishing such rules. In response, states reduced disincentives that discouraged couples from remaining together in households that receive welfare grants. Under the old AFDC rules, welfare was generally available only to single-parent families, with limited funds for two-parent families; since 2002, thirty-six states have eliminated two-parent family eligibility requirements, and another eleven have partially eliminated them. As of 2002, twenty-two states operated separate programs for two-parent families and funded them solely with state dollars. Families served are exempt from federal participation and work requirements. Nine states offer welfare recipients financial incentives, including a $100 monthly bonus, to marry. Other incentives are excluding a spouse's earnings in determining financial eligibility or grant amounts and forgiving child support arrearages owed by a noncustodial parent to the state if the parents marry or reunite.

1. U.S. Department of Health and Human Services, Administration for Children and Families, www.acf.hhs.gov/healthymarriage (accessed February 2005).

2. Theodora Ooms, Stacey Bouchet, and Mary Parke, *Beyond Marriage Licenses: Efforts in States to Strengthen Marriage and Two-Parent Families* (Washington: Center for Law and Social Policy, 2004).

3. U.S. Department of Health and Human Services, Administration for Children and Families, "Promoting Responsible Fatherhood," www.hhs.gov/news/press/2002pres/fathers.html (accessed February 2005).

4. Ronald B. Mincy and Hillard W. Pouncy, "The Responsible Fatherhood Field: Evolution and Goals," in *Handbook of Father Involvement: Multidisciplinary Perspectives*, edited by Katherine S. Tamis-Lamonda and Natasha Cabrera (Mahwah, N.J.: Lawrence Erlbaum Associates, 2002).

5. William J. Doherty and Jared R. Anderson, "Community Marriage Initiatives," *Family Relations* 53 (2004): 425–32.

and subsequently on marriage and couples education programs.[39] (See box for more details about state and federal marriage programs.)

The economic implications of single-parenthood have featured conspicuously in state debates about family policy. In 1999, for example, Oklahoma governor Frank Keating launched the nation's largest marriage initiative, supported with $10 million of federal welfare funds, to cut the state's high divorce

---

At the federal level, concern about marriage was driven primarily by increasing rates of births to unmarried women and corresponding claims on public assistance.

---

and out-of-wedlock birth rates. Keating's move came on the heels of a 1998 report showing that his state's economy was flagging partly because high rates of family breakdown were driving many Oklahomans into poverty. Likewise, Louisiana first authorized covenant marriage (see box) in 1997, following legislative debate highlighting the costs of poverty resulting from divorce.[40]

At the federal level, concern about marriage was driven primarily by increasing rates of births to unmarried women and corresponding claims on public assistance. Activists who had already been working to promote marriage understandably welcomed this novel role for the federal government. But both liberals and conservatives expressed reservations. Among conservatives, the debate was over whether federal efforts should be fo-

cused on reducing illegitimacy or mandating work for welfare recipients. Those endorsing the latter view argued that there was little evidence to support the claim that efforts to reduce out-of-wedlock births could work.[41] Liberal concern was similar. The National Organization for Women, for example, has objected that marriage-promotion efforts divert welfare funds from basic economic supports for mother-headed families, intrude on private decisions, place some women at greater risk of domestic violence by coercing them to stay in bad or dangerous marriages, waste public funds on ineffective policies, limit state flexibility by earmarking welfare funds for specified programs, and generally lack public support.[42] These and similar concerns continue to be expressed. But leading policy analysts Will Marshall and Isabel Sawhill see a political consensus emerging over the complex challenges facing American families—single, teen, and unwed parenting; economic insecurity; health care; and balancing home and work. They call for a comprehensive family policy to address all such issues.[43]

Much of the contemporary federal concern about marriage and unmarried fertility is based on arguments similar to those first advanced in 1965 by Daniel Patrick Moynihan, then assistant secretary of labor for President Johnson.[44] Moynihan claimed that female-headed households were a primary cause of poverty and welfare dependency among black Americans. In 1984, in *Losing Ground: American Social Policy: 1950–1980*, welfare critic Charles Murray elaborated on that theme, arguing that welfare encouraged dependency by making it economically rational for a poor mother to remain single and unemployed rather than marry. The problem of welfare dependency became a central issue in the welfare reform debate that led to a major overhaul of federal legislation in 1996.

As political scientist R. Kent Weaver writes: Murray's "conservative diagnoses and prescriptions for welfare reform were part of a broader conservative renaissance that began in the 1970s and gained momentum with the election of Ronald Reagan to the presidency in 1980. . . . Conservatives were far from united on their prescriptions for what to do about AFDC [Aid to Families with Dependent Children] . . . but did succeed in making the reduction of welfare dependency the focus of welfare debates in the 1990s."[45]

Tackling welfare dependency would require dealing with issues of out-of-wedlock births, moving welfare recipients into the labor force, and making fathers contribute—financially, at least—to raising their children. These issues, raised by Congress in initial deliberations about welfare reform during the 1980s and 1990s, continue to be debated today. Many states have undertaken marriage-strengthening efforts supported largely with federal welfare funds. Although such efforts may reflect a more general federal interest in marriage, the most significant initiatives target poor women and, to some extent, men.

The welfare reform bill signed into law by President Bill Clinton in 1996 featured four family-formation objectives. The first was to provide assistance to needy families to allow children to be cared for in their own homes or those of relatives. The second was to end the dependence of needy parents on government benefits by promoting job preparation, work, and marriage. The third was to prevent and reduce the incidence of out-of-wedlock pregnancies and establish annual numerical goals toward that end. The final goal was to encourage the formation and maintenance of two-parent families.[46] Congress gave states wide latitude to implement innovative strategies, such as limiting additional welfare support to households in which an additional child is born or limiting cash benefits to teenage mothers. Congress also provided funding for abstinence education.

Promoting two-parent families and discouraging out-of-wedlock births are now acknowledged federal objectives. A state's performance in meeting these statutory goals has consequences in terms of the welfare funds that flow to it from Washington. States may use block grant funds in "any manner reasonably calculated" to achieve any of the program's goals, and they have used these funds to create new fatherhood and marriage-promotion programs or enlarge existing ones.

Conclusions and Recommendations

The seemingly endless array of contemporary public and private efforts to promote marriage, reduce out-of-wedlock births, encourage responsible fatherhood, and persuade unmarried parents to marry would have made little sense to Americans living just fifty years ago. For them, marriage was the central and defining feature of adult identity; for them, such goals were elemental moral principles. Not so for today's Americans, who find themselves far removed from such a marriage-centered culture and struggling to redefine the role that marriages and families play in society.

Sociologists refer to historical moments such as our own, when technology has advanced much more rapidly than the institutions surrounding it, as periods of culture lag. The technological advance in this case was effective fertility control. When scientists discovered how to control the link between sex and reproduction, they set off prodigious changes in the institutions of marriage and the family. Many Americans are now engaged in the contemporary marriage debate precisely because they are struggling to understand the meaning of the wrenching dislocations in American social and family life over the past half-century.

As other articles in this volume show, champions of marriage have thus far had few victories. Perhaps it is still too early. More likely, the related goals of promoting marriage and discouraging divorce or out-of-wedlock births will fare about as well as other national attempts to alter large social trends.

At the moment, most marriage-promotion efforts focus on individuals and the choices they make. It may be possible to convince poor women that it is best to get married before having children. It may be possible to convince them that marriage is better than cohabitation. It may be possible to teach couples how to resolve problems that jeopardize their relationships. Evidence suggests that most poor women already understand many of these things.[47] Given how little researchers and professionals know about helping couples get or stay married, however, our expectations of policies in these areas should be modest, at best. Despite the lack of effective strategies to accomplish these goals, there nevertheless appears to be an emerging political, cultural, and scientific consensus about the consequences of different family structures for children's well-being. Increasingly, Americans appear to understand that the best arrangement for children is with two loving parents even if we have yet to develop ways always to achieve that goal. Our current efforts reflect this uncertainty about how to strengthen families.

Attempts directed toward changing or "fixing" individuals reflect a psychological behaviorist assumption that the root "problem" lies within the person, not his or her society or environment. If one adopts this perspective, then the obvious solution is something like education or training—couples education, for example, or counseling. Again, if one adopts this perspective, then the assessment of such solutions lies in measuring individual change, as studied through such strategies as random-assignment experiments. But if the problem is viewed as larger than the individual, and if it is seen as endemic to an entire historical era, then it cannot be addressed solely at the individual level. One way to begin to address it would be to engage in a prolonged and sometimes painful national discussion. Such a discussion would take place in public among lawmakers, clergy, teachers, journalists, opinion leaders, and intellectuals—and in private between partners, between parents, and among family members. Such a national conversation would interpret and make sense of the changing roles played by marriage and families in society. This is how social change is managed and understood. And this, I believe, is how to understand today's debate over the value of marriage.

Endnotes

1. Nancy F. Cott, *Public Vows: A History of Marriage and the Nation* (Harvard University Press, 2000).

2. Matthew D. Bramlett and William D. Mosher, *Cohabitation, Marriage, Divorce, and Remarriage in the United States*, Vital and Health Statistics, Series 23, no. 22 (Hyattsville, Md.: Centers for Disease Control and Prevention, National Center for Health Statistics, July 2002).

3. Julie DaVanzo and M. Amar Rahman, "American Families: Trends and Correlates," *Population Index* 59 (1993): 350–86; Sara S. McLanahan and Lynne M. Casper, "Growing Diversity and Inequality in the American Family," in *State of the Union: America in the 1990s*, vol. 2, *Social Trends*, edited by Reynolds Farley (New York: Russell Sage Foundation, 1995), pp. 1–45; Lynne M. Casper and Suzanne M. Bianchi, *Continuity and Change in the American Family* (Thousand Oaks, Calif.: Sage, 2002), pp. 7–8.

4. Steven Nock, "The Divorce of Marriage and Parenthood," *Journal of Family Therapy* 22, no. 2 (2000): 245–63; Hendrick Hertog, *Man and Wife in America: A History* (Harvard University Press, 2000).

5. John D'Emilio and Estelle B. Freedman, *Intimate Matters: A History of Sexuality in America* (New York: Harper and Row, 1988), p. 251; George A. Akerlof and Janet L. Yellen, "An Analysis of Out-of-Wedlock Childbearing in the United States," *Quarterly Journal of Economics* 2 (1996): 277–317.

6. Charles F. Westoff and Norman B. Ryder, *The Contraceptive Revolution* (Princeton University Press, 1977).

7. *Griswold* v. *Connecticut*, 381 U.S. 479 (1965); *Eisenstadt* v. *Baird*, 405 U.S. 438 (1972); *Roe* v. *Wade*, 410 U.S. 113 (1973); *Lawrence* v. *Texas*, 539 U.S. 558 (2003).

8. Mary Ann Glendon, *The Transformation of Family Law* (University of Chicago Press, 1989), p. 96; Harry D. Krause and David D. Meyer, *Family Law* (Eagan, Minn.: Thomson/West, 2003), p. 96.

9. *Levy* v. *Louisiana*, 391 U.S. 68 (1968); *Glona* v. *American Guarantee and Liability Insurance Co.*, 391 U.S. 73 (1968); *Weber* v. *Aetna Casualty and Surety Co.*, 406 U.S. (1972); *Gomes* v. *Perez*, 209 U.S. 535 (1973); *Jiminez* v. *Weinberger*, 417 U.S. 628 (1974); *Matthews* v. *Lucas*, 427 U.S. 495 (1976); *Trimble* v. *Gordon*, 430 U.S. 762 (1977); *Fiallo* v. *Bell*, 430 U.S. 787 (1977); *Lalli* v. *Lalli*, 439 U.S. 259 (1978).

10. Hertog, *Man and Wife in America* (see note 4).

11. Larry L. Bumpass and Hsien-Hen Lu, "Trends in Cohabitation and Implications for Children's Family Contexts in the United States," *Population Studies* 54 (2000): 29–41.

12. Steven L. Nock, "A Comparison of Marriages and Cohabiting Relationships," *Journal of Family Issues* 16 (1995): 53–76.

13. Ibid.

14. Emile Durkheim, *Suicide: A Study in Sociology* (trans. John A. Spaulding and George Simpson), edited with an introduction by George Simpson (New York: Free Press, 1997) (originally published in French, 1897).

15. Ibid.; David C. Ribar, "What Do Social Scientists Know about the Benefits of Marriage? A Review of Quantitative Methodologies," Office of Planning, Research, and Evaluation, Administration for Children and Families (U.S. Department of Health and Human Services, 2003), p. 1.

16. Linda J. Waite, "Does Marriage Matter?" *Demography* 32 (1995): 483–507; Linda J. Waite and Maggie Gallagher, *The Case for Marriage: Why Married People Are Happier, Healthier, and Better Off Financially* (New York: Doubleday, 2000).

17. Noreen Goldman, "Marriage Selection and Mortality Patterns: Inferences and Fallacies," *Demography* 30, no. 2 (1993): 189–208; Ribar, "What Do Social Scientists Know?" (see note 15).

18. Reviews are found in John E. Murray, "Marital Protection and Marital Selection: Evidence from a Historical-Prospective Sample of American Men," *Demography* 37, no. 4 (2000): 511–21; and Lee Lillard and Constantijn Panis, "Marital Status and Mortality: The Role of Health," *Demography* 33 (1996): 313–27.

19. Steven L. Nock, *Marriage in Men's Lives* (Oxford University Press, 1998).

20. Waite and Gallagher, *The Case for Marriage* (see note 16).

21. Antony W. Dnes, "Marriage as a Signal," in *The Law and Economics of Marriage and Divorce,* edited by Antony W. Dnes and Robert Rowthorn (Cambridge University Press, 2002).

22. Philip N. Cohen, "Cohabitation and the Declining Marriage Premium for Men," *Work and Occupations* 29 (August 2002): 346–63.

23. Andrew J. Cherlin, "The Deinstitutionalization of American Marriage," *Journal of Marriage and the Family* 66 (November 2004): 848–61; Paul R. Amato, "Tension between Institutional and Individual Views of Marriage," *Journal of Marriage and the Family* 66 (November 2004): 959–65.

24. Steven L. Nock and Paul W. Kingston, "The Family Work Day," *Journal of Marriage and the Family* 46 (1984): 333–43.

25. Steven L. Nock and Margaret F. Brinig, "Weak Men and Disorderly Women: Divorce and the Division of Labor," in *The Law and Economics of Marriage and Divorce,* edited by Anthony W. Dnes and Robert Rowthorn (Cambridge University Press, 2002); Steven L. Nock, "The Marriages of Equally Dependent Spouses," *Journal of Family Issues* 22, no. 6 (2001): 755–75.

26. Gary S. Becker, *A Treatise on the Family* (Harvard University Press, 1981); Margaret F. Brinig, Carl E. Schneider, and Lee E. Teitlebaum, *Family Law in Action: A Reader* (Cincinnati: Anderson Publishing Company, 1999).

27. Durkheim, *Suicide* (see note 14); Nock, *Marriage in Men's Lives* (see note 19); Steven L. Nock. "Time and Gender in Marriage," *Virginia Law Review* 86, no. 8 (2000): 1971–87; Waite and Gallagher, *The Case for Marriage* (see note 16).

28. Robert A. Nakosteen and Michael A. Zimmer, "Men, Money, and Marriage: Are High Earners More Prone than Low Earners to Marry?" *Social Science Quarterly* 79 (1997): 66–82; Nock, *Marriage in Men's Lives* (see note 19); Robert F. Schoeni, "Marital Status and Earnings in Developed Countries," *Journal of Population Economics* 8 (1995): 351–59; Sanders Korenman and David Neumark, "Does Marriage Really Make Men More Productive?" *Journal of Human Resources* 26 (1991): 282–307; Kermit Daniel, "The Marriage Premium," in *The New Economics of Human Behavior,* edited by Mariano Tommasi and Kathryn Ierulli (Cambridge University Press, 1995), pp. 113–25.

29. Shoshana Grossbard-Schectman, *On the Economics of Marriage: A Theory of Marriage, Labor, and Divorce* (Boulder, Colo.: Westview Press, 1993); Sanders Korenman and David Neumark, "Marriage, Moth-

erhood, and Wages," *Journal of Human Resources* 27 (Spring 1992): 233–55; Michelle Budig and Paula England, "The Wage Penalty for Motherhood," *American Sociological Review* 66 (April 2001): 204–25.

30. Cherlin, "The Deinstitutionalization of American Marriage" (see note 23); Kathryn Edin, "What Do Low-Income Single Mothers Say about Marriage?" *Social Problems* 47 (February 2000): 112–33.

31. James House, Karl Landis, and Debra Umberson, "Social Relationships and Health," *Science* 241 (July 29, 1988): 540–45.

32. Lillard and Panis, "Marital Status and Mortality: The Role of Health" (see note 18); Lee Lillard and Linda Waite, "Till Death Do Us Part: Marital Disruption and Mortality," *American Journal of Sociology* 100 (1995): 1131–56; Eugene Litwak, Peter Messeri, and others, "Organizational Theory, Social Support, and Mortality Rates: A Theoretical Convergence," *American Sociological Review* 54 (1989): 49–66; Murray, "Marital Protection and Marital Selection" (see note 18).

33. Janis K. Kiecolt-Glaser and Tamara Newton, "Marriage and Health: His and Hers," *Psychological Bulletin* 127 (July 2001): 472–503.

34. Ingrid Waldron, Mary E. Hughes, and Tracy L. Brooks, "Marriage Protection and Marriage Selection—Prospective Evidence for Reciprocal Effects of Marital Status and Health," *Social Science and Medicine* 43 (1996): 113–23; Inez Young and others, "A Longitudinal Study of Health Selection in Marital Transitions," *Social Science and Medicine* 46 (1998): 425–35; see Waite and Gallagher, *The Case for Marriage*, chapter 4 (see note 16), for a review of sex differences.

35. W. Bradford Wilcox, *Soft Patriarchs, New Men: How Christianity Shapes Fathers and Husbands* (University of Chicago Press, 2004), p. 36.

36. Christian Smith, *American Evangelicalism: Embattled and Thriving* (University of Chicago Press, 1998); Robert Wuthnow, *The Restructuring of American Religion* (Princeton University Press, 1988).

37. Karen Armstrong, *The Battle for God* (New York: Ballantine, 2000), p. 312; R. Kent Weaver, *Ending Welfare as We Know It* (Brookings, 2000), pp. 104–05.

38. See the Coalition for Marriage, Families and Couples Education, www.smartmarriages.com (accessed February 2005); Center for Law and Social Policy, www.clasp.org (accessed February 2005); Institute for American Values, www.americanvalues.org/index.html (accessed February 2005); Brookings Institution, www.brookings.edu/default.htm; Heritage Foundation, www.heritage.org/research/family/index.cfm; Urban Institute, www.urban.org/; and the National Marriage Project at Rutgers University, marriage.rutgers.edu/default.htm (accessed February 2005).

39. Theodora Ooms, Stacey Bouchet, and Mary Parke, *Beyond Marriage Licenses: Efforts in States to Strengthen Marriage and Two-Parent Families* (Washington: Center for Law and Social Policy, 2004).

40. Paula Roberts, *I Can't Give You Anything but Love: Would Poor Couples with Children Be Better Off Economically if They Married?* Policy Brief no. 5 (Center for Law and Social Policy, 2004). See also Laura Sanchez, Steven L. Nock, and James D. Wright, "The Implementation of Covenant Marriage Legislation in Louisiana," *Virginia Journal of Social Policy and the Law* 9, no. 1 (2001): 192–223. The Oklahoma Marriage Initiative—including its history, funding, and objectives—is described and detailed on its website: www.okmarriage.org (accessed February 2005). See testimony of Howard Hendrick, secretary of health and human services, Oklahoma, before the U.S. Senate Finance Committee, May 16, 2002, regarding

issues in TANF reauthorization (finance.senate.gov/hearings/testimony/051602hhtest.pdf [accessed February 2005]).

41. Ron Haskins, "Liberal and Conservative Influences on the Welfare Reform Legislation of 1996," in *For Better and For Worse: Welfare Reform and the Well-Being of Children and Families*, edited by Greg J. Duncan and P. Lindsey Chase-Lansdale (New York: Russell Sage Foundation, 2001), pp. 9–34.

42. NOW (National Organization for Women) Legal Defense and Education Fund, "Welfare and Poverty: Marriage Promotion" and "Looking for Love in All the Wrong Places: The Case against Government Marriage Promotion," both at www.nowldef.org/html/issues/wel/marriagepromotion.shtml (accessed February 5, 2005).

43. Will Marshall and Isabel V. Sawhill, "Progressive Family Policy in the Twenty-First Century," in *The Future of the Family*, edited by Daniel P. Moynihan, Timothy M. Smeeding, and Lee Rainwater (New York: Russell Sage Foundation, 2004), pp. 198–230.

44. Daniel Patrick Moynihan, *The Negro Family: The Case for National Action* (Office of Policy Planning and Research, U.S. Department of Labor, 1965).

45. Weaver, *Ending Welfare as We Know It* (see note 37), pp. 104–05.

46. The Personal Responsibility and Work Opportunity Reconciliation Act of 1996 (PL 104-193); see www.access.gpo.gov/nara/publaw/104publ.html (accessed February 2005).

47. Kathryn Edin and Laura Lein, *Making Ends Meet: How Single Mothers Survive Welfare and Low-Wage Work* (New York: Russell Sage Foundation, 1997); Sharon Hays, *Flat Broke with Children: Women in the Age of Welfare Reform* (Oxford University Press, 2003).

American Marriage in the Early Twenty-First Century

Andrew J. Cherlin

Summary

During the past century the U.S. family system has seen vast changes—in marriage and divorce rates, cohabitation, childbearing, sexual behavior, and women's work outside the home. Andrew Cherlin reviews these historic changes, noting that marriage remains the most common living arrangement for raising children, but that children, especially poor and minority children, are increasingly likely to grow up in single-parent families and to experience family instability.

Cherlin describes the economic and cultural forces that have transformed family life. Job market changes have drawn married women into the work force and deprived less-educated men of the blue-collar jobs by which they traditionally supported their families. And effective contraception and legalized abortion have eroded the norm of marriage before childbearing.

Cherlin notes that sentiment in favor of marriage appears to be stronger in the United States than in other developed countries. The share of U.S. adults who are likely to marry is higher, but so is the share likely to divorce. U.S. children are also more likely to live in single-parent families at some time in their childhood.

Although nearly all Americans, whether poor or well-to-do, hold to marriage as an ideal, today marriage is increasingly optional. To a greater extent than ever before, individuals can choose whether to form a family on their own, in a cohabiting relationship, or in a marriage.

Given U.S. patterns of swift transitions into and out of marriage and high rates of single parenthood, American policymakers eager to promote marriage are unlikely to be able to raise U.S. family stability to levels typical of other developed countries. Consequently, a family policy that relies too heavily on marriage will not help the many children destined to live in single-parent and cohabiting families—many of them poor—during their formative years. Assistance must be directed to needy families, regardless of their household structure. Policymakers must craft a careful balance of marriage-based and marriage-neutral programs to provide adequate support to American children.

www.futureofchildren.org

Andrew J. Cherlin is Griswold Professor of Public Policy at Johns Hopkins University.

The decline of American marriage has been a favorite theme of social commentators, politicians, and academics over the past few decades. Clearly the nation has seen vast changes in its family system—in marriage and divorce rates, cohabitation, childbearing, sexual behavior, and women's work outside the home. Marriage is less dominant as a social institution in the United States than at any time in history. Alternative pathways through adulthood—childbearing outside of marriage, living with a partner without ever marrying, living apart but having intimate relationships—are more acceptable and feasible than ever before. But as the new century begins, it is also clear that despite the jeremiads, marriage has not faded away. In fact, given the many alternatives to marriage now available, what may be more remarkable is not the decline in marriage but its persistence. What is surprising is not that fewer people marry, but rather that so *many* still marry and that the desire to marry remains widespread. Although marriage has been transformed, it is still meaningful. In this article I review the changes in American marriage, discuss their causes, compare marriage in the United States with marriage in the rest of the developed world, and comment on how the transformation of marriage is likely to affect American children in the early twenty-first century.

Changes in the Life Course

To illuminate what has happened to American marriage, I begin by reviewing the great demographic changes of the past century, including changes in age at marriage, the share of Americans ever marrying, cohabitation, nonmarital births, and divorce.

Recent Trends

Figure 1 shows the median age at marriage—the age by which half of all marriages occur—for men and women from 1890 to 2002. In 1890 the median age was relatively high, about twenty-six for men and twenty-two for women. During the first half of the twentieth century the typical age at marriage dropped—gradually at first, and then precipitously after World War II. By the 1950s it had reached historic lows: roughly twenty-three for men and twenty for women. Many people still think of the 1950s as the standard by which to compare today's families, but as figure 1 shows, the 1950s were the anomaly: during that decade young adults married earlier than ever before or since. Moreover, nearly all young adults— about 95 percent of whites and 88 percent of African Americans—eventually married.[1] During the 1960s, however, the median age at marriage began to climb, returning to and then exceeding that prevalent at the start of the twentieth century. Women, in particular, are marrying substantially later today than they have at any time for which data are available.

What is more, unmarried young adults are leading very different lives today than their earlier counterparts once did. The late-marrying young women and men of the early 1900s typically lived at home before marriage or paid for room and board in someone else's home. Even when they were courting, they lived apart from their romantic interests and, at least among women, the majority abstained from sexual intercourse until they were engaged or married. They were usually employed, and they often turned over much of their paycheck to their parents to help rear younger siblings. Few went to college; most had not even graduated from high school. As recently as 1940, only about one-third of adults in their late twenties had graduated from high school and just one in sixteen had graduated from college.[2]

Figure 1. Median Age at Marriage, 1890–2002

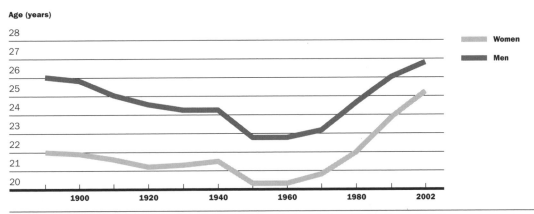

Source: U.S. Bureau of the Census, "Estimated Median Age at First Marriage, by Sex: 1890 to Present," 2003, www.census.gov/population/socdemo/hh-fam/tabMS-2.pdf (accessed July 23, 2004).

Today's unmarried young adults are much more likely to be living independently, in their own apartments. Five out of six young adults graduate from high school, and about one-third complete college.[3] They are more likely than their predecessors to spend their wages on themselves. Their sexual and intimate lives are also very different from those of earlier generations. The vast majority of unmarried young adults have had sexual intercourse. In fact, most women who married during the 1990s first had intercourse five years or more before marrying.[4]

About half of young adults live with a partner before marrying. Cohabitation is far more common today than it was at any time in the early- or mid-twentieth century (although it was not unknown among the poor and has been a part of the European family system in past centuries). Cohabitation today is a diverse, evolving phenomenon. For some people, it is a prelude to marriage or a trial marriage. For others, a series of cohabiting relationships may be a long-term substitute for marriage. (Thirty-nine percent of cohabiters in 1995 lived with children of one of the partners.) It is still rare in the United States for cohabiting relation-

ships to last long—about half end, through marriage or a breakup, within a year.[5]

Despite the drop in marriage and the rise in cohabitation, there has been no explosion of nonmarital births in the United States. Birth rates have fallen for unmarried women of all reproductive ages and types of marital status, including adolescents. But because birth rates have fallen faster for married women than for unmarried women, a larger share of women who give birth are unmarried. In 1950, only 4 percent of all births took place outside of marriage. By 1970, the figure was 11 percent; by 1990, 28 percent; and by 2003, 35 percent. In recent years, then, about one-third of all births have been to unmarried women—and that is the statistic that has generated the most debate.[6] Of further concern to many observers is that about half of all unmarried first-time mothers are adolescents. Academics, policymakers, and private citizens alike express unease about the negative consequences of adolescent childbearing, both for the parents and for the children, although whether those consequences are due more to poverty or to teen childbearing per se remains controversial.

When people think of nonmarital or "out-of-wedlock" childbearing, they picture a single parent. Increasingly, however, nonmarital births are occurring to cohabiting couples—about 40 percent according to the latest estimate.[7] One study of unmarried women giving birth in urban hospitals found that about half were living with the fathers of their children.

When people think of "out of wedlock" childbearing, they picture a single parent. Increasingly, however, nonmarital births are occurring to cohabiting couples.

Couples in these "fragile families," however, rarely marry. One year after the birth of the child, only 15 percent had married, while 26 percent had broken up.[8]

Marriage was not an option for lesbians and gay men in any U.S. jurisdiction until Massachusetts legalized same-sex marriage in 2004. Cohabitation, however, is common in this group. In a 1992 national survey of sexual behavior, 44 percent of women and 28 percent of men who said they had engaged in homosexual sex in the previous year reported that they were cohabiting.[9] The Census Bureau, which began collecting statistics on same-sex partnerships in 1990, does not directly ask whether a person is in a romantic same-sex relationship; rather, it gives people the option of saying that a housemate is an "unmarried partner" without specifying the nature of the partnership. Because some people may not wish to openly report a same-sex relationship

to the Census Bureau, it is hard to determine how reliable these figures are. The bureau reports, however, that in 2000, 600,000 households were maintained by same-sex partners. A substantial share—33 percent of female partnerships and 22 percent of male partnerships—reported the presence of children of one or both of the partners.[10]

As rates of entry into marriage were declining in the last half of the twentieth century, rates of exit via divorce were increasing—as they have been at least since the Civil War era. At the beginning of the twentieth century, about 10 percent of all marriages ended in divorce, and the figure rose to about one-third for marriages begun in 1950.[11] But the rise was particularly sharp during the 1960s and 1970s, when the likelihood that a married couple would divorce increased substantially. Since the 1980s the divorce rate has remained the same or declined slightly. According to the best estimate, 48 percent of American marriages, at current rates, would be expected to end in divorce within twenty years.[12] A few percent more would undoubtedly end in divorce after that. So it is accurate to say that unless divorce risks change, about half of all marriages today would end in divorce. (There are important class and racial-ethnic differences, which I will discuss below.)

The combination of more divorce and a greater share of births to unmarried women has increased the proportion of children who are not living with two parents. Figure 2 tracks the share of children living, respectively, with two parents, with one parent, and with neither parent between 1968 and 2002. It shows a steady decline in the two-parent share and a corresponding increase in the one-parent share. In 2002, 69 percent of children were living with two parents, including families where one biological (or adoptive)

Figure 2. Living Arrangements of U.S. Children, 1968–2002

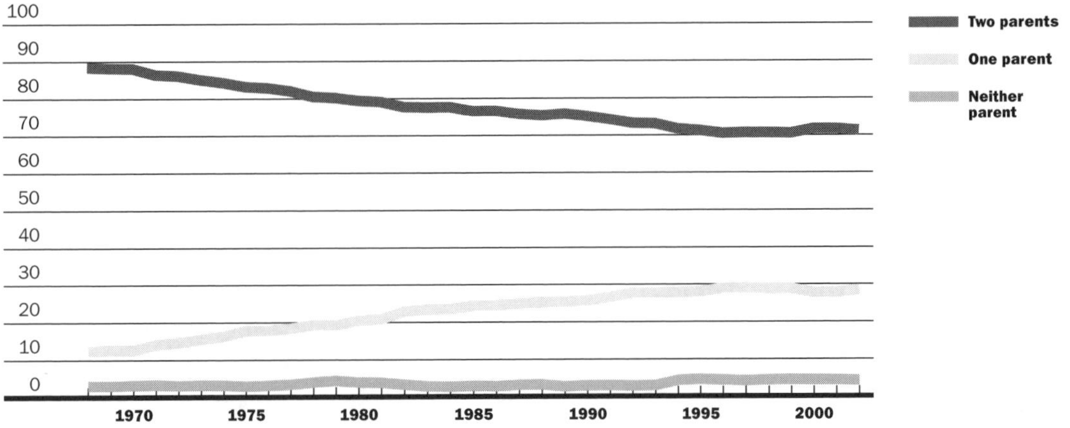

Percent

Source: U.S. Bureau of the Census, "Living Arrangements of Children under 18 Years Old: 1960 to Present," 2003, www.census.gov/population/socdemo/hh-fam/tabCH-1.pdf (accessed July 23, 2004).

parent had remarried. Not counting step- or adoptive families, 62 percent, according to the most recent estimate in 1996, were living with two biological parents.[13] Twenty-seven percent of American children were living with one parent; another 4 percent, with neither parent.[14] Most in the latter group were living with relatives, such as grandparents.

Where do all these changes leave U.S. marriage patterns and children's living arrangements in the early twenty-first century? As demographers have noted, many of the above trends have slowed over the past decade, suggesting a "quieting" of family change.[15] Marriage remains the most common living arrangement for raising children. At any one time, most American children are being raised by two parents. Marriage, however, is less dominant in parents' and children's lives than it once was. Children are more likely to experience life in a single-parent family, either because they are born to unmarried mothers or because their parents divorce. And children are more likely to experience instability in their living arrangements as par-

ents form and dissolve marriages and partnerships. Although children are less likely to lose a parent through death today than they once were, the rise in nonmarital births and in divorce has more than compensated for the decline in parental death.[16] From the adult perspective, the overall drop in birth rates and the increases in nonmarital childbearing and divorce mean that, at any one time, fewer adults are raising children than in the past.

Class and Racial-Ethnic Divergence

To complete this portrait of American marriage one must take note of class and racial-ethnic variations, for the overall statistics mask contrasting trends in the lives of children from different racial-ethnic groups and different social classes. In fact, over the past few decades, the family lives of children have been diverging across class and racial-ethnic lines.[17] A half-century ago, the family structures of poor and non-poor children were similar: most children lived in two-parent families. In the intervening years, the increase in single-parent families has been greater among the poor and near-poor.[18] Women at all levels of education have been postponing marriage, but less-educated women have postponed childbearing less than better-educated women have. The divorce rate in recent decades appears to have held steady or risen for women without a college education but fallen for college-edu-

The divorce rate in recent decades appears to have held steady or risen for women without a college education but fallen for college-educated women.

cated women.[19] As a result, differences in family structure according to social class are much more pronounced than they were fifty years ago.

Consider the share of mothers who are unmarried. Throughout the past half-century, single motherhood has been more common among women with less education than among well-educated women. But the gap has grown over time. In 1960, 14 percent of mothers in the bottom quarter of the educational distribution were unmarried, as against 4.5 percent of mothers in the top quarter—a difference of 9.5 percentage points. By 2000, the corresponding figures were 43 percent for the less-educated mothers and 7 percent for the more educated—a gap of 36 percentage points.[20] Sara McLanahan argues that societal changes such as greater opportunities for women in the labor market, a resurgence of feminist ideology, and the advent of effective birth control have

encouraged women to invest in education and careers. Those who make these investments tend to delay childbearing and marriage, and they are more attractive in the marriage market.[21] Put another way, women at the top and bottom of the educational distribution may be evolving different reproductive strategies. Among the less educated, early childbearing outside of marriage has become more common, as the ideal of finding a stable marriage and then having children has weakened, whereas among the better educated, the strategy is to delay childbearing and marriage until after investing in schooling and careers.

One result of these developments has been growth in better-educated, dual-earner married-couple families. Since the 1970s these families have enjoyed much greater income growth than have breadwinner-homemaker families or single-parent families. What we see today, then, is a growing group of more fortunate children who tend to live with two parents whose incomes are adequate or ample and a growing group of less fortunate children who live with financially pressed single parents. Indeed, both groups at the extremes—the most and the least fortunate children—have been expanding over the past few decades, while the group of children in the middle has been shrinking.[22]

The family lives of African American children have also been diverging from those of white non-Hispanic children and, to a lesser extent, Hispanic children. African American family patterns were influenced by the institution of slavery, in which marriage was not legal, and perhaps by African cultural traditions, in which extended families had more influence and power compared with married couples. As a result, the proportion of African American children living with single parents has been greater than that of white children for a century or more.[23] Nevertheless, African American women married at an earlier age than did white women through the first half of the twentieth century.[24]

But since the 1960s, the decline of marriage as a social institution has been more pronounced among African Americans than among whites. The best recent estimates suggest that at current rates only about two-thirds of African American women would be expected ever to marry.[25] Correspondingly, the share of African American children born outside of marriage has risen to 69 percent.[26] In fact, about three-fifths of African American children may never live in a married-couple family while growing up, as against one-fifth of white children.[27] The greater role of extended kin in African American families may compensate for some of this difference, but the figures do suggest a strikingly reduced role of marriage among African Americans.

The family patterns of the Hispanic population are quite diverse. Mexican Americans have higher birth rates than all other major ethnic groups, and a greater share of Mexican American births than of African American births is to married women.[28] Moreover, Mexican American families are more likely to include extended kin.[29] Consequently, Mexican Americans have more marriage-based, multigenerational households than do African Americans. Puerto Ricans, the second largest Hispanic ethnic group and the most economically disadvantaged, have rates of nonmarital childbearing second only to African Americans.[30] But Puerto Ricans, like many Latin Americans, have a tradition of consensual unions, in which a man and woman live together as married but without approval of the church or a license from the

state. So it is likely that more Puerto Rican "single" mothers than African American single mothers are living with partners.

Explaining the Trends

Most analysts would agree that both economic and cultural forces have been driving the changes in American family life over the past half-century. Analysts disagree about the relative weight of the two, but I will assume that both have been important.

Economic Influences

Two changes in the U.S. labor market have had major implications for families.[31] First, demand for workers increased in the service sector, where women had gained a foothold earlier in the century while they were shut out of manufacturing jobs. The rising demand encouraged women to get more education and drew married women into the workforce—initially, those whose children were school-aged, and later, those with younger children. Single mothers had long worked, but in 1996 major welfare reform legislation further encouraged work by setting limits on how long a parent could receive public assistance. The increase in women's paid work, in turn, increased demand for child care services and greatly increased the number of children cared for outside their homes.

The second work-related development was the decline, starting in the 1970s, in job opportunities for men without a college education. The flip side of the growth of the service sector was the decline in manufacturing. As factory jobs moved overseas and industrial productivity increased through automated equipment and computer-based controls, demand fell for blue-collar jobs that high school–educated men once took in hopes of supporting their families. As a result, average wages in these jobs fell. Even during the prosperous 1990s, the wages of men without a college degree hardly rose.[32] The decline in job opportunities had two effects. It decreased the attractiveness of non-college-educated men on the marriage market—made them less "marriageable" in William Julius Wilson's terms—and thus helped drive marriage rates down among the less well educated.[33] It also undermined the single-earner "family wage system" that had been the ideal in the first half of the twentieth century and increased the incentive for wives to take paying jobs.

Cultural Developments

But economic forces, important as they were, could not have caused all the changes in family life noted above. Declines in the availability of marriageable men, for example, were not large enough to account, alone, for falling marriage rates among African Americans.[34] Accompanying the economic changes was a broad cultural shift among Americans that eroded the norms both of marriage before childbearing and of stable, lifelong bonds after marriage.

Culturally, American marriage went through two broad transitions during the twentieth century. The first was described famously by sociologist Ernest Burgess as a change "from institution to companionship."[35] In institutional marriage, the family was held together by the forces of law, tradition, and religious belief. The husband was the unquestioned head of the household. Until the late nineteenth century, husband and wife became one legal person when they married—and that person was the husband. A wife could not sue in her own name, and her husband could dispose of her property as he wished. Until 1920 women could not vote; rather, it was assumed that almost all women would marry and that their husbands' votes would

represent their views. But as the forces of law and tradition weakened in the early decades of the twentieth century, the newer, companionate marriage arose. It was founded on the importance of the emotional ties between wife and husband—their companionship, friendship, and romantic love. Spouses drew satisfaction from performing the social roles of breadwinner, homemaker, and parent. After World War II, the spouses in companionate marriages, much to everyone's surprise, produced the baby boom: they had more children per family than any other generation in the twentieth century. The typical age at marriage fell to its lowest point since at least the late nineteenth century, and the share of all people who ever married rose. The decade of the 1950s was the high point of the breadwinner-homemaker, two-, three-, or even four-child family.

Starting around 1960, marriage went through a second transition. The typical age at marriage returned to, and then exceeded, the high levels of the early 1900s. Many young adults stayed single into their mid- to late twenties or even their thirties, some completing college educations and starting careers. Most women continued working for pay after they married. Cohabitation outside marriage became much more acceptable. Childbearing outside marriage became less stigmatized. The birth rate resumed its long decline and sank to an all-time low. Divorce rates rose to unprecedented levels. Same-sex partnerships found greater acceptance as well.

During this transition, companionate marriage waned as a cultural ideal. On the rise were forms of family life that Burgess had not foreseen, particularly marriages in which both husband and wife worked outside the home and single-parent families that came into being through divorce or through childbearing outside marriage. The roles of wives and husbands became more flexible and open to negotiation. And a more individualistic perspective on the rewards of marriage took root. When people evaluated how satisfied they were with their marriages, they began to think more in terms of developing their own sense of self and less in terms of gaining satisfaction through building a family and playing the roles of spouse and parent. The result was a transition from the companionate marriage to what we might call the individualized marriage.[36]

The Current Context of Marriage

To be sure, the "companionate marriage" and the "individualized marriage" are what sociologists refer to as ideal types. In reality, the distinctions between the two are less sharp than I have drawn them. Many marriages, for example, still follow the companionate ideal. Nevertheless, as a result of the economic and cultural trends noted above, marriage now exists in a very different context than it did in the past. Today it is but one among many options available to adults choosing how to shape their personal lives. More forms of marriage and more alternatives to it are socially acceptable. One may fit marriage into life in many ways: by first living with a partner, or sequentially with several partners, without explicitly considering whether to marry; by having children with one's eventual spouse or with someone else before marrying; by (in some jurisdictions) marrying someone of the same gender and building a shared marital world with few guidelines to rely on. Within marriage, roles are more flexible and negotiable, although women still do more of the household work and childrearing.

The rewards that people seek through marriage and other close relationships have also shifted. Individuals aim for personal growth

and deeper intimacy through more open communication and mutually shared disclosures about feelings with their partners. They may insist on changes in a relationship that no longer provides them with individualized rewards. They are less likely than in the past to focus on the rewards gained by fulfilling socially valued roles such as the

Marriage now exists in a very different context than it did in the past. Today it is but one among many options available to adults choosing how to shape their personal lives.

good parent or the loyal and supportive spouse. As a result of this changing context, social norms about family and personal life count for less than they did during the heyday of companionate marriage and far less than during the era of institutional marriage. Instead, personal choice and self-development loom large in people's construction of their marital careers.

But if marriage is now optional, it remains highly valued. As the practical importance of marriage has declined, its symbolic importance has remained high and may even have increased.[37] At its height as an institution in the mid-twentieth century, marriage was almost required of anyone wishing to be considered a respectable adult. Having children outside marriage was stigmatized, and a person who remained single through adulthood was suspect. But as other lifestyle options became more feasible and acceptable, the need to be married diminished. Nevertheless, marriage remains the preferred option for most people. Now, however, it is not a step taken lightly or early in young adulthood. Being "ready" to marry may mean that a couple has lived together to test their compatibility, saved for a down payment on a house, or possibly had children to judge how well

Women of all classes value companionship in marriage: shared lives, joint childrearing, friendship, romantic love, respect, and fair treatment.

they parent together. Once the foundation of adult family life, marriage is now often the capstone.

Although some observers believe that a "culture of poverty" has diminished the value of marriage among poor Americans, research suggests that the poor, the near-poor, and the middle class conceive of marriage in similar terms. Although marriage rates are lower among the poor than among the middle class, marriage as an ideal remains strong for both groups. Ethnographic studies show that many low-income individuals subscribe to the capstone view of marriage. In a study of low-income families that I carried out with several collaborators, a twenty-seven-year-old mother told an ethnographer:[38]

> I was poor all my life and so was Reginald. When I got pregnant, we agreed we would marry some day in the future because we loved each other and wanted to

raise our child together. But we would not get married until we could afford to get a house and pay all the utility bills on time. I have this thing about utility bills. Our gas and electric got turned off all the time when we were growing up and we wanted to make sure that would not happen when we got married. That was our biggest worry. . . . We worked together and built up savings and then we got married. It's forever for us.

The poor, the near-poor, and the middle class also seem to view the emotional rewards of marriage in similar terms. Women of all classes value companionship in marriage: shared lives, joint childrearing, friendship, romantic love, respect, and fair treatment. For example, in a survey conducted in twenty-one cities, African Americans were as likely as non-Hispanic whites to rate highly the emotional benefits of marriage, such as friendship, sex life, leisure time, and a sense of security; and Hispanics rated these benefits somewhat higher than either group.[39] Moreover, in the "fragile families" study of unmarried low- and moderate-income couples who had just had a child together, Marcia Carlson, Sara McLanahan, and Paula England found that mothers and fathers who scored higher on a scale of relationship supportiveness were substantially more likely to be married one year later.[40] Among the items in the scale were whether the partner "is fair and willing to compromise" during a disagreement, "expresses affection or love," "encourages or helps," and does not insult or criticize. In a 2001 national survey of young adults aged twenty to twenty-nine conducted by the Gallup Organization for the National Marriage Project, 94 percent of never-married respondents agreed that "when you marry, you want your spouse to be your soul mate, first and foremost." Only 16 percent

Figure 3. Total First Marriage Rates of Women, Selected European and English-Speaking Countries, 1990

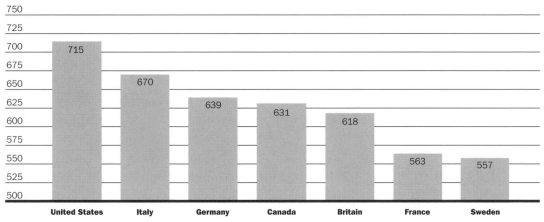

Marriages per 1,000 women

Sources: Alain Monnier and Catherine de Guibert-Lantoine, "The Demographic Situation of Europe and Developed Countries Overseas: An Annual Report," *Population; An English Selection* 8 (1996): 235–50; U.S. National Center for Health Statistics, "Advance Report of Final Marriage Statistics, 1989 and 1990," *Monthly Vital Statistics Report* 43, no. 12, supp. (Government Printing Office, 1995).

agreed that "the main purpose of marriage these days is to have children."[41]

As debates over same-sex marriage illustrate, marriage is also highly valued by lesbians and gay men. In 2003 the Massachusetts Supreme Court struck down a state law limiting marriage to opposite-sex couples, and same-sex marriage became legal in May 2004 (although opponents may eventually succeed in prohibiting it through a state constitutional amendment). Advocates for same-sex marriage argued that gay and lesbian couples should be entitled to marry so that they can benefit from the legal rights and protections that marriage brings. But the Massachusetts debate also showed the symbolic value of marriage. In response to the court's decision, the state legislature crafted a plan to enact civil unions for same-sex couples. These legally recognized unions would have given same-sex couples most of the legal benefits of marriage but would have withheld the status of being married. The court rejected this remedy, arguing that allowing civil unions but not mar-

riage would create a "stigma of exclusion," because it would deny to same-sex couples "a status that is specially recognized in society and has significant social and other advantages." That the legislature was willing to provide legal benefits was not sufficient for the judges, nor for gay and lesbian activists, who rejected civil unions as second-class citizenship. Nor would it be enough for mainstream Americans, most of whom are still attached to marriage as a specially recognized status.

Putting U.S. Marriage in International Perspective

How does the place of marriage in the family system in the United States compare with its place in the family systems of other developed nations? It turns out that marriage in the United States is quite distinctive.

A Greater Attachment to Marriage

Marriage is more prevalent in the United States than in nearly all other developed Western nations. Figure 3 shows the total first marriage rate for women in the United

States and in six other developed nations in 1990. (Shortly after 1990, the U.S. government stopped collecting all the information necessary to calculate this rate.) The total first marriage rate provides an estimate of the proportion of women who will ever marry.[42] It must be interpreted carefully because it yields estimates that are too low if calculated at a time when women are postponing marriage until older ages, as they were in 1990 in

Not only is marriage stronger demographically in the United States than in other developed countries, it also seems stronger as an ideal.

most countries. Thus, all the estimates in figure 3 are probably too low. Nevertheless, the total first marriage rate is useful in comparing countries at a given time point, and I have selected the nations in figure 3 to illustrate the variation in this rate in the developed world. The value of 715 for the United States—the highest of any country—implies that 715 out of 1,000 women were expected to marry. Italy had a relatively high value, while France and Sweden had the lowest. In between were Britain, Canada, and Germany.

Not only is marriage stronger demographically in the United States than in other developed countries, it also seems stronger as an ideal. In the World Values Surveys conducted between 1999 and 2001, one question asked of adults was whether they agreed with the statement, "Marriage is an outdated institution." Only 10 percent of Americans agreed—a lower share than in any developed nation except Iceland. Twenty-two percent of Canadians agreed, as did 26 percent of the British, and 36 percent of the French.[43] Americans seem more attached to marriage as a norm than do citizens in other developed countries.

This greater attachment to marriage has a long history. As Alexis de Tocqueville wrote in the 1830s, "There is certainly no country in the world where the tie of marriage is more respected than in America or where conjugal happiness is more highly or worthily appreciated."[44] Historian Nancy Cott has argued that the nation's founders viewed Christian marriage as one of the building blocks of American democracy. The marriage-based family was seen as a mini-republic in which the husband governed with the consent of the wife.[45] The U.S. government has long justified laws and policies that support marriage. In 1888, Supreme Court Justice Stephen Field wrote, "marriage, as creating the most important relation in life, as having more to do with the morals and civilization of a people than any other institution, has always been subject to the control of the legislature."[46]

The conspicuous historical exception to government support for marriage was the institution of slavery, under which legal marriage was prohibited. Many slaves nevertheless married informally, often using public rituals such as jumping over a broomstick.[47] Some scholars also think that slaves may have retained the kinship patterns of West Africa, where marriage was more a process that unfolded over time in front of the community than a single event.[48] The prospective husband's family, for example, might wait until the prospective wife bore a child to finalize the marriage.

The distinctiveness of marriage in the United States is also probably related to greater religious participation. Tocqueville observed, "there is no country in the world where the Christian religion retains a greater influence over the souls of men than in America."[49] That statement is still true with respect to the developed nations today: religious vitality is greatest in the United States.[50] For instance, in the World Values Surveys, 60 percent of Americans reported attending religious services at least monthly, as against 36 percent of Canadians, 19 percent of the British, and 12 percent of the French.[51] Americans look to religious institutions for guidance on marriage and family life more than do the citizens of most Western countries. Sixty-one percent of Americans agreed with the statement, "Generally speaking, do you think that the churches in your country are giving adequate answers to the problems of family life?" Only 48 percent of Canadians, 30 percent of the British, and 28 percent of the French agreed.[52]

Moreover, family policies in many European nations have long promoted births, whereas American policies generally have not. This emphasis on pronatalism has been especially prominent in France, where the birth rate began to decline in the 1830s, decades before it did in most other European nations.[53] Since then, the French government has been concerned about losing ground in population size to potential adversaries such as Germany.[54] (The Germans felt a similar concern, which peaked in the Nazis' pronatalist policies of the 1930s and early 1940s.)[55] As a result, argues one historian, French family policy has followed a "parental logic" that places a high priority on supporting parents with young children—even working wives and single parents.[56] These policies have included family allowances prorated by the number of children, maternity insurance, and maternity leave with partial wage replacement. In contrast, policies in Britain and the United States followed a "male breadwinner logic" of supporting married couples in which the husband worked outside the home and the wife did not.[57] Pronatalist pressure has never been strong in the United States, even though the decline in the U.S. birth rate started in the early 1800s, because of the nation's openness to increasing its population through immigration.

More Transitions Into and Out of Marriage

In addition to its high rate of marriage, the United States has one of the highest rates of divorce of any developed nation. Figure 4 displays the total divorce rate in 1990 for the countries shown in figure 3. The total divorce rate, which provides an estimate of the number of marriages that would end in divorce, has limits similar to those of the total marriage rate but is likewise useful in international comparisons.[58] Figure 4 shows that the United States had a total divorce rate of 517 divorces per 1,000 marriages, with just over half of all marriages ending in divorce. Sweden had the second highest total divorce rate, and other Scandinavian countries had similar levels. The English-speaking countries of Britain and Canada were next, followed by France and Germany. Italy had a very low level of predicted divorce.

Both entry into and exit from marriage are indicators of what Robert Schoen has called a country's "marriage metabolism": the number of marriage- and divorce-related transitions that adults and their children undergo.[59] Figure 5, which presents the sum of the total first marriage rate and the total divorce rate, shows that the United States has by far the highest marriage metabolism of any of the developed countries in question.[60] Italy, despite its high marriage rate, has the lowest metabolism because of its very low divorce rate. Sweden, despite its high divorce rate,

Figure 4. Total Divorce Rates, Selected European and English-Speaking Countries, 1990

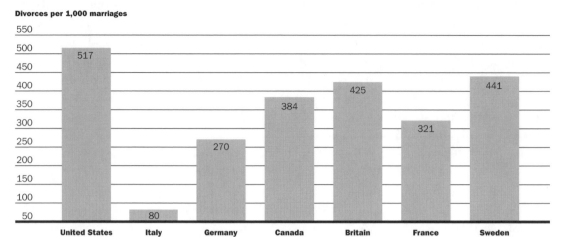

Divorces per 1,000 marriages

United States	517
Italy	80
Germany	270
Canada	384
Britain	425
France	321
Sweden	441

Sources: Monnier and de Guibert-Lantoine, "The Demographic Situation of Europe and the Developed Countries Overseas" (see figure 3); U.S. National Center for Health Statistics, "Advance Report of Final Divorce Statistics, 1989 and 1990," *Monthly Vital Statistics Report* 43, no. 9, supp. (Government Printing Office, 1995).

has a lower metabolism than the United States because of its lower marriage rate. In other words, what makes the United States most distinctive is the combination of high marriage and high divorce rates—which implies that Americans typically experience more transitions into and out of marriages than do people in other countries.

A similar trend is evident in movement into and out of cohabiting unions. Whether in marriage or cohabitation, Americans appear to have far more transitions in their live-in relationships. According to surveys from the mid-1990s, 5 percent of women in Sweden had experienced three or more unions (marriages or cohabiting relationships) by age thirty-five. In the rest of Europe, the comparable figure was 1 to 3 percent.[61] But in the United States, according to a 1995 survey, 9 percent of women aged thirty-five had experienced three or more unions, nearly double the Swedish figure and far higher than that of other European nations.[62] By 2002, the U.S. figure had climbed to 12 percent.[63] No other comparable nation has such a high

level of multiple marital and cohabiting unions.

American children are thus more likely to experience multiple transitions in living arrangements than are children in Europe. Another study using the same comparative data from the mid-1990s reported that 12 percent of American children had lived in three or more parental partnerships by age fifteen, as against 3 percent of children in Sweden, which has the next highest figure.[64] As transitions out of partnerships occur, children experience a period of living in a single-parent family. And although American children, in general, are more likely to live in a single-parent family while growing up than are children elsewhere, the trend differs by social class. As Sara McLanahan shows in a comparison of children whose mothers have low or moderate levels of education, American children are much more likely than those in several European nations to have lived with a single mother by age fifteen. The cross-national difference is less pronounced among children whose mothers are highly educated.[65]

Figure 5. Marriage Metabolism, Selected European and English-Speaking Countries, 1990

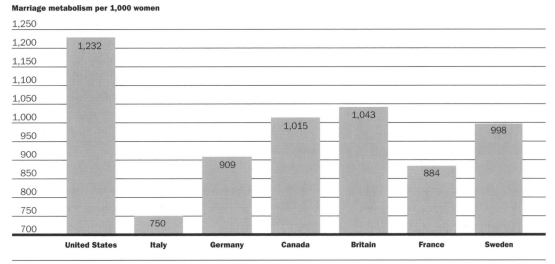

Marriage metabolism per 1,000 women

Sources: See figures 3 and 4.

Also contributing to the prevalence of single-parent families in the United States is the relatively large share of births to unmarried, noncohabiting women—about one in five.[66] In most other developed nations with numerous nonmarital births, a greater share of unmarried mothers lives with the fathers of their children. In fact, the increases in nonmarital births in Europe in recent decades largely reflect births to cohabiting couples rather than births to single parents.[67] As noted, the United States is seeing a similar trend toward births to cohabiting couples, but the practice is still less prevalent in the United States than in many European nations.

Greater Economic Inequality

Children in the United States experience greater inequality of economic well-being than children in most other developed nations. One recent study reported that the gap between the cash incomes of children's families in the lowest and highest 10 percent was larger in the United States than in twelve other developed countries.[68] The low ranking of the United States is attributable both to the higher share of births to single parents and to the higher share of divorce. But even when the comparison is restricted to children living in single-parent families, children in the United States have the lowest relative standard of living. For example, one comparative study reported that 60 percent of single-mother households in the United States were poor, as against 45 percent in Canada, 40 percent in the United Kingdom, 25 percent in France, 20 percent in Italy, and 5 percent in Sweden.[69] The differences are caused by variations both in the income earned by single parents and in the generosity of government cash transfers. In other words, having a high share of single-parent families predisposes the United States to have a higher poverty rate, but other countries compensate better for single parenthood through a combination of social welfare spending and supports for employed parents, such as child care.

More Controversy over Gay and Lesbian Partnerships

Other developed countries tend to be more open to gay and lesbian partnerships than is the United States. Two European nations, Belgium and the Netherlands, have legalized same-sex marriage. By 2005, courts in seven Canadian provinces had ruled that laws restricting marriage to opposite-sex couples were discriminatory, and the Canadian federal government had introduced a bill to legalize gay marriage nationwide. Many other developed nations, including all the Scandinavian countries and Germany, have amended their family laws to include legal recognition of same-sex partnerships.[70]

France enacted its somewhat different form of domestic partnership, the *pacte civil de solidarité* (PACS), in 1999. Originally conceived in response to the burden placed on gay couples by the AIDS epidemic, the 1999 legislation was not restricted to same-sex partnerships.[71] In fact, it is likely that more opposite-sex partners than same-sex partners have chosen this option.[72] The PACS does not provide all the legal benefits of marriage. It is a privately negotiated contract between two persons who are treated legally as individuals unless they have children. Even when they have children, the contract does not require one partner to support the other after a dissolution, and judges are reluctant to award joint custody. Moreover, individuals in a same-sex PACS do not have the right to adopt children or to use reproductive technology such as in vitro fertilization.

For the most part, the issue of marriage has been less prominent in European than in North American debates about same-sex partnerships. To this point, no serious movement for same-sex marriage has appeared in Britain.[73] The French debate, consistent with the nation's child-oriented social policies, has focused more on the kinship rights and relationships of the children of the partners than on whether the legal form of partnership should include marriage.[74] In 2004, the mayor of Bègles, France, created a furor—similar to that seen in the United States following the granting of marriage licenses in San Francisco—by marrying a gay couple. But marriage remains less central to the politics of same-sex partnerships in France and elsewhere in Europe than it is in North America.

Marriage Transformed

Marriage remains an important part of the American family system, even if its dominance has diminished. Sentiment in favor of marriage appears to be stronger in the United States than elsewhere in the developed world, and the share of adults who are likely to marry is higher—as is, however, their propensity to get divorced. Increasingly, gay and lesbian activists are arguing, with some success, that they, too, should be allowed to marry. Even poor and near-poor Americans, who are statistically less likely to marry, hold to marriage as an ideal. But the contemporary ideal differs from that of the past in two important ways.

The Contemporary Ideal

First, marriage is now more optional in the United States than it has ever been. Until recently, family formation rarely occurred outside of marriage. Now, to a greater extent than ever before, one can choose whether to have children on one's own, in a cohabiting relationship, or in a marriage. Poor and working-class Americans have radically separated the timing of childbearing and marriage, with many young adults having children many years before marrying. At current rates, perhaps one-third of African Americans will never marry. To be sure, some of the increase in seemingly single-parent families reflects a rise in the number of cohabiting couples who are having children, but these cohabiting relationships often prove unstable. How frequently the option of marriage becomes a reality depends heavily on one's race, ethnicity, or social class. African Americans and less well-educated Americans, for example, still value marriage highly but attain it less frequently than whites and better-educated Americans.

Second, the rewards of marriage today are more individualized. Being married is less a required adult role and more an individual achievement—a symbol of successful self-development. And couples are more prone to dissolve a marriage if their individualized rewards seem inadequate. Conversely, marriage is less centered on children. Today, married couples in the United States are having fewer children than couples have had at any time in the nation's history except during the Great Depression.

The changes in marriage, however, have not been solely cultural in origin. It is still the norm that a man must be able to provide a steady income to be seen as a good prospect for marriage. He no longer need earn all the family's income, but he must make a substantial, stable contribution. As the labor market position of young men without a college education has eroded, their attractiveness in the marriage market has declined. Many of their potential partners have chosen to have children outside marriage early in adulthood rather than to wait for the elusive promise of finding a spouse. Moreover, the introduction of the birth control pill and the legalization of abortion have allowed young women and men to become sexually active long before they think about marriage.

When the American family system is viewed in international perspective, it is most distinctive for the many transitions into and out of marital and cohabiting unions. Americans are more likely to experience multiple unions over the course of their lives than are Europeans. Moreover, cohabiting relationships in the United States still tend to be rather short, with a median duration (until either marriage or dissolution) of about one year. The median duration of cohabiting unions is about four years in Sweden and France and two or more years in most other European nations.[75] All this means that American children probably face greater instability in their living arrangements than children anywhere else in the developed world. Recent research has suggested that changes in family structure, regardless of the beginning and ending configurations, may cause problems for children.[76] Some of these apparent problems may reflect preexisting family difficulties, but some cause-and-effect association between instability and children's difficulties probably exists. If so, the increase in instability over the past decades is a worrisome trend that may not be receiving the attention it deserves.

Positive Developments

This is not to suggest that all the trends in marriage in America have been harmful to children. Those who live with two parents or with one well-educated parent may be doing better than comparable children a few decades ago. As noted, income growth has been greater in dual-career families, and divorce rates may have fallen among the college educated. In addition, the time spent with their parents by children in two-parent families has gone up, not down, and the comparable time spent by children with single parents has not changed, even though mothers' work outside the home has increased.[77] Working mothers appear to compensate for time spent outside the home by cutting back on housework and leisure—and, for those who are married, relying on modest but noticeable increases in husbands' housework—to preserve time with children.[78]

Meanwhile, the decline in fertility means that there are fewer children in the home to compete for their parents' attention. Middle-class parents engage in an intensive childrearing style that sociologist Annette Lareau calls "concerted cultivation": days filled with organized activities and parent-child discussions designed to enhance their children's talents, opinions, and skills.[79] While some social critics decry this parenting style, middle-class children gain skills that will be valuable to them in higher education and in the labor market. They learn how to communicate with professionals and other adults in positions of authority. They develop a confident style of interaction that Lareau calls "an emerging sense of entitlement," compared with "an emerging sense of constraint" among working-class and lower-class youth.

Marriage and Public Policy

Because marriage has been, and continues to be, stronger in the United States than in much of Europe, American social welfare policies have focused more on marriage than have those of many European countries. That emphasis continues. George W. Bush's administration advocates marriage-promotion programs as the most promising way to assist families. No European country has pursued a comparable policy initiative. Moreover, the issue of gay marriage has received more attention in the United States than in most of Europe. This greater emphasis on marriage in public policy reflects the history and culture of the United States. Policies that build on and support marriage are likely to be popular with American voters because they resonate with American values. Europe's more generous public spending on children, regardless of their parents' marital status, is rooted in concerns about low population growth that have never been strong in the United States. Such public spending on single-parent families also reflects the lesser influence of religion in Europe. So it is understandable that American policymakers wishing to generate support for new family policy initiatives might turn to marriage-based programs.

Yet the relatively high value placed on marriage in the United States coexists with an unmatched level of family instability and large numbers of single-parent families. This, too, is part of the American cultural heritage. The divorce rate appears to have been higher in the United States than in most of Europe since the mid-nineteenth century.[80]

This emblematic American pattern of high marriage and divorce rates, cohabiting unions of short duration, and childbearing among unpartnered women and men makes it unrealistic to think that policymakers will be able to reduce rates of multiple unions and of single parenthood in the United States to typical European levels. Consequently, a family policy that relies too heavily on marriage will not help the many children destined to live in single-parent and cohabiting-parent families—many of them economically disadvantaged—for some or all of their formative years. Only assistance directed to needy families, regardless of their household structure, will reach them. Such policies are less popular in the United States, as the widespread disdain for cash welfare and the popularity of the 1996 welfare reform legislation demonstrate. Moreover, some American policymakers worry that programs that support all parents without regard to partnership status may decrease people's incentive to marry.[81] The dilemma for policymakers is how to make the trade-off between marriage-based and marriage-neutral programs. A careful balance of both is needed to provide adequate support to American children.

Endnotes

1. W. C. Rodgers and A. Thornton, "Changing Patterns of First Marriage in the United States," *Demography* 22 (1985): 265–79; Joshua R. Goldstein and Catherine T. Kenney, "Marriage Delayed or Marriage Forgone? New Cohort Forecasts of First Marriage for U.S. Women," *American Sociological Review* 66 (2001): 506–19.

2. U.S. Bureau of the Census, "Percent of People 25 Years Old and Over Who Have Completed High School or College, by Race, Hispanic Origin and Sex: Selected Years 1940 to 2002," 2003, table A-2, www.census.gov/population/socdemo/education/tabA-2.pdf (accessed June 24, 2004).

3. Ibid.

4. U.S. National Center for Health Statistics, "Fertility, Family Planning, and Women's Health: New Data from the 1995 National Survey of Family Growth," *Vital and Health Statistics* 23, no. 19 (1997), available at www.cdc.gov/nchs/data/series/sr_23/sr23_019.pdf (accessed July 13, 2004).

5. Larry L. Bumpass and Hsien-Hen Lu, "Trends in Cohabitation and Implications for Children's Family Contexts in the United States," *Population Studies* 54 (2000): 29–41. They note that 49 percent of women aged thirty to thirty-four years old in the 1995 National Survey of Family Growth reported ever cohabiting.

6. U.S. National Center for Health Statistics, "Number and Percent of Births to Unmarried Women, by Race and Hispanic Origin: United States, 1940–99," *Vital Statistics of the United States, 1999*, vol. 1, *Natality*, table 1-17 (available at www.cdc.gov/nchs/data/statab/t991x17.pdf [accessed January 12, 2005]); and U.S. National Center for Health Statistics, "Births: Preliminary Data for 2002," *National Vital Statistics Report* 53, no. 9, www.cdc.gov/nchs/data/nvsr/nvsr53/nvsr53_09.pdf (accessed January 12, 2005). For 2003, the figures were 34.6 percent overall, 23.5 percent for non-Hispanic whites, 68.5 percent for non-Hispanic blacks, and 45 percent for Hispanics.

7. Ibid.

8. Marcia Carlson, Sara McLanahan, and Paula England, "Union Formation in Fragile Families," *Demography* 41 (2004): 237–61

9. Dan Black and others, "Demographics of the Gay and Lesbian Population in the United States: Evidence from Available Systematic Data," *Demography* 37 (2000): 139–54.

10. U.S. Bureau of the Census, "Married-Couple and Unmarried-Partner Households: 2000" (Government Printing Office, 2003).

11. Andrew Cherlin, *Marriage, Divorce, Remarriage* (Harvard University Press, 1992).

12. Matthew Bramlett and William D. Mosher, *Cohabitation, Marriage, Divorce and Remarriage in the United States*, series 22, no. 2 (U.S. National Center for Health Statistics, Vital and Health Statistics, 2002), available at www.cdc.gov/nchs/data/series/sr_23/sr23_022.pdf (accessed June 2003).

13. U.S. Bureau of the Census. "Detailed Living Arrangements of Children by Race and Hispanic Origin, 1996," 2001, www.census.gov/population/socdemo/child/p70–74/tab01.pdf (accessed June 28, 2004). The data are from the 1996 Survey of Income and Program Participation, wave 2.

14. Some of the one-parent families contain an unmarried cohabiting partner, whom the Census Bureau normally does not count as a "parent." According to the 1996 estimates cited in the previous note, about 2.5 percent of children live with a biological or adoptive parent who is cohabiting.

15. Lynne Casper and Suzanne M. Bianchi, *Continuity and Change in the American Family* (Thousand Oaks, Calif.: Sage, 2002).

16. David Ellwood and Christopher Jencks, "The Uneven Spread of Single-Parent Families: What Do We Know? Where Do We Look for Answers?" in *Social Inequality*, edited by Kathryn M. Neckerman (New York: Russell Sage Foundation, 2004), pp. 3–118.

17. Sara McLanahan, "Diverging Destinies: How Children Are Faring under the Second Demographic Transition," *Demography* 41 (2004): 607–27.

18. Ellwood and Jencks, "The Uneven Spread of Single-Parent Families" (see note 16).

19. Steven P. Martin, "Growing Evidence for a 'Divorce Divide'? Education and Marital Dissolution Rates in the U.S. since the 1970s," Working Paper on Social Dimensions of Inequality (New York: Russell Sage Foundation, 2004).

20. McLanahan, "Diverging Destinies" (see note 17).

21. Ibid.

22. Isabel Sawhill and Laura Chadwick, *Children in Cities: Uncertain Futures* (Brookings, 1999); and Donald J. Hernandez, *America's Children: Resources from Family, Government, and Economy* (New York: Russell Sage Foundation, 1993).

23. S. Philip Morgan and others, "Racial Differences in Household and Family Structure at the Turn of the Century," *American Journal of Sociology* 98 (1993): 798–828.

24. Cherlin, *Marriage, Divorce, Remarriage* (see note 11).

25. Goldstein and Kenney, "Marriage Delayed or Marriage Forgone?" (see note 1).

26. U.S. National Center for Health Statistics, "Births: Preliminary Data" (see note 6).

27. Bumpass and Lu, "Trends in Cohabitation" (see note 5).

28. U.S. National Center for Health Statistics, "Revised Birth and Fertility Rates for the 1990s and New Rates for the Hispanic Populations, 2000 and 2001: United States," *National Vital Statistics Reports* 51, no. 12 (Government Printing Office, 2003); and U.S. National Center for Health Statistics, "Births: Final Data for 2000," *National Vital Statistics Report* 50, no. 5 (Government Printing Office, 2002).

29. Frank D. Bean and Marta Tienda, *The Hispanic Population of the United States* (New York: Russell Sage Foundation, 1987).

30. U.S. National Center for Health Statistics, "Births: Final Data for 2000" (see note 28).

31. McLanahan, "Diverging Destinies" (see note 17).

32. Elise Richer and others, *Boom Times a Bust: Declining Employment among Less-Educated Young Men* (Washington: Center for Law and Social Policy, 2003); available at www.clasp.org/DMS/Documents/1058362464.08/Boom_Times.pdf (accessed July 13, 2004).

33. William J. Wilson, *The Truly Disadvantaged: The Inner City, the Underclass, and Public Policy* (University of Chicago Press, 1987).

34. Robert D. Mare and Christopher Winship, "Socioeconomic Change and the Decline in Marriage for Blacks and Whites," in *The Urban Underclass*, edited by Christopher Jencks and Paul Peterson (Brookings, 1991), pp. 175–202; and Daniel T. Lichter, Diane K. McLaughlin, and David C. Ribar, "Economic Restructuring and the Retreat from Marriage," *Social Science Research* 31 (2002): 230–56.

35. Ernest W. Burgess and Harvey J. Locke, *The Family: From Institution to Companionship* (New York: American Book Company, 1945).

36. Andrew J. Cherlin, "The Deinstitutionalization of American Marriage," *Journal of Marriage and the Family* 66 (2004): 848–61.

37. Ibid.

38. Linda Burton of Pennsylvania State University directed the ethnographic component of the study. For a general description, see Pamela Winston and others, "Welfare, Children, and Families: A Three-City Study Overview and Design," 1999, www.jhu.edu\~welfare\ overviewanddesign.pdf (accessed July 10, 2004).

39. M. Belinda Tucker, "Marital Values and Expectations in Context: Results from a 21-City Survey," in *The Ties That Bind: Perspectives on Marriage and Cohabitation*, edited by Linda J. Waite (New York: Aldine de Gruyter, 2000), pp. 166–87.

40. Carlson, McLanahan, and England, "Union Formation" (see note 8).

41. Barbara Dafoe Whitehead and David Popenoe, "Who Wants to Marry a Soul Mate?" in *The State of Our Unions, 2001*, The National Marriage Project, Rutgers University, pp. 6–16, 2001, available at marriage. rutgers.edu/Publications/SOOU/NMPAR2001.pdf (accessed February 12, 2004).

42. The estimate assumes that the age-specific marriage rates in the year of calculation (in this case, 1990) will remain unchanged in future years. Since this assumption is unrealistic, the total marriage rate is unlikely to predict the future accurately. But it does demonstrate the rate of marriage implied by current trends.

43. Ronald Inglehart and others, *Human Beliefs and Values: A Cross-Cultural Sourcebook Based on the 1999–2002 Values Surveys* (Mexico City: Siglo Veintiuno Editores, 2004).

44. Alexis de Tocqueville, *Democracy in America*, vol. 1 (New York: Knopf, Everyman's Library, 1994), p. 304.

45. Nancy Cott, *Public Vows: A History of Marriage and the Nation* (Harvard University Press, 2000).

46. Quoted in ibid., pp. 102–03.

47. Herbert G. Gutman, *The Black Family in Slavery and Freedom, 1750–1925* (New York: Pantheon, 1976).

48. Jacqueline Jones, *Labor of Love, Labor of Sorrow: Black Women and the Family from Slavery to the Present* (New York: Basic Books, 1985).

49. Tocqueville, *Democracy in America* (see note 44), p. 303.

50. Grace Davie, "Patterns of Religion in Western Europe: An Exceptional Case," in *The Blackwell Companion to the Sociology of Religion*, edited by Richard K. Fenn (Oxford: Blackwell, 2001), pp. 264–78; and Seymour Martin Lipset, "American Exceptionalism Reaffirmed," *Tocqueville Review* 10 (1990): 3–35.

51. Inglehart and others, *Human Beliefs and Values* (see note 43).

52. Ibid.

53. See the discussion in Ron J. Lesthaeghe, *The Decline of Belgian Fertility, 1800–1970* (Princeton University Press, 1977), p. 304.

54. Alisa Klaus, "Depopulation and Race Suicide: Maternalism and Pronatalist Ideologies in France and the United States," in *Mothers of a New World: Maternalist Politics and the Origins of the Welfare State*, edited by Seth Koven and Sonya Michel (New York: Routledge, 1993), pp. 188–212.

55. Paul Ginsborg, "The Family Politics of the Great Dictators," in *Family Life in the Twentieth Century*, edited by David I. Kertzer and Marzio Barbagli (Yale University Press, 2003), pp. 188–97.

56. Susan Pedersen, *Family, Dependence, and the Origins of the Welfare State: Britain and France, 1914–1945* (Cambridge University Press, 1993).

57. Ibid.

58. The total divorce rate is formed by summing duration-specific divorce rates prevalent in the year of observation—in this case, 1990. It therefore assumes that the duration-specific rates of 1990 will remain the same in future years. It shares the limits of the total marriage rate (see note 42).

59. Robert Schoen and Robin M. Weinick, "The Slowing Metabolism of Marriage: Figures from 1988 U.S. Marital Status Life Tables," *Demography* 39 (1993): 737–46. Schoen and Weinick used life table calculations to establish the marriage and divorce probabilities for American men and women. Unfortunately, only total marriage rates and total divorce rates are available for other countries. Consequently, I calculated a total divorce rate for the United States from published duration-specific divorce rates for 1990. I then summed the total first marriage rate and total divorce rate for the United States and the other countries displayed in figure 4. Although this procedure is not as accurate as using rates generated by life tables, the difference is unlikely to alter the relative positions of the countries in the figure.

60. Strictly speaking, I should use the total divorce rate for people in first marriages (as opposed to including people in remarriages), but the available data do not allow for that level of precision.

61. Alexia Fürnkranz-Prskawetz and others, "Pathways to Stepfamily Formation in Europe: Results from the FFS," *Demographic Research* 8 (2003): 107–49.

62. Author's calculation from the 1995 National Survey of Family Growth microdata file.

63. Author's calculation from the 2002 National Survey of Family Growth microdata file.

64. Patrick Heuveline, Jeffrey M. Timberlake, and Frank F. Furstenberg Jr., "Shifting Childrearing to Single Mothers: Results from 17 Western Countries," *Population and Development Review* 29 (2003): 47–71. The figures quoted appear in note 6.

65. McLanahan, "Diverging Destinies" (see note 17).

66. About one-third of all births are to unmarried mothers, and Bumpass and Lu report that about 60 percent of unmarried mothers in 1995 were not cohabiting (0.33 x 0.60 = 0.198). Bumpas and Lu, "Trends in Cohabitation" (see note 5).

67. Kathleen Kiernan, "European Perspectives on Nonmarital Childbearing," in *Out of Wedlock: Causes and Consequences of Nonmarital Fertility*, edited by Lawrence L. Wu and Barbara Wolfe (New York: Russell Sage Foundation, 2001), pp. 77–108.

68. Lars Osberg, Timothy M. Smeeding, and Jonathan Schwabish, "Income Distribution and Public Social Expenditure: Theories, Effects, and Evidence," in *Social Inequality*, edited by Kathryn M. Neckerman (New York: Russell Sage Foundation, 2004), pp. 821–59.

69. Poverty was defined as having a family income of less than half of the median income for all families. Bruce Bradbury and Markus Jäntti, "Child-Poverty across the Industrialized World: Evidence from the Luxembourg Income Study," in *Child Well-Being, Child Poverty and Child Policy in Modern Nations: What Do We Know?* edited by Koen Vleminckx and Timothy M. Smeeding (Bristol, England: Policy Press, 2000), pp. 11–32.

70. Marzio Barbagli and David I. Kertzer, "Introduction," and Paulo Ronfani, "Family Law in Europe," in *Family Life in the Twentieth Century*, edited by David I. Kertzer and Marzio Barbagli (Yale University Press, 2003), respectively, pp. xi–xliv and 114–51.

71. Claude Martin and Irène Théry, "The Pacs and Marriage and Cohabitation in France," *International Journal of Law, Policy and the Family* 15 (2001): 135–58.

72. Patrick Festy, "The 'Civil Solidarity Pact' (PACS) in France: An Impossible Evaluation," *Population et Sociétés*, no. 369 (2001): 1–4.

73. John Eekelaar, "The End of an Era?" *Journal of Family History* 28 (2003): 108–22.

74. Eric Fassin, "Same Sex, Different Politics: 'Gay Marriage' Debates in France and the United States," *Popular Culture* 13 (2001): 215–32.

75. Kathleen Kiernan, "Cohabitation in Western Europe," *Population Trends* 96 (Summer 1999): 25–32.

76. See, for example, Lawrence L. Wu and Brian C. Martinson, "Family Structure and the Risk of Premarital Birth," *American Sociological Review* 59 (1993): 210–32; Jake M. Najman and others, "Impact of Family Type and Family Quality on Child Behavior Problems: A Longitudinal Study," *Journal of the American Academy of Child and Adolescent Psychiatry* 36 (1997): 1357–65.

77. John F. Sandberg and Sandra D. Hofferth, "Changes in Children's Time with Parents, U.S. 1981–1997," *Demography* 38 (2001): 423–36.

78. Suzanne M. Bianchi, "Maternal Employment and Time with Children: Dramatic Change or Surprising Continuity?" *Demography* 37 (2000): 401–14.

79. Annette Lareau, *Unequal Childhoods: Class, Race, and Family Life* (University of California Press, 2003).

80. Gören Therborn, *Between Sex and Power: Family in the World, 1900–2000* (London: Routledge, 2004).

81. This proposition is similar to what David Ellwood has called the "assistance-family structure conundrum." David T. Ellwood, *Poor Support: Poverty and the American Family* (New York: Basic Books, 1988).

For Love *and* Money? The Impact of Family Structure on Family Income

Adam Thomas and Isabel Sawhill

Summary

What do the half-century decline in U.S. marriage and the attendant rise in single parenthood mean for the economic well-being of children, especially children living in single-parent families?

Adam Thomas and Isabel Sawhill show how differing living arrangements can be expected to affect families' economic well-being. Married-parent and cohabiting households, for example, can benefit from economies of scale and from having two adult earners. The availability of child support for single-parent families and the marriage penalties in the tax and transfer system reduce but rarely completely offset the economic benefits of marriage.

Consistent with these expectations, national data on family income show that across all races and for a variety of income measures, children in lone-parent families (single-parent households with no cohabiter) have less family income and are more likely to be poor than children in married-parent families. Cohabiting families are generally better off economically than lone-parent families, but considerably worse off than married-parent families.

Thomas and Sawhill acknowledge the possibility that the link between family structure and family resources may not be causal. But new research that simulates marriages between existing single mothers and unattached men with similar characteristics suggests that family structure does affect family resources and that child poverty rates would drop substantially if these mothers were to marry.

It does not necessarily follow, however, that policymakers ought to, or even can, do anything about family structure. Marriage is not an economic cure-all for the complex problem of child poverty. It would be a mistake for policymakers to focus on promoting marriage to the exclusion of encouraging and rewarding work or addressing problems such as early out-of-wedlock childbearing. Still, Thomas and Sawhill conclude that a continuation of recent declines in single parenthood, linked most recently to declines in teen and out-of-wedlock births, offers great promise for improving the economic welfare of U.S. children.

www.futureofchildren.org

Adam Thomas is a Ph.D. candidate at the John F. Kennedy School of Government, Harvard University. Isabel Sawhill is vice president and director of the Economic Studies program at the Brookings Institution and a senior editor of *The Future of Children*.

Adam Thomas and Isabel Sawhill

The American family has undergone considerable change over the past several decades. Between 1970 and 2002, the share of children living in two-parent families fell from 85 percent to 69 percent, while the share living in single-parent families more than doubled, from 11 percent to 27 percent. It is now estimated that more than half of all children in the United States will spend all or part of their childhoods in single-parent families.[1] Among such families, cohabitation—a single parent and his or her children living with an unmarried partner—has become increasingly common. About two-fifths of all children born in the early 1990s will spend at least some time in a cohabiting household.[2] Many analysts and policymakers view the decline in marriage and the attendant rise in single parenthood with concern because children in single-parent families tend to have substantially fewer financial resources and are more likely to be poor than children in married-parent families.[3]

Implicit in this concern is the belief that living arrangements affect children's economic well-being. But such a claim raises many questions. Have the decline in two-parent families and the increase in single-parent families increased poverty among children, or could poverty be a cause rather than a result of single parenthood? If policymakers could reverse the decline in marriage, what might be the economic effects of an increased marriage rate among low-income families with children? How does the increasing prevalence of cohabitation affect children's economic status? This article will take up these questions, examining evidence on the implications of changes in family structure for the incomes of families with children.

In general, our review suggests that increases in single parenthood have in fact reduced children's economic well-being. We also find that children in cohabiting households tend to fare better economically than those in lone-parent households (single-parent households with no cohabiter), but worse than those in married-parent households. We conclude that increases in marriage could be expected to improve children's economic prospects. But we also conclude that it would be a mistake for policymakers to focus on marriage to the exclusion of employment-based antipoverty strategies or of programs to address out-of-wedlock childbearing, especially among teens.

How Might Family Structure Affect Family Income?

Before turning our attention to the question of *whether* families' living arrangements affect their incomes, we first consider the reasons *why* one might expect them to do so. We focus here on economic effects; in another article in this volume, Paul Amato discusses the cognitive, social, and emotional effects of alternative living arrangements.

Potential Earning Power

One obvious reason why two-parent families might have relatively higher incomes is that they contain one more potential adult earner than single-parent families. But how often do both parents in a two-parent household work? Is it possible that marriage causes secondary earners to work fewer hours or to stop working entirely, thereby diminishing—or in some cases even completely offsetting—the potentially positive effects of marriage on family income? Many researchers have investigated the effects of marriage on work.

Although American women as a whole have increasingly joined the U.S. labor force over the past several decades, the group whose labor force participation rate has increased most rapidly is married women with children.[4] In more than 60 percent of marriages, both spouses now work, with the wife earning more than the husband in about a quarter of dual-earner couples. Although marriage historically has tended to reduce a couple's hours worked, usually the wife's, that effect has diminished over time. Today, it may largely be limited to groups that are relatively well-off, such as white women and wives whose husbands have high earnings.[5]

Child Support from an Absent Parent

How much worse off a single-parent household is than a married-parent household depends in part on how much economic help the absent parent gives in supporting the children. Formal child support payments are the most important source of such income.

In 2001, 59 percent of custodial parents had child support awards, but only 38 percent received any support from the absent parent.[6] The average amount received that year by families due child support was $3,160.[7] If a typical single mother were to marry a man with a minimum-wage job, and if that man contributed most of his $9,000 in annual after-tax income to the household, then the custodial parent would clearly be better off marrying than getting child support. So although child support payments improve the economic position of single-parent families relative to married couples, they are no substitute for marriage, because most noncustodial parents provide no support at all, and those who do generally provide limited amounts.

Nonetheless, it is worth emphasizing that to the extent child support collections increase over time, as they have in recent years, they will lower the relative economic gains to the

mother and her children associated with marrying the child's father. From the noncustodial parent's perspective, the reverse is true; the more a father is required to support his biological children whether he lives with them or not, the more likely he is to avoid having a child outside of marriage. In addition, once the child is born, the father is more likely to marry, or remain married to, the mother, because he will be required to support the family in any case. In the end, al-

---

Although child support can ameliorate the loss of income from a second parent, it is typically a small portion of that income and thus does not leave the family as well off as if the parents were married.

---

though child support can ameliorate the loss of income from a second parent, it is typically a small portion of that income and thus does not leave the family as well off as if the parents were married.

Economies of Scale

Another way in which marriage could make a family better off is through economies of scale. Some expenses—such as rent, for example—do not increase much when another adult joins the household. In 2003, the federal poverty threshold for a single-parent family with two children was $14,824, while the threshold for a two-parent family with two children was $18,660. According to this standard, adding a second adult to a family raises the income needed to escape poverty by less than $4,000. If marriage increases the income available to the family by more than $4,000, the family will, from an "income-to-needs" perspective, be better off.

Household Specialization

In his landmark 1981 work, *A Treatise on the Family*, Gary Becker set forth a model of household production suggesting that marriage has important implications for families' economic well-being. Efficient households, he wrote, "have a pronounced division of labor among members."[8] Becker's thesis was

> *Becker's thesis was that a household is most productive when one spouse specializes in "home production"; the other, in work outside the home.*

that a household is most productive when one spouse specializes in "home production"; the other, in work outside the home. As Becker notes, in the most common such division of labor, the wife specializes in domestic work, while the husband specializes in labor-market activities. A key implication of Becker's work (its potentially sexist aspects aside) is that marriage may make spouses more productive than their unmarried counterparts. Freed from the need to spend time caring for children or preparing meals, married men may be able to command relatively higher wages. In addition, once married, men may be more motivated to be good breadwinners.

Many studies have investigated the "wage premium" for married men. Robert Lerman finds that, after controlling for such characteristics as work experience and education, married men's weekly wages are between 16

and 35 percent higher than those of separated, divorced, and never-married men.[9] It is possible that married men have higher wages not because marriage enables or motivates them to earn more but because men with greater earning power, being more attractive marriage partners, are "selected" into marriage. Several studies reviewed by Lerman find that some of the wage difference—perhaps as much as half—can be attributed to such "selection," but that the rest is a direct effect of marriage.[10] Among the many studies reviewed by Lerman, a midpoint estimate would suggest that marriage directly raises the wages of men between 5 and 10 percent.

If Becker is correct that household specialization leads to a marriage premium, one would expect the premium to be declining because married women's work effort has been rising. And some analysts do indeed find evidence of such a decline.[11] Overall, however, it appears that marriage may still have some effect on men's wages, though precisely how large it is or how long it will last, given the increasing share of wives who work, is uncertain. Becker's theory would also suggest that wives who specialize in raising their children are better mothers than mothers who work. If that is true, these noneconomic benefits could be even more important than any income gained from having a second earner in the family. Reviewing the vast literature on the question of how maternal employment outside the home affects children is beyond the scope of this paper.[12] Suffice it to say that there is no clear evidence that, on average, such employment is deleterious to children. Opinions on this matter vary, however, and much depends on how many hours the mother works, the availability of good substitute care, the age of the children, and a variety of other factors.[13]

Marriage Penalties and Bonuses

The government tax and transfer system in the United States effectively imposes penalties on many married couples. Because federal tax rates are higher for families with relatively higher incomes and because couples' incomes are generally combined when their tax liability is calculated, a husband and wife may end up owing more in taxes together than they would if they were not married. Likewise, because means-tested government transfer programs generally lower benefits as income rises, adding a new spouse's earnings to a single-parent family's income may reduce the benefits available to that family.[14] Some couples, however, may experience a bonus after marrying. For example, when a mother on welfare marries a man with substantial earnings, he gains additional dependents and the advantages of income splitting, thereby reducing their joint tax liability.

The marriage penalties and bonuses in the tax and transfer system are treated in detail in the article by Adam Carasso and Eugene Steuerle in this volume. Among other things, they show that single-parent households receiving a wide variety of benefits, including housing subsidies, welfare benefits, and child care subsidies, could be made worse off if marriage pushes their incomes from $10,000 to about $40,000. Few households, however, receive all these benefits simultaneously. Although tax cut legislation in 2001 reduced the marriage penalties and increased the marriage bonuses facing many families, Carasso and Steuerle find that married couples still face penalties more often than bonuses from the combined tax and transfer system.

Cohabitation vs. Marriage

Thus far we have focused on how the living arrangements of married-parent and lone-parent households might affect their respective incomes. How does cohabitation fit into this discussion? Some of our conclusions about the economic effects of marriage would also seem to hold true for cohabiting families. For instance, the income of a cohabiter is sometimes taken into account in calculating certain means-tested benefits. However, cohabiters are less likely to report this income in practice, and the income of a cohabiter is not considered in determining tax liabilities. Thus, the penalties built into the tax and transfer system loom larger for married-parent families than for cohabiting families.

Like married-parent families, cohabiting families also benefit from economies of scale. Most important, they have two potential earners. Although the addition of a second potential earner to the household may be partly offset by the loss of certain means-tested benefits or of child support payments to the lone parent (but only if she cohabits with the child's biological father), the net economic benefits of cohabitation are almost always positive.

Because cohabitation does not signify the same degree of commitment as does marriage, and is in fact usually less durable, it produces less specialization. Any wage premium associated with cohabitation is thus likely to be smaller than that associated with marriage.[15] There is, however, a greater likelihood that both partners will work. The long-term commitment symbolized by a marriage vow ("'til death do us part") makes it likely that a stay-at-home wife will be more willing than a cohabiting single parent would be to give up a career to devote time to her children. Cohabiters are also less likely than married couples to pool resources, and they have less of a claim on each other's assets and fewer legal rights to various benefits. Some studies thus suggest that measures of family

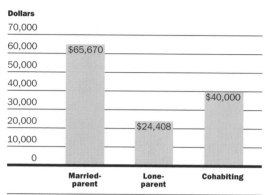

Figure 1. Median Official Incomes of Families with Children, 2003

Source: Authors' analysis of Current Population Survey, March 2004.

Figure 2. Median Adjusted per Capita Incomes of Families with Children, 2003

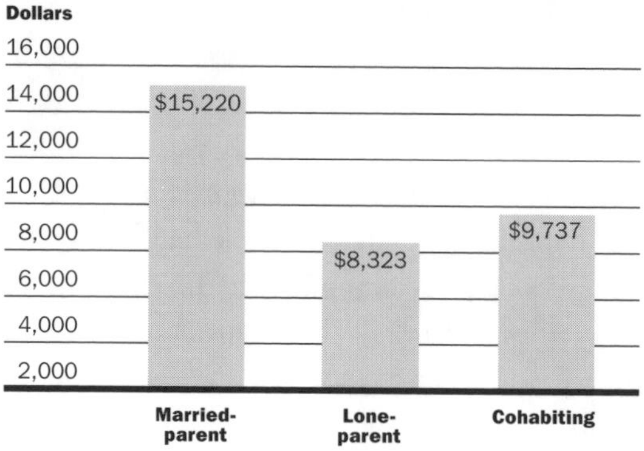

Source: Authors' analysis of Current Population Survey, March 2004.

income and child poverty that assume full income sharing among cohabiters overstate the resources available to children in some cohabiting households.[16]

Summary

Living in either a married-couple family or a cohabiting family should in theory produce greater economic gains than living in a single-parent family. Whether there should be any gains to marrying relative to cohabiting is less clear.

Because our interest is in the well-being of children, we have focused on the net gains to single-parent households when they enter into different living arrangements. But it should be noted that men who live with, or marry into, such families do not always gain—a fact that may partially explain the prevalence of single-parent families.

Family Structure and Family Income: A First Look

Figures 1 and 2 compare the incomes of single-parent families with those of married-parent and cohabiting families using two different measures of income. The first, which

we call "official income," reflects family income as reported by the Census Bureau. That official measure, however, does not take into account many factors that have important ramifications for families' economic well-being, including federal tax liabilities, earned income tax credit benefits, food stamp benefits, out-of-pocket work-related child care expenses, and family size. In figure 2, we therefore report results for a second measure, which we call "adjusted per capita income," that incorporates these factors.[17] We prefer the adjusted measure both because it paints a more accurate picture of the disposable resources available to the family and because it takes into account family size by dividing adjusted income by the total number of family members.[18]

The official and adjusted income measures tell roughly the same story, though household disparities are somewhat smaller when adjusted for family size. In both figures 1 and 2, the financial resources of married-parent families are substantially greater than those of lone-parent families. The median official income for lone-parent families is a little more than one-third that of married-parent

Table 1. Income and Poverty Measures for Families with Children, by Race and Ethnicity, 2003

Measure and family type	Total	White	Black	Hispanic
Per capita adjusted family income (dollars)				
Married-parent	15,220	17,240	12,051	8,342
Lone-parent	8,323	10,686	6,113	6,399
Cohabiting	9,737	11,313	9,162	7,388
Adjusted child poverty rate (percent)				
Married-parent	7.6	4.0	12.1	18.3
Lone-parent	34.0	21.7	45.6	41.6
Cohabiting	21.5	18.3	22.0	27.6

Source: Authors' analysis of Current Population Survey, March 2004.

families. The median adjusted per capita income of lone-parent families is about 55 percent of that of married-parent families. The median adjusted income of cohabiting families is slightly less than 65 percent of that of married-parent families.[19]

In table 1, we extend our exploration of the variation in adjusted per person income by family type by looking at race and ethnicity. The top panel of the table shows that, as expected, blacks and Hispanics tend to have less adjusted family income per person than whites across all family types. Among blacks, the median lone-parent family has slightly more than half as much adjusted income as the median two-parent family, while a cohabiting family has about three-quarters as much adjusted income as the typical two-parent family. The results for whites are qualitatively similar, although the differences across family types are somewhat less dramatic than they are among blacks. Income differences are likewise smaller among Hispanics than they are among either whites or blacks.

The bottom panel of table 1 examines child poverty rates by race and family types, using our adjusted measure of income. Child poverty rates vary considerably across races,

with children in white families much less likely to be poor than their black and Hispanic counterparts. Within each race, child poverty rates are substantially higher among lone-parent families than among married-parent families. Child poverty is less common among cohabiting families than among lone-parent families, but more common than it is among married-parent families. As a whole, children in lone-parent families are more than four times as likely to be poor as children in married-parent families, while children in cohabiting families are almost three times as likely to be poor as children in married-parent families.

Overall, these findings paint a consistent picture: children in lone-parent and cohabiting households tend to have fewer economic resources available to them, and are more likely to be poor, than children in married-parent families. Children in cohabiting households tend to be better off economically than children in lone-parent households. These findings apply for all races and across a variety of measures.

Do these findings necessarily mean that differences in family structure have *created* these economic disparities? Might it not be that the sorts of people who are most likely to divorce or have children out of wedlock are also the sorts of people who are most likely to have limited incomes, regardless of their living arrangements? Could it be that economic distress helps to bring about marital dissolution? If the answers to such questions are yes, then one would expect to see a correlation between family structure and family economic well-being, even if the former had no effect on the latter.

Does Marriage Reduce Child Poverty and Increase Family Income? A Closer Look at the Evidence

Earlier, we described a host of different ways in which particular living arrangements might affect families' economic resources. We concluded that marriage, especially, and cohabitation, to a lesser extent, produce economic benefits for children. We then presented data showing that the incomes of the three groups tracked our expectations. But we have not shown that a particular living arrangement affects income. As we noted earlier, even if family composition itself had no real effect on income, the incomes and poverty rates of married-parent, cohabiting, and lone-parent families might differ widely because of "selection." Perhaps those people with the most economic resources are the most likely to marry, those with relatively limited resources are the most likely to cohabit, and those with the fewest resources are the most likely to become lone parents.

In light of this problem, how can one be certain whether family structure is helping to drive the differences in the incomes of married-parent, cohabiting, and lone-parent families? The short answer is that we cannot be absolutely sure. But researchers have tried to account for the phenomenon of selection,

and their findings generally suggest that living arrangements do have an impact on families' incomes. In the following sections, we review this evidence by summarizing studies that have estimated the economic consequences of divorce, of out-of-wedlock childbearing, and of marriage.

The Estimated Effects of Divorce

In their 1994 book, *Growing Up with a Single Parent*, Sara McLanahan and Gary Sandefur chart income changes in stable and unstable families during a child's adolescence (a family is "unstable" if parents divorce or separate during that time). McLanahan and Sandefur find that among whites, the incomes of stable families increased from an average of $61,559 when the child was twelve to an average of $66,696 when the child was seventeen, while the incomes of unstable families dropped from an average of $62,367 when the child was twelve to an average of $36,662 when the child was seventeen.[20] Among blacks, the incomes of stable families increased from an average of $39,040 when the child was twelve to an average of $40,934 when the child was seventeen, while the incomes of unstable families fell from an average of $28,197 when the child was twelve to an average of $18,894 when the child was seventeen.

The large difference in the average initial incomes of the stable and unstable black families makes it difficult to interpret the income data on black families. Perhaps there were systematic differences between families that this analysis did not capture. Given the substantially lower average initial income level of the unstable black families, it is difficult to rule out the possibility that economic distress actually *induced* marital disruption for many of these families. But for white families, the similarity between the two groups' initial incomes and the magnitude of the difference in their later incomes are rather striking.[21] Thus, we are more confident about the generalizability of these findings for whites than for blacks.

The Estimated Effects of Out-of-Wedlock Childbearing

During the 1960s and 1970s, most of the rise in single parenthood was related to divorce. But over the past quarter-century, by far the most important cause of the rise in single-parent families has been out-of-wedlock childbearing.[22] A large body of evidence demonstrates that children born to unmarried mothers are more likely to be poor than are other children.[23] Some studies have attempted to control for the possibility that these mothers would have been poor regardless of whether they had had a child outside marriage. For instance, one group of researchers finds that even after controlling for race, family background, age, education, and employment status, women who have had a child out of wedlock are between 2 and 2.7 times more likely to be poor than other women.[24]

Over the past decade the growth in the share of children born outside marriage has slowed dramatically, in part because of a sharp decline in teen pregnancy and birth rates. Births per 1,000 teens aged fifteen to nineteen fell from 61.8 in 1991 to 41.7 in 2003. This decline has substantially reduced the number of children living in poor single-parent families. One recent study finds that the number of poor children would have increased by almost half a million and the 2002 poverty rate for children under six would have been nearly a full percentage point higher had teen birth rates not declined.[25]

The Estimated Effects of Marriage

Other studies have assessed the extent to which the decline in marriage and the spread of single parenthood over time have contributed to the growth of child poverty. Some of these studies use "shift-share techniques" to address questions of the following sort: "if the share of children living in single-parent families had remained constant since the 1960s, how would this have affected child poverty?" With some exceptions, these studies generally find that most, and in some cases all, of the increase in child poverty over the past thirty to forty years can be explained by changes in family structure.[26] Some of these studies, however, find that growing economic inequality and limited income growth can also explain an important portion of the increase in child poverty during this period. Indeed, John Iceland finds that the association between economic factors and child poverty has in fact been stronger than the association between family structure and child poverty over time. He concludes that this was particularly true during the 1990s, when he finds no significant association between family structure and child poverty.[27]

Moreover, to say that changes in living arrangements can *explain* poverty increases is not necessarily the same as saying that they *cause* these increases. Indeed, one could argue that it is unreasonable to assume, as most of these analyses implicitly do, that the poverty rates of two-parent families would remain the same if many single parents were to marry. In a study that addresses this issue by controlling for family attributes that might affect families' economic well-being, Robert Lerman finds that living in a married-parent family confers large economic benefits relative to living in a single-parent family and more modest but still significant benefits relative to living in a cohabiting family. In one analysis, he finds that living in a married-parent family raises needs-adjusted income by 65 percent relative to living in a lone-parent family and by 20 percent relative to living in a cohabiting household.[28]

Even if marriage has historically affected family income and child poverty, however, there is no guarantee that increasing the marriage rate today would reduce poverty and improve family incomes in the future. Indeed, William Julius Wilson has hypothesized that there are not enough suitable men to allow for large increases in marriage within low-income black communities.[29] And even if the marriage rate could be increased, the newly married families could differ from current and past married families in important ways that could make them more vulnerable to poverty. Several studies have therefore taken up the question of what would happen to the incomes and poverty rates of families with children if parents who are now single were to get married.

One such paper was published by Robert Lerman in 1996; we published another in 2002; and Wendy Sigle-Rushton and Sara McLanahan published a third in 2003.[30] All three simulate hypothetical marriages by "pairing up" single women and men in various large data sets and then estimate how these simulated marriages would affect family incomes and child poverty. One advantage of these studies is that they correct for much of the selection bias found in other studies by matching women with men who are deemed to be suitable partners and then counting only the actual income that these men have to bring into a combined household.[31] A second advantage is that because these analyses simulate marriages only for women for whom a potential husband can be identified, they address the critique that there are not enough "marriageable males" to allow for substantially more marriages to take place. A third advantage is that they sometimes adjust

for the loss of benefits and the higher taxes that result from marriage.[32] Thus, they provide some of the most powerful evidence to date of what could happen to the existing population if many single men and women were to marry. The methodologies and findings of these analyses are summarized in the box opposite.

Lerman used 1989 data and "married off" enough single mothers to return the marriage rate to that prevailing in 1971. His simulated increase in the marriage rate reduced the black child poverty rate in 1989 from 43.3 percent to 37.1 percent and the white child poverty rate from 11.7 percent to 9.8 percent. Among all children, the poverty rate fell from 17.1 percent to 14.7 percent. Among families participating in a simulated marriage, the new marriages pulled 43 percent of poor black children and 18 percent of poor white children out of poverty. Lerman also found that the simulation reduced income inequality among children by 26 percent.[33]

Our analysis was similar to Lerman's, although we used more recent data (1998) and replicated marriage patterns prevailing in 1970. We also made postmarriage adjustments to a wider range of benefits and taxes.[34] Like Lerman, we found that raising the marriage rate would reduce child poverty considerably. In our simulation, the 1998 child poverty rate fell from 16.9 percent to 13.5 percent. Among families participating in the simulation, marriage reduced the number of poor children by 65.4 percent while raising average per capita income by 43.2 percent and the average income-to-needs ratio by 57.9 percent.[35]

Neither Lerman's simulation nor our initial analysis dealt with the issue of cohabitation. But we conducted a sensitivity analysis that

Summary of Marriage Simulation Studies

Lerman (1996)

Data: Current Population Survey, March 1972 and March 1990.

Goal: Set the proportion of mothers who were single in 1989 equal to the corresponding portion in 1971.

Family income adjustments: Single mothers lose welfare benefits after marriage. In some analyses, men's and women's postmarriage earnings are adjusted.

Key findings

Family income: Depending on the assumptions about men's and women's earnings responses to marriage, income inequality among children is reduced by between 24 and 46 percent as a result of the simulation.

Poverty: Assuming no changes in earnings, the black child poverty rate falls from 43.3 to 37.1 percent and the white child poverty rate falls from 11.7 to 9.8 percent. If one assumes typical postmarriage earnings responses, the simulation's antipoverty effects are larger.

Thomas and Sawhill (2002)

Data: Current Population Survey, March 1999.

Goal: Set the proportion of children in female-headed families in 1998 equal to the corresponding proportion in 1970.

Family income adjustments: Tax liabilities, child care expenses, food stamps, earned income tax credit benefits, SSI benefits, and cash-assistance welfare benefits are recalculated after marriage. Men's and women's earnings are assumed to remain unchanged after marriage.

Key findings

Family income: Average per capita family income increases by 43.2 percent and average income-to-needs ratio (see note 35) increases by 57.9 percent among children whose mothers participate in the simulation.

Poverty: Overall adjusted child poverty rate falls from 16.9 to 13.5 percent as a result of the simulation. This result is robust to sensitivity tests in which the implications of cohabitation are considered. Among families participating in the simulation, the child poverty rate drops from 37.8 to 13.1 percent. Antipoverty effects are about a third larger for white children than for black children.

Sigle-Rushton and McLanahan (2003)

Data: Fragile Families and Child Well-Being Survey.

Goal: Simulate marriages between unwed mothers and the fathers of their children.

Family income adjustments: Postmarriage income is calculated by combining the self-reported earnings of both parents (because earnings information was recorded in bands, a midpoint estimate was used).

Key findings

Family income: Median family earnings of the lowest-earning women in the simulation increase from $0 to $8,250. Among unwed women who are slightly better off initially, median family earnings increase from about $2,000 to about $17,500.

Poverty: Poverty rate among mothers participating in the simulation falls from 86 to 46 percent. This reduction is calculated under the assumption that unmarried parents were not sharing any income before marriage. To the extent that this assumption is incorrect, the antipoverty effects of this simulation may be overstated.

Note: Studies are cited in note 30.

assumed that the incomes and poverty rates of all cohabiting families participating in the simulation would remain unchanged after marrying. In this second simulation, poverty fell almost as much as it did in the original analysis. Another implication of our simulation is that the "marriageable male" hypothesis holds some salience for blacks. The anti-poverty effects in our simulation were about a third lower for blacks than for whites because we were unable to identify well-

Cohabiting families are generally better off economically than lone-parent families, but they still tend to be considerably worse off than married-parent families.

matched mates for some single black mothers. On the whole, however, both black and white families experienced large reductions in child poverty and large gains in family income.

Sigle-Rushton and McLanahan simulated marriages between unwed parents participating in the Fragile Families and Child Well-Being Study. After combining the earnings of the unmarried parents in their data, they found that the new marriages pulled about 47 percent of the poor unwed mothers above the federal poverty line, although a larger share (about 53 percent) remained in poverty.[36] These findings, together with others in their study, led them to conclude that labor market policies that encourage and reward full-time work might be more cost-

effective for alleviating poverty than policies that promote marriage. Overall, however, Sigle-Rushton and McLanahan's simulation, like the others reviewed above, reduced child poverty dramatically among affected families.

Conclusions

Differing living arrangements can be expected to affect families' economic well-being for a variety of reasons. Most important, married and cohabiting families can benefit from economies of scale and from having two adult earners in the household. The availability of child support for single-parent families and the marriage penalties in the tax and transfer system reduce somewhat the economic benefits associated with marriage, but usually not enough to offset the gains from sharing expenses and having a second earner in the family. Consistent with these expectations, the data show that across all races and for a variety of income measures, children in lone-parent families have less family income and are more likely to be poor than children in married-parent families. Cohabiting families are generally better off economically than lone-parent families, but they still tend to be considerably worse off than married-parent families.

Interpreting these data is tricky. Researchers can never be sure, beyond all doubt, that x causes y. But most of the evidence suggests that single parenthood reduces children's economic prospects and that marriage improves them. Some evidence suggests that this conclusion is more likely to be true for white children than for black children, but it would be a mistake to conclude that black children do not gain at all.

One might ask why single parenthood remains so common among low-income populations if marriage confers relatively large economic benefits on single parents and their children. It bears reiteration that relationships are always two-way streets: marriage may be economically beneficial for mothers and their children, but what about for their potential husbands? A recent study finds that men generally have no financial gains when they cohabit or marry, which would seem to be a potentially important piece of this story.[37] Another obvious consideration is that innumerable noneconomic factors drive peoples' decisions about marriage (or at least, we hope they do).

A more fundamental puzzle appears in the ethnographic literature on single parenthood. Despite the consistent research findings of social scientists that married families have higher income than single-parent families, ethnographers sometimes report that single mothers tend to list as a primary reason for being unmarried their belief that marriage would not improve—and might in fact detract from—their economic well-being.[38] This suggests that many women may prefer a more stable (if somewhat lower) income than would be available to them if they were to marry. Another possibility is that these mothers may simply prefer to be independent and make their own decisions, even at the price of having less income.

A few final caveats are in order. First, although family structure may have important economic implications for families with children, it does not necessarily follow that policymakers ought to, or even can, do anything about it. The debate over marriage policy is a heated one, and we will not attempt to review it here. We would, however, suggest that the debate ought to be informed by the understanding that living arrangements have important implications for children's economic well-being. As for whether policymakers can do anything about family structure, the challenge of crafting policies that effectively influence trends in family formation is considerable, as several other articles in this volume make clear.

Finally, we would stress that it is possible to overstate the potentially ameliorative effects of marriage. In a 2003 analysis, for example, researchers found that among women who have had children out of wedlock, marriage only partially alleviates the economic predicament created by their unwed childbearing.[39] Moreover, there may be better weapons in the fight against poverty. Sigle-Rushton and McLanahan's conclusion that it may be more cost-effective to encourage and reward work than to entice unwed parents to marry highlights an important lesson. Although marriage is significant, it is not an economic cure-all for the complex problem of child poverty. It would be a mistake for policymakers to focus on marriage to the exclusion of pursuing labor-market strategies or addressing other critical problems such as early out-of-wedlock childbearing.

Fortunately, the news on this latter front is good. After rising for decades, the share of children living in single-parent families has fallen in recent years. This change in trajectory is a result of a drop in the divorce rate and, most important, a slowing in the spread of out-of-wedlock childbearing, led by a steep decline in teenage pregnancy.[40] In light of the findings reviewed in this article, we believe that these trends augur well for children's futures. Our reading of the evidence suggests that continued declines in single parenthood may portend even greater improvements in the economic welfare of children in the United States.

Endnotes

1. The cross-sectional estimates cited here are based on the authors' tabulations of data from U.S. Bureau of the Census, "Living Arrangements of Children under 18 Years Old: 1960 to Present," tables CH-1 to CH-3, September 2004, www.census.gov/population/socdemo/hh-fam/ (accessed September 19, 2003). The estimated childhood probability of living in a single-parent family was taken from U.S. House of Representatives, Committee on Ways and Means, *2000 Green Book: Background Material on Data and Programs within the Jurisdiction of the Committee on Ways and Means*, 106 Cong. 2 sess. See the article by Andrew Cherlin in this volume for a more detailed discussion of trends in family formation, both in the United States and abroad.

2. Larry Bumpass and Hsien-Hen Lu, "Trends in Cohabitation and Implications for Children's Family Contexts in the United States," *Population Studies* 54 (2000): 29–41.

3. Robert I. Lerman, "Marriage and the Economic Well-Being of Families with Children: A Review of the Literature," Working Paper (Washington: Urban Institute, July 2002); Sara McLanahan and Gary Sandefur, *Growing Up with a Single Parent: What Hurts, What Helps* (Harvard University Press, 1994); Linda J. Waite, "Does Marriage Matter?" *Demography* 32, no. 4 (1995): 483–506.

4. Daphne Spain and Suzanne M. Bianchi, *Balancing Act: Motherhood, Marriage, and Employment among American Women* (New York: Russell Sage Foundation, 1997).

5. For additional information, see Anne E. Winkler, "Earnings of Husbands and Wives in Dual-Earner Families," *Monthly Labor Review* 121, no. 4 (1998): 42–48; Audrey Light, "Gender Differences in the Marriage and Cohabitation Income Premium," *Demography* 41, no. 2 (2004): 263–84; Lee Lillard and Linda Waite, "Marriage, Divorce, and the Work and Earning Careers of Spouses," Working Paper 9906 (University of Michigan Retirement Research Center, April 2000); and Philip N. Cohen and Suzanne M. Bianchi, "Marriage, Children, and Women's Employment: What Do We Know?" *Monthly Labor Review* 122, no. 21 (1999): 22–31.

6. Data from Timothy S. Grall, "Custodial Mothers and Fathers and Their Child Support: 2001," Current Population Reports (U.S. Bureau of the Census, October 2003), table A.

7. U.S. Bureau of the Census, "Table 1. Child Support Payments Due and Actually Received, by Sex: 2001" (www.census.gov/hhes/www/childsupport/ chldsu01.pdf [October 29, 2004]). Calculation includes families that were due support but received none.

8. Gary Becker, *A Treatise on the Family* (Harvard University Press, 1991), p. 32.

9. Lerman, "Marriage and the Economic Well-Being" (see note 3).

10. McKinley Blackburn and Sanders Korenman, "The Declining Marital-Status Earnings Differential," *Journal of Population Economics* 7, no. 3 (1994): 247–70; Hyunbae Chun and Injae Lee, "Why Do Married Men Earn More: Productivity or Marriage Selection?" *Economic Inquiry* 39, no. 2 (2001): 307–19; Kermit Daniel, "The Marriage Premium," in *The Economics of Human Behavior*, edited by Mariano Tommasi and Kathryn Ierulli (Cambridge University Press, 1995), pp. 113–25; Sanders Korenman and David Neumark, "Does Marriage Really Make Men More Productive?" *Journal of Human Resources* 26, no. 2 (1991): 282–307.

11. Jeffrey S. Gray, "The Fall in Men's Returns to Marriage: Declining Productivity Effects or Changing Selection?" *Journal of Human Resources* 32, no. 2 (1997): 481–504.

12. Isabel V. Sawhill, "Families at Risk," in *Setting National Priorities: The 2000 Election and Beyond*, edited by Henry J. Aaron and Robert D. Reischauer (Brookings, 1999), pp. 97–135.

13. Jeanne Brooks-Gunn, Allison Sidle Fuligni, and Lisa J. Berlin, eds., *Early Childhood Development in the 21st Century: Profiles of Current Research* (Teachers College Press, 2003).

14. Further complications arise for two reasons. First, some programs discriminate more explicitly against two-parent families, for example, in the provision of welfare, housing, or child care subsidies. Second, many of these programs do not distinguish between cohabiting and married parents, but rather between lone parents and two-parent households. An important exception is the earned income tax credit.

15. On wage premiums, see Daniel, "The Marriage Premium" (see note 10); and Philip N. Cohen, "Racial-Ethnic and Gender Differences in Returns to Cohabitation and Marriage: Evidence from the Current Population Survey," Working Paper 35 (U.S. Bureau of the Census, Population Division, May 1999).

16. For instance, Anne E. Winkler finds that, in general, cohabiters tend not to pool income. Anne E. Winkler, "Economic Decision-Making by Cohabiters: Findings Regarding Income Pooling," *Applied Economics* 29, no. 8 (1997): 1079–90. In another study, Kurt J. Bauman explores the question of whether the source of household income affects the likelihood that families will experience material hardship. He finds that, holding household income constant, a family is more likely to experience hardship if some of its resources come from a cohabiter. Kurt J. Bauman, "Shifting Family Definitions: The Effect of Cohabitation and Other Nonfamily Household Relationships on Measures of Poverty," *Demography* 36, no. 3 (1999): 315–25. A more recent study, by Thomas DeLeire and Ariel Kalil, reinforces this conclusion. They find that cohabiters living with children spend a larger share of their incomes on alcohol and tobacco, and a smaller share on health care and education, than do married parents. See Thomas DeLeire and Ariel Kalil, "How Do Cohabiting Couples with Children Spend Their Money?" unpublished paper (University of Chicago, April 2002). Note that we make this same assumption when we estimate the incomes and poverty rates of cohabiting families in the next section of this paper. Our results might therefore reasonably be considered to be upper-bound estimates of the resources accessible to children in cohabiting households.

17. For additional information on our income-adjustment methodology, see Isabel Sawhill and Adam Thomas, "A Hand Up for the Bottom Third: Toward an Agenda for Low-Income Working Families," Working Paper (Brookings Institution Children's Roundtable, May 2001).

18. Although these income estimates adjust for family size, they ignore the economies of scale reaped by larger families. Because families with two adults have greater economies of scale available to them than do single-parent families, these estimates actually understate the economic advantages of marriage and cohabitation relative to single parenthood.

19. For cohabiting households, we add the income of the cohabiter to the income of the single-parent family. Likewise, in our analyses of poverty rates among cohabiting families, we adjust cohabiting families' poverty thresholds to reflect the presence of the cohabiter in the household (the Census Bureau ignores the presence of cohabiters when calculating family income and poverty thresholds). We adopt the Census Bureau's Adjusted POSSLQ method for identifying cohabiting households. A thorough discussion of this methodology can be found in Lynne M. Casper and Philip N. Cohen, "How Does POSSLQ Measure Up? Historical Estimates of Cohabitation," Working Paper 36 (U.S. Bureau of the Census, Population Division, May 1999).

20. McLanahan and Sandefur, *Growing Up* (see note 3).

21. The fact that the results are crisper for whites than for blacks is consistent with earlier work by Mary Jo Bane, who found that divorce leads to poverty much more often among whites than among blacks. See Mary Jo Bane, "Household Composition and Poverty," in *Fighting Poverty: What Works and What Doesn't*, edited by Sheldon H. Danziger and Daniel H. Weinberg (Harvard University Press, 1986), pp. 209–31. A number of other studies have taken up the question of whether divorce affects children's family incomes. These studies have drawn on a diverse assortment of methods and data sources. Unfortunately, though, most fail to report separate results for black and white families. In general, the thrust of these studies' findings is that divorce tends to reduce children's family incomes. See Lerman, "Marriage and the Economic Well-Being" (see note 3); Marianne Page and Ann Huff Stevens, "Will You Miss Me When I Am Gone? The Economic Consequences of Absent Parents," Working Paper 8786 (Cambridge, Mass.: National Bureau of Economic Research, July 2002); Pamela J. Smock, Wendy D. Manning, and Sanjiv Gupta, "The Effect of Marriage and Divorce on Women's Economic Well-Being," *American Sociological Review* 64, no. 6 (1999): 794–812.

22. David T. Ellwood and Christopher Jencks, "The Spread of Single Parent Families in the United States since 1960," Working Paper RWP04-008 (John F. Kennedy School of Government, Harvard University, June 2004).

23. Stephen G. Bronars and Jeff Grogger, "The Economic Consequences of Unwed Motherhood: Using Twin Births as a Natural Experiment," *American Economic Review* 85, no. 5 (1994): 1141–56; Daniel T. Lichter, Deborah Roemke Graefe, and J. Brian Brown, "Is Marriage a Panacea? Union Formation among Economically Disadvantaged Unwed Mothers," *Social Problems* 50, no. 1 (2003): 60–86; Isabel Sawhill, "Welfare Reform and Reducing Teen Pregnancy," *Public Interest*, no. 138 (2000): 40–51.

24. Lichter, Graefe, and Brown, "Is Marriage a Panacea?" (see note 23).

25. U.S. House of Representatives, Committee on Ways and Means, *Steep Decline in Teen Birth Rate Significantly Responsible for Reducing Child Poverty and Single-Parent Families*, Committee Issue Brief (April 23, 2004).

26. The following studies get somewhat different results, depending on the period investigated, the variables included in the analysis, the ordering of the variables, the data used, and the specifics of the methodology, but most find that family structure changes were associated with large changes in child poverty: Maria Cancian and Deborah Reed, "Changes in Family Structure: Implications for Poverty and Related Policy," in *Understanding Poverty in America: Progress and Problems*, edited by Sheldon Danziger and Robert Haveman (Harvard University Press and Russell Sage Foundation, 2001), pp. 69–96; Sheldon Danziger and Peter Gottschalk, *America Unequal* (New York: Russell Sage Foundation, 1995); David Eggebeen and Daniel Lichter, "Race, Family Structure, and Changing Poverty among American Children," *American Sociological Review* 56, no. 6 (1991): 801–17; Peter Gottschalk and Sheldon Danziger, "Family Structure, Family Size, and Family Income: Accounting for Changes in the Economic Well-Being of Children, 1968–1986," in *Uneven Tides: Rising Inequality in America*, edited by Sheldon Danziger and Peter Gottschalk (New York: Russell Sage Foundation, 1993), pp. 167–93; Robert I. Lerman, "The Impact of Changing U.S. Family Structure on Child Poverty and Income Inequality," *Economica* 63, no. 250 (1996): S119–S139; Sawhill, "Families at Risk" (see note 12). Some studies find that there is a considerably weaker correlation over time between family structure and *overall* poverty than between family structure and *child*

poverty. See, for instance: Sheldon Danziger and Peter Gottschalk, *Diverging Fortunes: Trends in Poverty and Inequality* (New York: Russell Sage Foundation, 2004); Danziger and Gottschalk, *America Unequal* (see above in this note); and John Iceland, "Why Poverty Remains High: The Role of Income Growth, Economic Inequality, and Changes in Family Structure, 1949–1999," *Demography* 40, no. 3 (2003): 499–519. Iceland's analysis covers a somewhat longer period than do the other studies cited above.

27. Some of the studies cited in the previous note incorporate changes in family income and economic inequality into their analyses. All find that these factors have had an important association with child poverty over time. See Danziger and Gottschalk, *America Unequal*; Danziger and Gottschalk, *Diverging Fortunes*; and Iceland, "Why Poverty Remains High" (all from note 26).

28. Robert I. Lerman, "Married and Unmarried Parenthood and Economic Well-Being: A Dynamic Analysis of a Recent Cohort," Working Paper (Washington: Urban Institute, July 2002).

29. William Julius Wilson, *The Truly Disadvantaged* (University of Chicago Press, 1987).

30. See Lerman, "The Impact of Changing U.S. Family Structure" (see note 26); Adam Thomas and Isabel Sawhill, "For Richer or for Poorer: Marriage as an Antipoverty Strategy," *Journal of Policy Analysis and Management* 21, no. 4 (2002): 587–99; Wendy Sigle-Rushton and Sara McLanahan, "For Richer or Poorer? Marriage as an Anti-Poverty Strategy in the United States," Working Paper 01-17-FF (Princeton University, Center for Research on Child Wellbeing, June 2003).

31. If the men whom the Census Bureau reports as living alone are actually cohabiting or paying child support that is not reported, these studies may overstate the resources available to a new family.

32. On the other hand, the figures reported here do not include a wage premium for married men (results from analyses incorporating the estimated effects of a wage premium are reported in the next endnote).

33. In some analyses, Lerman simulates wage changes after marriage, which in turn generates larger antipoverty effects. In these analyses, the black 1989 child poverty rate fell from 43.3 percent to 29.1 percent, the white 1989 child poverty rate fell from 11.7 percent to 9.6 percent, and the overall child poverty rate fell from 17.1 percent to 12.9 percent. Among families participating in a simulated marriage, 80 percent of poor black children and 67 percent of poor white children were pulled out of poverty as a result of the new marriages.

34. After a marriage is simulated, Lerman subtracts the mother's entire welfare benefit from the new family's income. In our study we recalculate a range of benefits—including food stamps, supplemental security income, cash assistance, and earned income tax credit amounts—using a somewhat more sophisticated set of procedures.

35. A family's income-to-needs ratio is calculated as its income divided by its poverty threshold. A ratio of less than one implies that a family is poor, while a ratio of two implies that a family's income is twice its poverty threshold, and so forth.

36. They also point out that many of the unwed parents in their data were already living together and were therefore presumably sharing at least some of their resources with each other before marrying, which suggests that the antipoverty effects of their marriage simulation may be overstated.

37. Audrey Light, "Gender Differences in the Marriage and Cohabitation Income Premium," Working Paper (Ohio State University, August 2003).

38. Kathryn Edin, "Few Good Men," *American Prospect* 11, no. 4 (2000): 26–31.

39. Lichter, Graefe, and Brown, "Is Marriage a Panacea?" (see note 23).

40. Ellwood and Jencks, "Spread of Single Parent Families" (see note 22); John S. Santelli and others, "Can Changes in Sexual Behaviors among High School Students Explain the Decline in Teen Pregnancy Rates in the 1990s?" *Journal of Adolescent Health* 35, no. 2 (2004): 80–90.

The Impact of Family Formation Change on the Cognitive, Social, and Emotional Well-Being of the Next Generation

Paul R. Amato

Summary

How have recent changes in U.S. family structure affected the cognitive, social, and emotional well-being of the nation's children? Paul Amato examines the effects of family formation on children and evaluates whether current marriage-promotion programs are likely to meet children's needs.

Amato begins by investigating how children in households with both biological parents differ from children in households with only one biological parent. He shows that children growing up with two continuously married parents are less likely to experience a wide range of cognitive, emotional, and social problems, not only during childhood but also in adulthood. Although it is not possible to demonstrate that family structure causes these differences, studies using a variety of sophisticated statistical methods suggest that this is the case.

Amato then asks what accounts for the differences between these two groups of children. He shows that compared with other children, those who grow up in stable, two-parent families have a higher standard of living, receive more effective parenting, experience more cooperative co-parenting, are emotionally closer to both parents, and are subjected to fewer stressful events and circumstances.

Finally, Amato assesses how current marriage-promotion policies will affect the well-being of children. He finds that interventions that increase the share of children who grow up with both parents would improve the overall well-being of U.S. children only modestly, because children's social or emotional problems have many causes, of which family structure is but one. But interventions that lower only modestly the overall *share* of U.S. children experiencing various problems could nevertheless lower substantially the *number* of children experiencing them. Even a small decline in percentages, when multiplied by the many children in the population, is a substantial social benefit.

www.futureofchildren.org

Paul R. Amato is professor of sociology at Pennsylvania State University.

Paul R. Amato

Perhaps the most profound change in the American family over the past four decades has been the decline in the share of children growing up in households with both biological parents. Because many social scientists, policymakers, and members of the general public believe that a two-parent household is the optimal setting for children's development, the decline in such households has generated widespread concern about the well-being of American children. This concern has generated interest among policymakers in programs and interventions to increase the share of children growing up in stable, two-parent families. Not everyone, however, agrees with these policies; many observers believe that it is either inappropriate, or futile, for government to attempt to affect children's family structures.

My goal in this article is to inform this debate by addressing three questions. First, how do children in households with only one biological parent differ in terms of their cognitive, social, and emotional well-being from children in households with both biological parents? Second, what accounts for the observed differences between these two groups of children? And finally, how might current policies to strengthen marriage, decrease divorce, and lower nonmarital fertility affect the well-being of children in the United States?

Research on the Effects of Family Structure on Children

The rise in the divorce rate during the 1960s and 1970s prompted social scientists to investigate how differing family structures affect children. Their research focus initially was on children of divorced parents, but it expanded to include out-of-wedlock children and those in other nontraditional family structures.

Parental Divorce

Early studies generally supported the assumption that children who experience parental divorce are prone to a variety of academic, behavioral, and emotional problems.[1] In 1971, psychologists Judith Wallerstein and Joan Kelly began an influential long-term study of 60 divorced families and 131 children. According to the authors, five years after divorce, one-third of the children were adjusting well and had good relationships with both parents. Another group of children (more than one-third of the sample) were clinically depressed, were doing poorly in school, had difficulty maintaining friendships, experienced chronic problems such as sleep disturbances, and continued to hope that their parents would reconcile.[2]

Despite these early findings, other studies in the 1970s challenged the dominant view that divorce is uniformly bad for children. For example, Mavis Hetherington and her colleagues studied 144 preschool children, half from recently divorced maternal-custody families and half from continuously married two-parent families. During the first year of the study, the children with divorced parents exhibited more behavioral and emotional problems than did the children with continuously married parents. Two years after divorce, however, children with divorced parents no longer exhibited an elevated number of problems (although a few difficulties lingered for boys). Despite this temporary improvement, a later wave of data collection revealed that the remarriage of the custodial mother was followed by additional problems among the children, especially daughters.[3]

Trying to make sense of this research literature can be frustrating, because the results of individual studies vary considerably: some suggest serious negative effects of divorce, others suggest modest effects, and yet others suggest no effects. Much of this inconsistency is due to variations across studies in the types of samples, the ages of the children, the outcomes examined, and the methods of analysis. To summarize general trends across such a large and varied body of research, social scientists use a technique known as meta-analysis. By calculating an effect size for each study (which reflects the difference between two groups expressed in a common metric), meta-analysis makes it possible to pool results across many studies and adjust for variations such as those noted.[4]

In 1991, Bruce Keith and I published the first meta-analysis dealing with the effects of divorce on children.[5] Our analysis summarized the results of ninety-three studies published in the 1960s, 1970s, and 1980s and confirmed that children with divorced parents are worse off than those with continuously married parents on measures of academic success (school grades, scores on standardized achievement tests), conduct (behavior problems, aggression), psychological well-being (depression, distress symptoms), self-esteem (positive feelings about oneself, perceptions of self-efficacy), and peer relations (number of close friends, social support from peers), on average. Moreover, children in divorced families tend to have weaker emotional bonds with mothers and fathers than do their peers in two-parent families. These results supported the conclusion that the rise in divorce had lowered the average level of child well-being.

Our meta-analysis also indicated, however, that the estimated effects of parental divorce on children's well-being are modest rather than strong. We concluded that these modest differences reflect widely varying experiences within both groups of children. Some children growing up with continuously married parents are exposed to stressful circumstances, such as poverty, serious conflict between parents, violence, inept parenting, and mental illness or substance abuse, that increase the risk of child maladjustment. Correspondingly, some children with divorced parents cope well, perhaps because their parents are able to separate amicably and engage in cooperative co-parenting following marital dissolution.

Children in divorced families tend to have weaker emotional bonds with mothers and fathers than do their peers in two-parent families.

In a more recent meta-analysis, based on sixty-seven studies conducted during the 1990s, I again found that children with divorced parents, on average, scored significantly lower on various measures of well-being than did children with continuously married parents.[6] As before, the differences between the two groups were modest rather than large. Nevertheless, the more recent meta-analyses revealed that children with divorced parents continued to have lower average levels of cognitive, social, and emotional well-being, even in a decade in which divorce had become common and widely accepted.

Other studies have shown that the differences in well-being between children with divorced and children with continuously married parents persist well into adulthood. For example, adults who experience parental divorce as a child have lower socioeconomic attainment, an increased risk of having a non-marital birth, weaker bonds with parents, lower psychological well-being, poorer marital quality, and an elevated risk of seeing their own marriage end in divorce.[7] Overall, the evidence is consistent that parental divorce during childhood is linked with a wide range of problems in adulthood.

Children Born outside Marriage

Children born outside marriage have been studied less frequently than have children of divorce. Nevertheless, like children with divorced parents, children who grow up with a single parent because they were born out of wedlock are more likely than children living with continuously married parents to experience a variety of cognitive, emotional, and behavioral problems. Specifically, compared with children who grow up in stable, two-parent families, children born outside marriage reach adulthood with less education, earn less income, have lower occupational status, are more likely to be idle (that is, not employed and not in school), are more likely to have a nonmarital birth (among daughters), have more troubled marriages, experience higher rates of divorce, and report more symptoms of depression.[8]

A few studies have compared children of unmarried single parents and divorced single parents. Despite some variation across studies, this research generally shows that the long-term risks for most problems are comparable in these two groups. For example, Sara McLanahan and Gary Sandefur, using the National Survey of Families and Households, found that 31 percent of youth with divorced parents dropped out of high school, compared with 37 percent of youth born outside marriage (the corresponding figure for youth with continuously married parents was 13 percent). Similarly, 33 percent of daughters with di-

vorced parents had a teen birth, compared with 37 percent of daughters born outside marriage (the corresponding figure for daughters with continuously married parents was 11 percent).[9] Other studies that have compared offspring in these two groups yield similar results with respect to occupational attainment, earned income, depression, and the risk of seeing one's own marriage end in divorce.[10]

Although it is sometimes assumed that children born to unwed mothers have little contact with their fathers, about 40 percent of unmarried mothers are living with the child's father at the time of birth.[11] If one-third of all children are born to unmarried parents, and if 40 percent of these parents are cohabiting, then about one out of every eight infants lives with two biological but unmarried parents. Structurally, these households are similar to households with two married parents. And young children are unlikely to be aware of their parents' marital status. Nevertheless, cohabiting parents tend to be more disadvantaged than married parents. They have less education, earn less income, report poorer relationship quality, and experience more mental health problems.[12] These considerations suggest that children living with cohabiting biological parents may be worse off, in some respects, than children living with two married biological parents.

Consistent with this assumption, Susan L. Brown found that children living with cohabiting biological parents, compared with children living with continuously married parents, had more behavioral problems, more emotional problems, and lower levels of school engagement (that is, caring about school and doing homework).[13] Parents' education, income, psychological well-being, and parenting stress explained most—but not all—of these differences. In other words, unmarried cohabiting parents, compared with married parents, had fewer years of education, earned less income, had lower levels of psychological well-being, and reported more stress in parenting. These factors, in turn, partly accounted for the elevated number of problems among their children.

The risk of relationship dissolution also is substantially higher for cohabiting couples with children than for married couples with children.[14] For example, the Fragile Families Study indicates that about one-fourth of cohabiting biological parents are no longer living together one year after the child's birth.[15] Another study of first births found that 31 percent of cohabiting couples had broken up after five years, as against 16 percent of married couples.[16] Growing up with two continuously cohabiting biological parents is rare. Using the 1999 National Survey of American Families, Brown found that only 1.5 percent of all children lived with two cohabiting parents at the time of the survey.[17] Similarly, an analysis of the 1995 Adolescent Health Study (Add Health) revealed that less than one-half of 1 percent of adolescents aged sixteen to eighteen had spent their entire childhoods living with two continuously cohabiting biological parents.[18]

Unresolved questions remain about children born to cohabiting parents who later marry. If cohabiting parents marry after the birth of a child, is the child at any greater risk than if the parents marry before having the child? Correspondingly, do children benefit when their cohabiting parents get married? To the extent that marriage increases union stability and binds fathers more strongly to their children, marriage among cohabiting parents may improve children's long-term well-being. Few studies, however, have addressed this issue.

Death of a Parent

Some children live with a single parent not because of divorce or because they were born outside marriage but because their other parent has died. Studies that compare children who experienced the death of a parent with children separated from a parent for other reasons yield mixed results. The Amato and Keith meta-analysis found that children who experienced a parent's death scored lower on

The risk of relationship dissolution also is substantially higher for cohabiting couples with children than for married couples with children.

several forms of well-being than did children living with continuously married parents. Children who experienced a parent's death, however, scored significantly *higher* on several measures of well-being than did children with divorced parents.[19] McLanahan and Sandefur found that children with a deceased parent were no more likely than children with continuously married parents to drop out of high school. Daughters with a deceased parent, however, were more likely than teenagers living with both parents to have a nonmarital birth.[20] Another study found that although adults whose parents divorced or never married during their childhood had lower levels of socioeconomic attainment than did adults who grew up with continuously married parents, adults who experienced the death of a parent as a child did not differ from those with two continuously married parents.[21] In contrast, Amato found that *all* causes of separation from a parent during childhood, including parental death, were linked with increased symptoms of depression in adulthood.[22] Although the research findings are mixed, these studies suggest that experiencing the death of a parent during childhood puts children at risk for a number of problems, but not as much as does divorce or out-of-wedlock birth.

Discordant Two-Parent Families

Most studies in this literature have compared children living with a single parent with a broad group of children living with continuously married parents. Some two-parent families, however, function better than others. Marriages marked by chronic, overt conflict and hostility are "intact" structurally but are not necessarily good environments in which to raise children. Some early studies compared children living with divorced parents and children living with two married but discordant parents. In general, these studies found that children in high-conflict households experience many of the same problems as do children with divorced parents. In fact, some studies show that children with discordant married parents are worse off than children with divorced parents.[23]

A more recent generation of long-term studies has shown that the effects of divorce vary with the degree of marital discord that precedes divorce. When parents exhibit chronic and overt conflict, children appear to be better off, in the long run, if their parents split up rather than stay together. But when parents exhibit relatively little overt conflict, children appear to be better off if their parents stay together. In other words, children are particularly at risk when low-conflict marriages end in divorce.[24] In a twenty-year study, Alan Booth and I found that the majority of marriages that ended in divorce fell into

the low-conflict group. Spouses in these marriages did not fight frequently or express hostility toward their partners. Instead, they felt emotionally estranged from their spouses, and many ended their marriages to seek greater happiness with new partners. Although many parents saw this transition as positive, their children often viewed it as unexpected, inexplicable, and unwelcome. Children and parents, it is clear, often have different interpretations of family transitions.[25]

Stepfamilies

Although rates of remarriage have declined in recent years, most divorced parents eventually remarry. Similarly, many women who have had a nonmarital birth eventually marry men who are not the fathers of their children. Adding a stepfather to the household usually improves children's standard of living. Moreover, in a stepfamily, two adults are available to monitor children's behavior, provide supervision, and assist children with everyday problems. For these reasons, one might assume that children generally are better off in stepfamilies than in single-parent households. Studies consistently indicate, however, that children in stepfamilies exhibit more problems than do children with continuously married parents and about the same number of problems as do children with single parents.[26] In other words, the marriage of a single parent (to someone other than the child's biological parent) does not appear to improve the functioning of most children.

Although the great majority of parents view the formation of a stepfamily positively, children tend to be less enthusiastic. Stepfamily formation is stressful for many children because it often involves moving (generally to a different neighborhood or town), adapting to new people in the household, and learning new rules and routines. Moreover, early relationships between stepparents and stepchildren are often tense. Children, especially adolescents, become accustomed to a substantial degree of autonomy in single-parent households. They may resent the monitoring and supervision by stepparents and react with hostility when stepparents attempt to exert authority. Some children experience loyalty conflicts and fear that becoming emotionally close to a stepparent implies betraying the nonresident biological parent. Some become jealous because they must share parental time and attention with the stepparent. And for some children, remarriage ends any lingering hopes that the two biological parents will one day reconcile.[27] Finally, stepchildren are overrepresented in official reports of child abuse.[28] Of course, the great majority of stepparents are not abusive. Moreover, survey data have not supported the notion that children in stepfamilies are more likely to be abused than are children in two-parent families.[29] Nevertheless, even a slight trend in this direction would represent an additional risk for children in stepfamilies.

Although relationships in many stepfamilies are tense, stepparents are still able to make positive contributions to their stepchildren's lives. If stepfamilies survive the early "crisis" stage, then close and supportive relationships between stepparents and stepchildren often develop. Research suggests that these relationships can serve as important resources for children's development and emotional well-being.[30]

The increase in nonmarital cohabitation has focused attention on the distinction between married-couple stepfamilies and cohabiting-couple "stepfamilies." Christine Buchanan, Eleanor Maccoby, and Sanford Dornbusch found that adolescents had fewer emotional and behavior problems following divorce if their mothers remarried than if they cohabited with a partner.[31] Similarly, two studies of African American families found that children were better off in certain respects if they lived with stepfathers than with their mother's cohabiting partners.[32] In contrast, Susan Brown found no significant differences between children in married and cohabiting stepfamilies.[33] Although these data suggest that children may be better off if single mothers marry their partners rather than cohabit, the small number of studies on this topic makes it difficult to draw firm conclusions.

Variations by Gender of Child

Several early influential studies found that boys in divorced families had more adjustment problems than did girls.[34] Given that boys usually live with their mothers following family disruption, the loss of contact with the same-gender parent could account for such a difference. In addition boys, compared with girls, may be exposed to more conflict, receive less support from parents and others (because they are believed to be tougher), and be picked on more by custodial mothers (because sons may resemble their fathers). Subsequent studies, however, have failed to find consistent gender differences in children's reactions to divorce.

The meta-analyses on children of divorce provide the most reliable evidence on this topic. The Amato and Keith meta-analysis of studies conducted before the 1990s revealed one significant gender difference: the estimated negative effect of divorce on social adjustment was stronger for boys than girls. In other areas, however, such as academic achievement, conduct, and psychological adjustment, no differences between boys and girls were apparent.[35] In my meta-analysis of studies conducted in the 1990s, the estimated effect of divorce on children's conduct problems was stronger for boys than for girls, although no other gender differences were apparent.[36] Why the earlier studies suggest a gender difference in social adjustment and the more recent studies suggest a gender difference in conduct problems is unclear. Nevertheless, taken together, these meta-analyses provide some limited support for the notion that boys are more susceptible than girls to the detrimental consequences of divorce.

Variations by Race of Child

Compared with whites, African Americans have a higher rate of marital disruption and a substantially higher rate of nonmarital births. Because relatively little research has focused on this topic, however, it is difficult to reach firm conclusions about racial differences in children's well-being in single-parent households. Some research suggests that the academic deficits associated with living with a single mother are less pronounced for black than for white children.[37] One study found that growing up in a single-parent family predicted lower socioeconomic attainment among white women, white men, and black women, but not among black men.[38] McLanahan and Sandefur found that white offspring from single-parent families were more likely to drop out of high school than were African American offspring from single-parent families.[39] African American children may thus adjust better than white children to life in single-parent families, although the explanation for this difference is not clear. Other studies, however, have found few racial differences in the estimated effects of growing up with a single parent on long-term outcomes.[40]

Some studies suggest that stepfathers play a particularly beneficial role in African American families. One study found that in African American families (but not European American families), children who lived with stepfathers were less likely to drop out of high school or (among daughters) have a nonmarital birth.[41] Similarly, a study of African Americans living in high-poverty neighborhoods found that girls living with their mothers and stepfathers were less likely than girls living with single mothers to become sexually active or pregnant. Interestingly, the protective effect of a stepfather held only when mothers were married and not when they were cohabiting.[42] Another study yielded comparable results: among African Americans, adolescents living with stepfathers were better off in many respects than were adolescents living with single mothers, but adolescents living with cohabiting parents were worse off than those living with single mothers.[43] The reasons for these racial differences are not clear, and future research is required to understand how interpersonal dynamics differ in white and African American stepfamilies.

Why Do Single-Parent Families Put Children at Risk?

Researchers have several theories to explain why children growing up with single parents have an elevated risk of experiencing cognitive, social, and emotional problems. Most refer either to the economic and parental resources available to children or to the stressful events and circumstances to which these children must adapt.

Economic Hardship

For a variety of reasons documented elsewhere in this volume, most children living with single parents are economically disadvantaged. It is difficult for poor single parents to afford the books, home computers, and private lessons that make it easier for their children to succeed in school. Similarly, they cannot afford clothes, shoes, cell phones, and other consumer goods that give their children status among their peers. Moreover, many live in rundown neighborhoods with high crime rates, low-quality schools, and few community services. Consistent with these observations, many studies have shown that economic resources explain some of the differences in well-being between children with single parents and those with continuously married parents.[44] Research showing that children do better at school and exhibit fewer behavioral problems when nonresident fathers pay child support likewise suggests the importance of income in facilitating children's well-being in single-parent households.[45]

Quality of Parenting

Regardless of family structure, the quality of parenting is one of the best predictors of children's emotional and social well-being. Many single parents, however, find it difficult to function effectively as parents. Compared with continuously married parents, they are less emotionally supportive of their children, have fewer rules, dispense harsher discipline, are more inconsistent in dispensing discipline, provide less supervision, and engage in more conflict with their children.[46] Many of these deficits in parenting presumably result from struggling to make ends meet with limited financial resources and trying to raise children without the help of the other biological parent. Many studies link inept parenting by resident single parents with a variety of negative outcomes among children, including poor academic achievement, emotional problems, conduct problems, low self-esteem, and problems forming and maintaining social relationships. Other studies show that depression among custodial mothers, which usually detracts from effective parenting, is related to poor adjustment among offspring.[47]

Although the role of the resident parent (usually the mother) in promoting children's well-being is clear, the nonresident parent (usually the father) can also play an important role. In a meta-analysis of sixty-three studies of non-resident fathers and their children, Joan Gilbreth and I found that children had higher academic achievement and fewer emotional and conduct problems when non-resident fathers were closely involved in their lives.[48] We also found that studies of nonresident fathers in the 1990s were more likely than earlier studies to report positive effects of father involvement. Nonresident fathers

---

Regardless of family structure, the quality of parenting is one of the best predictors of children's emotional and social well-being.

---

may thus be enacting the parent role more successfully now than in the past, with beneficial consequences for children. Nevertheless, analysts consistently find that many nonresident fathers are minimally engaged with their children. Between one-fourth and one-third of nonresident fathers maintain frequent contact with their children, and a roughly equal share of fathers maintains little or no contact.[49] Interviews with children reveal that losing contact with fathers is one of the most painful outcomes of divorce.[50]

Children also thrive when their parents have a cooperative co-parental relationship. When parents agree on the rules and support one another's decisions, children learn that parental authority is not arbitrary. Parental agreement also means that children are not subjected to inconsistent discipline when they misbehave. Consistency between parents helps children to learn and internalize social norms and moral values. Another benefit of a positive co-parental relationship is the modeling of interpersonal skills, such as showing respect, communicating clearly, and resolving disputes through negotiation and compromise. Children who learn these skills by observing their parents have positive relationships with peers and, later, with intimate partners. When children's parents live in sep-

> *Conflict between nonresident parents appears to be particularly harmful when children feel that they are caught in the middle.*

arate households, however, cooperative co-parenting is not the norm. Although some parents remain locked in conflict for many years, especially if a divorce is involved, most gradually disengage and communicate little with one another. At best, most children living with single parents experience "parallel" parenting rather than cooperative co-parenting.[51]

Exposure to Stress

Children living with single parents are exposed to more stressful experiences and circumstances than are children living with continuously married parents. Although scholars define stress in somewhat different ways, most assume that it occurs when external demands exceed people's coping resources. This results in feelings of emotional distress, a reduced capacity to function in school, work, and family roles, and an increase in physiological indicators of arousal.[52] Economic hardship, inept parenting, and loss of

contact with a parent (as noted earlier) can be stressful for children. Observing conflict and hostility between resident and nonresident parents also is stressful.[53] Conflict between nonresident parents appears to be particularly harmful when children feel that they are caught in the middle, as when one parent denigrates the other parent in front of the child, when children are asked to transmit critical or emotionally negative messages from one parent to the other, and when one parent attempts to recruit the child as an ally against the other.[54] Interparental conflict is a direct stressor for children, and it can also interfere with their attachments to parents, resulting in feelings of emotional insecurity.[55]

Moving is a difficult experience for many children, especially when it involves losing contact with neighborhood friends. Moreover, moves that require changing schools can put children out of step with their classmates in terms of the curriculum. Children with single parents move more frequently than other children do, partly because of economic hardship (which forces parents to seek less expensive accommodation in other areas) and partly because single parents form new romantic attachments (as when a single mother marries and moves in with her new husband). Studies show that frequent moving increases the risk of academic, behavioral, and emotional problems for children with single parents.[56] For many children, as noted, the addition of a stepparent to the household is a stressful change. And when remarriages end in divorce, children are exposed to yet more stressful transitions. Indeed, some studies indicate that the number of transitions that children experience while growing up (including multiple parental divorces, cohabitations, and remarriages) is a good predictor of their behavioral and emotional problems as adolescents and young adults.[57]

The "Selection" Perspective

Explanations that focus on economic hardship, the quality of parenting, and exposure to stress all assume that the circumstances associated with living in a single-parent household negatively affect children's well-being. A quite different explanation—and the main alternative to these views—is that many poorly adjusted individuals either never marry in the first place or see their marriages end in divorce. In other words, these people carry traits that "select" them into single parenthood. Parents can transmit these problematic traits to their children either through genetic inheritance or inept parenting. For example, a mother with an antisocial personality may pass this genetic predisposition to her children. Her personality also may contribute to her marriage's ending in divorce. Her children will thus be at risk of exhibiting antisocial behavior, but the risk has little to do with the divorce. The discovery that concordance (similarity between siblings) for divorce among adults is higher among identical than fraternal twins suggests that genes may predispose some people to engage in behaviors that increase the risk of divorce.[58] If parents' personality traits and other genetically transmitted predispositions are causes of single parenthood as well as childhood problems, then the apparent effects on children of growing up with a single parent are spurious.

Because researchers cannot conduct a true experiment and randomly allocate children to live with single or married parents, it is difficult to rule out the selection perspective. Nevertheless, many studies cast doubt on it. For example, some have found significant differences between children with divorced and continuously married parents even after controlling for personality traits such as depression and antisocial behavior in parents.[59] Others have found higher rates of problems among children with single parents, using statistical methods that adjust for unmeasured variables that, in principle, should include parents' personality traits as well as many genetic influences.[60] And a few studies have found that the link between parental divorce and children's problems is similar for adopted and biological children—a finding that cannot be explained by genetic transmission.[61] Another study, based on a large sample of twins, found that growing up in a single-parent family predicted depression in adulthood even with genetic resemblance controlled statistically.[62] Although some degree of selection still may be operating, the weight of the evidence strongly suggests that growing up without two biological parents in the home increases children's risk of a variety of cognitive, emotional, and social problems.

Implications of Policies to Increase the Share of Children in Two-Parent Families

Since social science research shows so clearly the advantages enjoyed by children raised by continuously married parents, it is no wonder that policymakers and practitioners are interested in programs to strengthen marriage and increase the proportion of children who grow up in such families. Realistically speaking, what could such programs accomplish? In what follows, I present estimates of how they could affect the share of children in the United States who experience various types of problems during adolescence.

Adolescent Family Structure and Well-Being in the Add Health Study

To make these estimates, I used the Adolescent Health Study—a national long-term sample of children in junior high and high schools—relying on data from Wave I, conducted in 1995. Table 1 is based on adoles-

Table 1. Family Structure and Adolescent Well-Being: Share of Adolescents Reporting Problems in Various Scenarios

Percent

Problem	Family structure, 1995			Estimated share if family structure were the same as in		
	Two parents	One parent	Combined	1980	1970	1960
Repeated grade	18.8	30.3	24.0	22.9	21.8	21.4
Suspended from school	21.2	39.8	29.6	27.9	26.0	25.4
Delinquency	36.4	44.7	40.1	39.4	38.5	38.3
Violence	36.0	44.1	39.6	38.9	38.1	37.8
Therapy	7.5	17.0	11.8	10.9	9.9	9.6
Smoked in last month	13.4	22.6	17.5	16.7	15.8	15.5
Thought of suicide	11.3	14.5	12.7	12.5	12.1	12.0
Attempted suicide	1.7	2.8	2.2	2.1	2.0	1.9

Source: National Study of Adolescent Health, 1995. See text for details.

cents' responses to questions about behavioral, emotional, and academic problems—specifically, whether they had repeated a grade, been suspended from school, engaged in delinquent behavior, engaged in a violent altercation, received counseling or therapy for an emotional problem, smoked cigarettes regularly during the last month, thought about suicide, or attempted suicide. Delinquency involved damaging property, shoplifting, breaking into a house or building to steal something, stealing something worth more than $50, or taking a car without the owner's permission. Violence was defined as engaging in a physical fight as a result of which the opponent had received medical attention (including bandaging a cut) or a fight involving multiple people or using a weapon to threaten someone. The results are based on responses from more than 17,000 children between the ages of twelve and eighteen, and the data have been weighted to make them nationally representative.[63]

Responses are shown separately for adolescents living with continuously married parents and for those living with one parent only.

The results are striking. Adolescents living with single parents consistently report encountering more problems than those living with continuously married parents. Thirty percent of the former reported that they had repeated a grade, as against 19 percent of the latter. Similarly, 40 percent of children living with single parents reported having been suspended from school, compared with 21 percent of children living with continuously married parents. Children in stable, two-parent families also were less likely to have engaged in delinquency or violence, seen a therapist for an emotional problem, smoked during the previous month, or thought about or attempted suicide. These findings are consistent with research demonstrating that children living with continuously married parents report fewer problems than do other children. The increase in risk associated with living without both parents ranged from about 23 percent (for being involved in a violent altercation) to 127 percent (for receiving emotional therapy).

To estimate the frequency of these problems in the larger population, I relied on the Add

Health finding that 55 percent of adolescents between the ages of twelve to eighteen lived with both biological parents at the time of the survey. Given that rates of divorce and non-marital births have not changed much since the mid-1990s, this figure is probably close to the current figure, and it is nearly identical to the estimate provided by Susan Brown from the 1999 National Survey of American Families. (Because most children in the sample were younger than eighteen and could still experience a parental divorce or death before reaching adulthood, these results are consistent with the projection that about half of all children will live continuously with both biological parents until adulthood.) The third column in table 1 shows the estimated share of adolescents in the U.S. population who experience each problem, based on the data in the first two columns.[64]

How would increasing the share of children growing up in stable, two-parent families affect the overall levels of these problems in the population? To provide estimates, I considered three levels of social change. The fourth column in table 1 provides estimates of adolescent outcomes if the share of adolescents living with two biological parents were the same as it was in 1980, the year in which the share of marriages ending in divorce reached its peak but before the large increase in nonmarital births during the 1980s and early 1990s. The fifth column provides estimates of adolescent outcomes if the share of adolescents living with continuously married parents were the same as it was in 1970, the year just before the massive increase in divorce rates during the 1970s. The final column provides estimates of adolescent outcomes if the share of adolescents living with continuously married parents were the same as it was in 1960, a period of relative family stability in the United States.[65]

Column four shows that if the share of adolescents living with two biological parents were the same today as it was in 1980, the share of adolescents repeating a grade would fall from 24 percent to about 23 percent. Similarly, if the share of adolescents living with two biological parents returned to its 1970 level, the share of adolescents repeating a grade would fall to about 22 percent. Finally, if the share of adolescents living with two biological parents increased to its 1960 level, the share of adolescents repeating a grade would fall to 21 percent.

How is it that increasing the share of children growing up with continuously married parents has such a relatively small effect on the share of children experiencing these problems? The explanation is that many children living with continuously married parents also experience these problems. In general, these findings, which are likely to disappoint some readers, are consistent with a broad, sociological understanding of human behavior. Most behaviors are determined by numerous social, cultural, individual, and biological factors. No single variable, such as family structure, has a monolithic effect on children's development and behavior. Although increasing the share of children growing up in stable, two-parent families would lower the incidence of all the problems shown in table 1, clearly it is not a panacea for the problems confronting our nation's youth.

Individual versus Public Health Perspectives

Whether one views the estimated changes in table 1 as small or big depends in large part on whether one adopts an individual perspective or a public health perspective. Attempts during the past twenty years by public health authorities to address cholesterol-related health problems help to illustrate this distinction. Many epidemiological and clinical studies have shown that a high level of blood cholesterol is a risk factor for cardiovascular disease. How large is the estimated effect of cholesterol on cardiovascular disease? Consider a group of male nonsmokers age fifty with normal blood pressure. Men in this group with high total cholesterol (defined as 250 mg/dL) have a 7 percent chance of suffering a heart attack during the next decade. In comparison, men in this group with low total cholesterol (defined as 190 mg/dL) have only a 4 percent chance. In other words, decreasing total cholesterol from a "dangerous" level to a "safe" level would lower the risk of having a heart attack for men in this group by 3 percentage points. Based on projections like these, public health authorities have encouraged people with high cholesterol to lower their cholesterol by eating fewer foods high in saturated fat and cholesterol, losing weight, and exercising more often. Physicians often recommend supplementing these lifestyle changes with cholesterol-lowering medications, such as statin drugs.[66]

Seen from a different perspective, however, 93 percent of men age fifty with high total cholesterol will *not* suffer a heart attack in the next decade. There are only 7 chances in 100 that a particular man will have a heart attack, and even if he lowers his cholesterol, he still has 4 chances in 100 of suffering a heart attack. In other words, all the required changes in lifestyle, plus the use of medications, will lower his chances of a heart attack by only 3 chances out of 100. An individual man with high cholesterol, therefore, may well wonder if is worth the effort to change his lifestyle and take medication. At the population level, however, with more than 9 million men in the United States in their early fifties, a 3 percentage point reduction in heart attacks would be seen as a major public

health achievement, because it would mean a quarter of a million fewer heart attacks in this group over a decade. [67]

The cholesterol example is relevant to understanding the effects of growing up without both parents in the household. The increase in the risk of cardiovascular disease associated with high blood cholesterol is comparable in many respects to the increase in the risk of behavioral, emotional, and academic problems associated with growing up in a single-parent household. For example, the increase in heart attacks associated with high blood cholesterol represents a 75 percent increase in risk—($[7 - 4]/4$) x 100—a figure comparable to the increased risk associated with single parenthood and repeating a grade, being suspended from school, receiving therapy, or attempting suicide. Adopting a public health view and considering the number rather than the percentage of adolescents who might be affected helps put these findings in perspective.

In 2002 there were about 29 million children in the United States between the ages of twelve and eighteen—the age range covered in table 1.[68] Table 2 indicates that nearly 7 million children in this age group will have repeated a grade. Increasing the share of adolescents living with two biological parents to the 1980 level, as illustrated in the second column of the table, suggests that some 300,000 fewer children would repeat a grade. Correspondingly, increasing the share of adolescents living with two biological parents to the 1970 level, as illustrated in the third column, would mean that 643,264 fewer children would repeat a grade. Finally, increasing the share of adolescents in two-parent families to the 1960 level suggests that nearly three-quarters of a million fewer children would repeat a grade. Similarly, increasing

Table 2. Well-Being of Adolescents Aged Twelve to Eighteen, 2002 Estimates

Problem	2002 estimate	Estimated change based on two-parent families in		
		1980	1970	1960
Repeated grade	6,948,530	−299,968	−643,264	−746,587
Suspended from school	8,570,096	−485,165	−1,040,410	−1,207,523
Delinquency	11,632,086	−216,498	−464,269	−538,841
Violence	11,490,072	−211,282	−453,082	−525,857
Therapy	3,412,678	−247,799	−531,392	−616,745
Smoked in last month	5,083,513	−239,974	−514,611	−597,269
Thought of suicide	3,692,358	−83,469	−178,995	−207,746
Attempted suicide	636,164	−28,693	−61,530	−71,413

Source: Author's estimates based on data from the National Study of Adolescent Health, 1995. See text for details.

marital stability to its 1980 level would result in nearly half a million fewer children suspended from school, about 200,000 fewer children engaging in delinquency or violence, a quarter of a million fewer children receiving therapy, about a quarter of a million fewer smokers, about 80,000 fewer children thinking about suicide, and about 28,000 fewer children attempting suicide. Seen from this perspective, restoring family stability to levels of a few decades ago could dramatically affect the lives of many children. Moreover, although the estimated decline in the share of children encountering these problems in table 1 is modest, increasing the number of children growing up with both parents would simultaneously improve *all* these outcomes, as well as many other outcomes not considered in these tables.

General Conclusion

My goal in this paper has been to inform the marriage debate by addressing three fundamental questions. First, how do children in households with only one biological parent differ from children in households with both biological parents, in terms of their cognitive, social, and emotional well-being? Research clearly demonstrates that children growing up with two continuously married parents are less likely than other children to experience a wide range of cognitive, emotional, and social problems, not only during childhood, but also in adulthood. Although it is not possible to demonstrate that family structure is the cause of these differences, studies that have used a variety of sophisticated statistical methods, including controls for genetic factors, suggest that this is the case. This distinction is even stronger if we focus on children growing up with two *happily married* biological parents.

Second, what accounts for the observed differences between these two groups of children? Compared with other children, those who grow up in stable, two-parent families have a higher standard of living, receive more effective parenting, experience more cooperative co-parenting, are emotionally closer to both parents (especially fathers), and are subjected to fewer stressful events and circumstances.

And third, how might current policies to strengthen marriage, decrease the rate of divorce, and lower nonmarital fertility affect the overall well-being of American children?

The projections in tables 1 and 2 suggest that increasing the share of children who grow up with continuously married parents would improve the overall well-being of U.S. children only modestly. The improvements are relatively small because problems such as being suspended from school, engaging in delinquent behavior, and attempting suicide have many causes, with family structure being but one.

What are the policy implications of these findings? First, interventions that increase the share of children growing up with two continuously married biological parents will have modest effects on the *percentage* of U.S. children experiencing various problems, but could have substantial effects on the *number* of children experiencing them. From a public health perspective, even a modest decline in percentages, when multiplied by the large number of children in the population, represents a substantial social benefit. That children living in stepfamilies do not tend to have better outcomes, on average, than children growing up in single-parent families suggests that interventions to strengthen marital quality and stability would be most profitable if focused on parents in first marriages. Similarly, interventions to strengthen relationships and encourage marriage among cohabiting couples with children would be most profitable if focused on couples with a first child, rather than couples with children from prior relationships.

U.S. policymakers also should acknowledge that returning to substantially lower rates of divorce and nonmarital childbearing, although a worthwhile goal, is not realistic, at least in the short term. Although policy interventions may lower the rate of divorce and nonmarital childbearing, many children will continue to grow up with a single parent. This stubborn fact means that policies for improving children's well-being cannot focus exclusively on promoting marriage and strengthening marital stability. These policies must be supplemented by others that improve economic well-being, strengthen parent-child bonds, and ease the stress experienced by children in single-parent and stepparent households. Such programs would provide parent education classes for divorcing parents, increase the minimum wage and the earned income tax credit for poor working parents, establish paternity and increase the payment of child support, and improve the quantity and quality of time that nonresident parents, especially fathers, spend with their children.

The importance of increasing the number of children growing up with two happily and continuously married parents and of improving the well-being of children now living in other family structures is self-evident. Children are the innocent victims of their parents' inability to maintain harmonious and stable homes. The importance of effective policies will become even clearer in the near future, as the baby boom generation reaches retirement age. As this happens, our society will become increasingly dependent on the emotional functioning, economic productivity, and leadership of a declining number of young adults. Although it is a cliché to say that children are the future, it has never been as true as it is today.

Endnotes

1. For examples, see Sheldon Glueck and Eleanor Glueck, *Family Environment and Delinquency* (Boston: Houghton Mifflin, 1962); J. F. McDermott, "Divorce and Its Psychiatric Sequelae in Children," *Archives of General Psychiatry* 23 (1970): 421–27.

2. Judith S. Wallerstein and Joan B. Kelly, *Surviving the Breakup: How Children and Parents Cope with Divorce* (New York: Basic Books, 1980).

3. E. Mavis Hetherington, "Divorce: A Child's Perspective," *American Psychologist* 34 (1979): 851–58; E. Mavis Hetherington, Martha Cox, and R. Cox, "Effects of Divorce on Parents and Children," in *Nontraditional Families*, edited by Michael Lamb (Hillsdale, N.J.: Lawrence Erlbaum, 1982), pp. 233–88.

4. The effect size for a study is defined as the standardized mean difference on some outcome between two groups of interest, that is, $(\bar{x}_1 - \bar{x}_2)/S_{pooled}$. For information on meta-analysis, see Harris M. Cooper and Larry V. Hedges, eds., *The Handbook of Research Synthesis* (New York: Russell Sage, 1994).

5. Paul R. Amato and Bruce Keith, "Consequences of Parental Divorce for Children's Well-Being: A Meta-Analysis," *Psychological Bulletin* 10 (1991): 26–46.

6. Paul R. Amato, "Children of Divorce in the 1990s: An Update of the Amato and Keith (1991) Meta-Analysis," *Journal of Family Psychology* 15 (2001): 355–70.

7. Paul R. Amato and Alan Booth, *A Generation at Risk: Growing Up in an Era of Family Upheaval* (Harvard University Press, 1997); Paul R. Amato and Juliana M. Sobolewski, "The Effects of Divorce and Marital Discord on Adult Children's Psychological Well-Being," *American Sociological Review* 66 (2001): 900–21; William S. Aquilino, "Impact of Childhood Family Disruption on Young Adults' Relationships with Parents," *Journal of Marriage and the Family* 56 (1994): 295–313; Alan Booth and Paul R. Amato, "Parental Predivorce Relations and Offspring Postdivorce Well-Being," *Journal of Marriage and the Family* 63 (2001): 197–212; Larry L. Bumpass, Theresa C. Martin, and James A. Sweet, "The Impact of Family Background and Early Marital Factors on Marital Disruption," *Journal of Family Issues* 12 (1991): 22–42; Andrew J. Cherlin, P. Lindsay Chase-Lansdale, and Christine McRae, "Effects of Divorce on Mental Health throughout the Life Course," *American Sociological Review* 63 (1998): 239–49; Sara McLanahan and Gary Sandefur, *Growing Up with a Single Parent: What Hurts, What Helps* (Harvard University Press, 1994); Lawrence L. Wu and B. C. Martinson, "Family Structure and the Risk of a Premarital Birth," *American Sociological Review* 58 (1993): 210–32.

8. McLanahan and Sandefur, *Growing Up with a Single Parent* (see note 7); Paul R. Amato, "Parental Absence during Childhood and Adult Depression," *Sociological Quarterly* 32 (1991): 543–56; Paul R. Amato and Bruce Keith, "Separation from a Parent during Childhood and Adult Socioeconomic Attainment," *Social Forces* 70 (1991): 187–206; William Aquilino, "The Life Course of Children Born to Unmarried Mothers: Childhood Living Arrangements and Young Adult Outcomes," *Journal of Marriage and the Family* 58 (1996): 293–310; Robert Haveman, Barbara Wolf, and Karen Pence, "Intergenerational Effects of Nonmarital and Early Childbearing," in *Out of Wedlock: Causes and Consequences of Nonmarital Fertility*, edited by Lawrence L. Wu and Barbara Wolfe (New York: Russell Sage Foundation, 2001), pp. 287–316; Jay D. Teachman, "Childhood Living Arrangements and the Intergenerational Transmission of Divorce," *Journal of Marriage and Family* 64 (2002): 717–29; Jay D. Teachman, "The Childhood Living Arrangements of Children and the Characteristics of Their Marriages," *Journal of Family Issues* 25 (2004): 86–96.

9. McLanahan and Sandefur, *Growing Up with a Single Parent* (see note 7).

10. Amato, "Parental Absence during Childhood and Adult Depression" (see note 8); Amato and Keith "Separation from a Parent" (see note 8); Teachman, "Childhood Living Arrangements" (see note 8).

11. Larry L. Bumpass and Hsien-Hen Lu, "Trends in Cohabitation and Implications for Children's Family Contexts in the United States," *Population Studies* 54 (2000): 29–41; Sara McLanahan and others, "Unwed Parents or Fragile Families? Implications for Welfare and Child Support Policy," in *Out of Wedlock: Causes and Consequences of Nonmarital Fertility,* edited by Lawrence L. Wu and Barbara Wolfe (New York: Russell Sage Foundation, 2001), pp. 202–28.

12. Susan Brown, "The Effect of Union Type on Psychological Well-Being: Depression among Cohabitors versus Marrieds," *Journal of Health and Social Behavior* 41 (2000): 241–55; Susan Brown and Alan Booth, "Cohabitation versus Marriage: A Comparison of Relationship Quality," *Journal of Marriage and the Family* 58 (1996): 668–78; Judith Seltzer, "Families Formed outside of Marriage," *Journal of Marriage and the Family* 62 (2000): 1247–68.

13. Susan Brown, "Family Structure and Child Well-Being: The Significance of Parental Cohabitation," *Journal of Marriage and the Family* 66 (2004): 351–67. For a general review of this literature, see Wendy Manning, "The Implications of Cohabitation for Children's Well-Being," in *Just Living Together: Implications of Cohabitation for Families, Children, and Social Policy,* edited by Alan Booth and Ann Crouter (Mahwah, N.J.: Lawrence Erlbaum Associates, 2002), pp. 21–152.

14. Nancy S. Landale and Susan M. Hauan, "The Family Life Course of Puerto Rican Children," *Journal of Marriage and the Family* 54 (1992): 912–24; Wendy Manning, Pamela Smock, and Debarun Majumdar, "The Relative Stability of Marital and Cohabiting Unions for Children," *Population Research and Policy Review* 23 (2004): 135–59.

15. M. Carlson, Sara McLanahan, and Paula England, "Union Formation and Dissolution in Fragile Families," Fragile Families Research Brief, no. 4 (Bendheim-Thoman Center for Research on Child Wellbeing, Princeton University, January 2003); see also Sara McLanahan, "Diverging Destinies: How Children Are Faring under the Second Demographic Transition," *Demography* 41 (2004): 606–27.

16. Lawrence L. Wu, Larry L. Bumpass, and Kelly Musick, "Historical and Life Course Trajectories of Nonmarital Childbearing," in *Out of Wedlock: Causes and Consequences of Nonmarital Fertility,* edited by Lawrence L. Wu and Barbara Wolfe (New York: Russell Sage Foundation, 2001), pp. 3–48.

17. Brown, "Family Structure and Child Well-Being" (see note 13).

18. The Add Health study was designed by J. Richard Udry, Peter S. Bearman, and Kathleen Mullan Harris and funded by grant R01-HD31921 from the NICHD, with cooperative funding from seventeen other agencies. Ronald R. Rindfuss and Barbara Entwisle provided assistance in the original study design. The analysis was conducted for this paper.

19. Amato and Keith, "Consequences of Parental Divorce" (see note 5).

20. McLanahan and Sandefur, *Growing Up with a Single Parent* (see note 7).

21. Amato and Keith, "Separation from a Parent" (see note 8).

22. Amato, "Parental Absence" (see note 8).

23. David Mechanic and Stephen Hansell, "Divorce, Family Conflict, and Adolescents' Well-Being," *Journal of Health and Social Behavior* 30 (1989): 105–16; James L. Peterson and Nichola Zill, "Marital Disruption, Parent-Child Relationships, and Behavior Problems in Children," *Journal of Marriage and the Family* 49 (1986): 295–307.

24. Amato and Booth, *A Generation at Risk* (see note 7); Booth and Amato, "Parental Predivorce Relations" (see note 7); Susan M. Jekielek, "Parental Conflict, Marital Disruption and Children's Emotional Well-Being," *Social Forces* 76 (1998): 905–35; Thomas L. Hanson, "Does Parental Conflict Explain Why Divorce Is Negatively Associated with Child Welfare?" *Social Forces* 77 (1999):1283–316.

25. Amato and Booth, *A Generation at Risk* (see note 7); Booth and Amato, "Parental Predivorce Relations" (see note 7); Paul R. Amato, "Good Enough Marriages: Parental Discord, Divorce, and Children's Well-Being," *Virginia Journal of Social Policy and the Law* 9 (2002): 71–94.

26. Paul R. Amato, "The Implications of Research on Children in Stepfamilies," in *Stepfamilies: Who Benefits? Who Does Not?* edited by Alan Booth and Judy Dunn (Hillsdale, N.J.: Lawrence Erlbaum, 1994); E. Mavis Hetherington and W. Glenn Clingempeel, "Coping with Marital Transitions," *Monographs of the Society for Research in Child Development*, vol. 57, nos. 2–3 (University of Chicago Press, 1992); E. Mavis Hetherington and K. M. Jodl, "Stepfamilies as Settings for Child Development," in *Stepfamilies: Who Benefits? Who Does Not?* edited by Alan Booth and Judy Dunn (Hillsdale, N.J.: Lawrence Erlbaum, 1994), pp. 55–79.

27. For a discussion of how stepchildren view stepparents, see E. Mavis Hetherington and John Kelly, *For Better or for Worse: Divorce Reconsidered* (New York: Norton, 2002).

28. Martin Daly and Margo Wilson, "Child Abuse and Other Risks of Not Living with Both Biological Parents," *Ethology and Sociobiology* 6 (1985): 197–220; Leslie Margolin and John L. Craft, "Child Sexual Abuse by Caretakers," 38 (1989): 450–55.

29. Richard Gelles and John W. Harrop, "The Risk of Abusive Violence among Children with Nongenetic Caretakers," *Family Relations* 40 (1991): 78–83.

30. Phyllis Bronstein and others, "Fathering after Separation or Divorce: Factors Predicting Children's Adjustment," *Family Relations* 43 (1994): 469–79; Margaret Crosbie-Burnett and Jean Giles-Sims, "Adolescent Adjustment and Stepparenting Styles," *Family Relations* 43 (1994): 394–99; Lynn White and Joan G. Gilbreth, "When Children Have Two Fathers: Effects of Relationships with Stepfathers and Noncustodial Fathers on Adolescent Outcomes," *Journal of Marriage and Family* 63 (2001): 155–67.

31. Christine M. Buchanan, Eleanor E. Maccoby, and Sanford M. Dornbusch, *Adolescents after Divorce* (Harvard University Press, 1996).

32. Mignon R. Moore and P. L. Chase-Lansdale, "Sexual Intercourse and Pregnancy among African-American Girls in High-Poverty Neighborhoods: The Role of Family and Perceived Community Environment," *Journal of Marriage and the Family* 63 (2001): 1146–57; Sandi Nelson, Rebecca L. Clark, and Gregory Acs, *Beyond the Two-Parent Family: How Teenagers Fare in Cohabiting Couple and Blended Families*, series B, no. B-31 (Washington: Urban Institute, 2001).

33. Brown, "The Effect of Union Type" (see note 12).

34. Hetherington, Cox, and Cox, "Effects of Divorce" (see note 3).

35. Amato and Keith, "Consequences of Parental Divorce" (see note 5).

36. Amato, "Children of Divorce" (see note 6).

37. E. Mavis Hetherington, K. A. Camara, and David L. Featherman, "Achievement and Intellectual Functioning of Children in One-Parent Households," in *Achievement and Achievement Motives*, edited by J. T. Spence (San Francisco: W. H. Freeman, 1983).

38. Amato and Keith, "Separation from a Parent" (see note 8).

39. McLanahan and Sandefur, *Growing Up with a Single Parent* (see note 7).

40. Amato, "Parental Absence" (see note 8).

41. McLanahan and Sandefur, *Growing Up with a Single Parent* (see note 7).

42. Moore and Chase-Lansdale, "Sexual Intercourse and Pregnancy" (see note 32).

43. Nelson, Clark, and Acs, *Beyond the Two-Parent Family* (see note 32).

44. McLanahan and Sandefur, *Growing Up with a Single Parent* (see note 7); Robert H. Aseltine, "Pathways Linking Parental Divorce with Adolescent Depression," *Journal of Health and Social Behavior* 37 (1996): 133–48; Donna R. Morrison and Andrew J. Cherlin, "The Divorce Process and Young Children's Well-Being: A Prospective Analysis," *Journal of Marriage and the Family* 57 (1995): 800–12; Ronald L. Simons and Associates, *Understanding Differences between Divorced and Intact Families* (Thousand Oaks, Calif.: Sage, 1996).

45. Valarie King, "Nonresident Father Involvement and Child Well-Being: Can Dads Make a Difference?" *Journal of Family Issues* 15 (1994): 78–96; Sara McLanahan and others, "Child Support Enforcement and Child Well-Being: Greater Security or Greater Conflict?" in *Child Support and Child Well-Being*, edited by Irwin Garfinkel, Sara McLanahan, and Philip K. Robins (Washington: Urban Institute Press, 1996), pp. 239–56.

46. Hetherington and Clingempeel, "Coping with Marital Transitions" (see note 26); Simons and Associates, *Understanding Differences* (see note 44); Nan Astone and Sara S. McLanahan, "Family Structure, Parental Practices, and High School Completion," *American Sociological Review* 56 (1991): 309–20; Elizabeth Thomson and others, "Family Structure, Gender, and Parental Socialization," *Journal of Marriage and the Family* 54 (1992): 368–78.

47. McLanahan and Sandefur, *Growing Up with a Single Parent* (see note 7); Hetherington and Clingempeel, "Coping with Marital Transition" (see note 26); Buchanan, Maccoby, and Dornbusch, *Adolescents after Divorce* (see note 31); Simons and Associates, *Understanding Differences* (see note 44).

48. Paul R. Amato and Joan Gilbreth, "Nonresident Fathers and Children's Well-Being: A Meta-Analysis," *Journal of Marriage and the Family* 61 (1999): 557–73.

49. Paul R. Amato and Juliana Sobolewski, "The Effects of Divorce on Fathers and Children: Nonresidential Fathers and Stepfathers," in *The Role of the Father in Child Development*, edited by Michael Lamb, 4th ed. (Hillsdale, N.J.: Erlbaum, 2003), pp. 341–67.

50. W. V. Fabricius, "Listening to Children of Divorce: New Findings that Diverge from Wallerstein, Lewis, and Blakeslee," *Family Relations* 52 (2003): 385–94.

51. Frank F. Furstenberg and Andrew Cherlin, *Divided Families: What Happens to Children When Parents Part* (Harvard University Press, 1991).

52. L. I. Pearlin and others, "The Stress Process," *Journal of Health and Social Behavior* 22 (1981): 337–56; Peggy A. Thoits, "Stress, Coping, and Social Support Processes: Where Are We? What Next?" *Journal of Health and Social Behavior,* extra issue (1995): 53–79.

53. Buchanan, Maccoby, and Dornbusch, *Adolescents after Divorce* (see note 31); Jeanne M. Tschann and others, "Conflict, Loss, Change and Parent-Child Relationships: Predicting Children's Adjustment during Divorce," *Journal of Divorce and Remarriage* 13 (1999): 1–22; Elizabeth A. Vandewater and Jennifer E. Lansford, "Influences of Family Structure and Parental Conflict on Children's Well-Being," *Family Relations* 47 (1998): 323–30.

54. Buchanan, Maccoby, and Dornbusch, *Adolescents after Divorce* (see note 31).

55. Patrick T. Davies and E. Mark Cummings, "Marital Conflict and Child Adjustment: An Emotional Security Hypothesis," *Psychological Bulletin* 116 (1994): 387–411.

56. McLanahan and Sandefur, *Growing Up with a Single Parent* (see note 7); Aseltine, "Pathways" (see note 44); Simons and Associates, *Understanding Differences* (see note 44); Buchanan, Maccoby, and Dornbusch, *Adolescents after Divorce* (see note 31); Michael S. Ellwood and Arnold L. Stolberg, "The Effects of Family Composition, Family Health, Parenting Behavior and Environmental Stress on Children's Divorce Adjustment," *Journal of Child and Family Studies* 2 (1993): 23–36; Irwin Sandler and others, "Stability and Quality of Life Events and Psychological Symptomatology in Children of Divorce," *American Journal of Community Psychology* 19 (1991): 501–20; Jay D. Teachman, Kathleen Paasch, and Karen Carver, "Social Capital and Dropping Out of School Early," *Journal of Marriage and the Family* 58 (1996): 773–83.

57. Wu and Martinson, "Family Structure" (see note 7); Paul R. Amato, "Reconciling Divergent Perspectives: Judith Wallerstein, Quantitative Family Research, and Children of Divorce," *Family Relations* 52 (2003): 332–39; Bryan Rodgers and Jan Pryor, *Divorce and Separation: The Outcomes for Children* (York, England: Joseph Rowntree Foundation, 1998).

58. M. McGue and D. T. Lykken, "Genetic Influence on Risk of Divorce," *Psychological Science* 3 (1992): 368–73; V. Jockin, M. McGue, and D. T. Lykken, "Personality and Divorce: A Genetic Analysis," *Journal of Personality and Social Psychology* 71 (1996): 288–99. For a strong statement of this position, see Judith Harris, *The Nurture Assumption: Why Children Turn Out the Way They Do* (New York: Touchstone, 1999).

59. Simons and Associates, *Understanding Differences* (see note 44); Amato, "Reconciling Divergent Perspectives" (see note 57).

60. See note 7. Cherlin and others used a fixed-effects model, which eliminates all unmeasured variables that do not change over time. McLanahan and Sandefur relied on biprobit analysis, a method that makes it possible to correlate error terms across equations, which is equivalent to adjusting for unmeasured variables that could affect family structure as well as children's outcomes.

61. David Brodzinsky, Jennifer C. Hitt, and Daniel Smith, "Impact of Parental Separation and Divorce on Adopted and Nonadopted Children," *American Journal of Orthopsychiatry* 63 (1993): 451–61; Thomas G. O'Connor and others, "Are Associations between Parental Divorce and Children's Adjustment Genetically Mediated? An Adoption Study," *Developmental Psychology* 36 (2000): 429–37.

62. K. S. Kendler and others, "Childhood Parental Loss and Adult Psychopathology in Women," *Archives of General Psychiatry* 49 (1992): 109–16.

63. In this analysis, I considered adoptive parents to be the same as biological parents. The "one parent" category includes adolescents living with one biological parent and a stepparent (or a cohabiting partner of the parent). This category also includes a small percentage of children living with neither parent at the time of the interview. I used logistic regression analysis to adjust the percentages in table 1 for variables that could be associated with family structure as well as child outcomes: mother's education, father's education, child's race (white, black, Latino, or other), child's age, child's gender, and whether the child was born in the United States. All of the differences reported in table 1 were statistically significant at $p < .01$.

64. The margin of error for these estimates, based on a 95 percent confidence interval, is about 1 percent.

65. To estimate the percentage of adolescents between the ages of thirteen and eighteen living with two biological parents in 1980, 1970, and 1960, I relied on retrospective data from the 1988 wave of the National Survey of Families and Households. The resulting figures are 64 percent, 74 percent, and 77 percent, respectively. The margin of error for these estimates, based on a 95 percent confidence interval, is about 2 percent. For details on the National Survey of Families and Households, see James Sweet, Larry Bumpass, and Vaughn Call, "The Design and Content of the National Survey of Families and Households," NSFH Working Paper 1 (Center for Demography and Ecology, University of Wisconsin-Madison, 1988). These estimates should not be equated with levels of program "effectiveness," because it is naive to assume that specific, short-term interventions could reverse family trends so strongly. It is possible, however, that a range of interventions, combined with a shift in the larger culture, could result in substantial changes in family structure over a decade or longer. Moreover, the figures used in table 1 are not completely unrealistic, because they correspond to levels of family stability that actually existed in recent U.S. history. Note also that these estimates are based only on changes in family structure and assume no changes in marital quality in two-parent families. If future policies also are capable of improving the quality of existing marriages, then the figures in tables 1 and 2 are underestimates of the total benefit to children.

66. The National Heart, Lung, and Blood Institute, *High Blood Cholesterol: What You Need to Know*, NIH Publication 01-3290 (May 2001). See also F. B. Hu, J. E. Manson, and W. C. Willett, "Types of Dietary Fat and Risk of Coronary Heart Disease: A Critical Review," *Journal of the American College of Nutrition* 20 (2001): 5–19; S. Lewington and S. MacMahon, "Blood Pressure, Cholesterol, and Common Causes of Death: A Review," *American Journal of Hypertension* 12 (1999): 96S–98S.

67. The estimates for ten-year risk of a heart attack vary with age and gender. The link between cholesterol and cardiovascular disease is stronger for men than for women, and stronger for older individuals than for younger individuals. The margin of error for these estimates, based on a 95 percent confidence interval, is about 1 percent.

68. U.S. Bureau of the Census, *Statistical Abstract of the United States* (Government Printing Office, 2003), table 11.

Gay Marriage, Same-Sex Parenting, and America's Children

William Meezan and Jonathan Rauch

Summary

Same-sex marriage, barely on the political radar a decade ago, is a reality in America. How will it affect the well-being of children? Some observers worry that legalizing same-sex marriage would send the message that same-sex parenting and opposite-sex parenting are interchangeable, when in fact they may lead to different outcomes for children.

To evaluate that concern, William Meezan and Jonathan Rauch review the growing body of research on how same-sex parenting affects children. After considering the methodological problems inherent in studying small, hard-to-locate populations—problems that have bedeviled this literature—the authors find that the children who have been studied are doing about as well as children normally do. What the research does not yet show is whether the children studied are typical of the general population of children raised by gay and lesbian couples.

A second important question is how same-sex marriage might affect children who are already being raised by same-sex couples. Meezan and Rauch observe that marriage confers on children three types of benefits that seem likely to carry over to children in same-sex families. First, marriage may increase children's material well-being through such benefits as family leave from work and spousal health insurance eligibility. It may also help ensure financial continuity, should a spouse die or be disabled. Second, same-sex marriage may benefit children by increasing the durability and stability of their parents' relationship. Finally, marriage may bring increased social acceptance of and support for same-sex families, although those benefits might not materialize in communities that meet same-sex marriage with rejection or hostility.

The authors note that the best way to ascertain the costs and benefits of the effects of same-sex marriage on children is to compare it with the alternatives. Massachusetts is marrying same-sex couples, Vermont and Connecticut are offering civil unions, and several states offer partner-benefit programs. Studying the effect of these various forms of unions on children could inform the debate over gay marriage to the benefit of all sides of the argument.

www.futureofchildren.org

William Meezan is dean of the College of Social Work at the Ohio State University. Jonathan Rauch is writer in residence in the Government Studies program at the Brookings Institution.

Although Americans are deeply divided over same-sex marriage, on one point most would agree: the issue has moved from the obscure fringes to the roiling center of the family-policy debate in a startlingly brief time. In May of 1970, Jack Baker and Mike McConnell applied for a marriage license in Hennepin County, Minnesota. They were turned down. For a generation, subsequent efforts in other venues met the same fate. In the 1990s, Hawaii's state supreme court seemed, for a time, likely to order same-sex marriage, but a state constitutional amendment preemptively overruled the court. Vermont's civil-union program, adopted in 2000 by order of Vermont's high court, offered state (though not federal) benefits to same-sex couples. That program, however, was seen as a substitute for full-fledged marriage. No state, it seemed, was prepared to grant legal matrimony to same-sex couples.

Last year, that taboo broke. Under order of its state supreme court, Massachusetts began offering marriage licenses to same-sex couples. More than forty states, by contrast, have enacted laws or, in some cases, constitutional amendments declaring they would *not* recognize same-sex marriage—a trend that escalated in 2004 when thirteen states passed constitutional amendments banning same-sex marriage.[1] The issue pits left against right and, perhaps more significant, old against young: Americans over age forty-four oppose same-sex marriage by a decisive majority, but a plurality of Americans under age thirty support it.[2] Today, across generations and geography, the country is divided over the meaning of marriage as it has not been since the days when states were at odds over interracial marriages and no-fault divorces—if then.

For many of its advocates, same-sex marriage is a civil rights issue, plain and simple. For many of its opponents, it is just as simply a moral issue. In reality, it is both, but it is also a family-policy issue—one of the most important, yet least studied, family-policy issues on the American scene today. The most controversial of its family-policy aspects is the question: how might same-sex marriage affect the well-being of American children?

Counting the Children

To begin thinking about gay marriage and children, it is useful to pose another question: which children? Consider three groups of children. First, there are those who are now being raised, or who would in the future be raised, by same-sex couples even if same-sex marriage were unavailable. No one knows just how many American children are being raised by same-sex couples today. The 2000 census counted about 594,000 households headed by same-sex couples, and it found children living in 27 percent of such households.[3] The census did not, however, count the number of children in each home. So all we can say is that, conservatively, at least 166,000 children are being raised by gay and lesbian couples.[4] Many of these children, whatever their number, would be directly affected by the introduction of same-sex marriage—a point we will return to later in this article.

On the obverse is a second group that is much larger but on which the effects, if any, of same-sex marriage are entirely unclear: children *not* being raised by same-sex couples—which is to say, children being raised by opposite-sex couples, married or unmarried, or by single parents. How might same-sex marriage affect these children? Or, to put it another way, how (if at all) might homosexual marriage affect heterosexual behavior?

Some opponents, such as the journalist Maggie Gallagher and Massachusetts Governor Mitt Romney, argue that same-sex marriage will signal governmental indifference to whether families contain both a mother and a father.[5] Such legal and cultural indifference, they fear, would further erode the norm of childrearing by both biological parents; more children would end up in fatherless homes. On the other hand, some advocates, such as Jonathan Rauch, argue that same-sex marriage will signal the government's (and society's) preference for marriage over other family arrangements, reinforcing marriage's status at a time when that status is under strain.[6] Same-sex marriage, in this view, would encourage marriage over nonmarriage and thus would benefit adults and children alike. Still others believe that same-sex marriage will have little or no effect of any sort on heterosexual families, if only because the number of gay and lesbian couples is small. There is, however, no evidence at all that bears directly on this question, at least in the American context, because until last year same-sex marriage had never been tried in the United States.[7]

In principle, a third class of children might be affected by same-sex marriage: additional children, so to speak, who might grow up with same-sex couples as a direct or indirect result of the legalization of same-sex marriage. Although even many opponents of same-sex marriage believe that gay and lesbian people should be allowed to foster and adopt children under certain circumstances, they worry that legalizing same-sex marriage would send an irrevocable cultural signal that same-sex parenting and opposite-sex parenting are interchangeable, when in fact they may not be equally good for children. In any case, the advent of same-sex marriage would probably make same-sex parenting easier

legally and more widely accepted socially, particularly for couples adopting children from the child welfare system. It is thus not surprising that questions about same-sex parenting come up time and again in discussions of same-sex marriage. To those questions we turn next.

What Are Same-Sex Families?

To speak of same-sex parenting is, almost by definition, to bundle together an assortment of family arrangements. Most children of opposite-sex parents got there the old-fashioned way, by being the biological children of both parents. Because same-sex couples cannot conceive together, their children arrive by a multiplicity of routes into families that assume a variety of shapes. In many cases (no one knows just how many), children living with gay and lesbian couples are the biological offspring of one member of the couple, whether by an earlier marriage or relationship, by arrangement with a known or anonymous sperm donor (in the case of lesbian couples), or by arrangement with a surrogate birth mother (in the case of male couples). Though, again, numbers are unavailable, male couples seem more likely than female couples to adopt children who are not biologically related to either custodial parent. It is worth noting that these different paths to parenthood lead to disparate destinations. The family dynamics of a female couple raising one partner's biological son from a previous marriage may be quite different from the dynamics of, say, a male couple raising a biologically unrelated son adopted from foster care.

Legal arrangements vary, too. Nonbiological parents in same-sex couples who seek to be legally recognized as parents must adopt, and the rules that govern adoption are as diverse as the state legislatures that pass adoption laws, the state agencies that promulgate adoption regulations, and the state courts that interpret them. All the states allow married couples to apply jointly—as couples—for adoption (but marriage is no guarantee that the adoption will be approved); and all the states allow unmarried individuals to apply for adoption. Only one state, Utah, denies adoption to unmarried couples (heterosexual and homosexual). And so marriage and adoption, though intertwined, are treated as distinct matters by the law and the courts.

> *As of this writing, the many same-sex couples whom researchers have studied share just one common trait: not one of them was legally married.*

Beyond that point, the rules diverge, especially for same-sex couples. Florida, uniquely, bans homosexual individuals from adopting. Mississippi explicitly bans adoption by same-sex couples. At the other end of the spectrum, as of mid-2004 nine states and the District of Columbia permitted same-sex couples to apply jointly for adoption, meaning that both members of the couple could be simultaneously granted parental status. In almost two dozen other states, courts in either the whole state or in some jurisdictions allow "second-parent" adoptions, under which one gay or lesbian partner can petition to become the second parent of the first partner's biological or previously adopted child. (For instance, a gay man could first adopt as a single parent, and then his partner could apply to become the child's other legal parent.) In the remaining states, same-sex couples are not el-

igible for either joint or second-parent adoption, which means that any children they might be raising are legally related to only one custodial parent.[8]

To study same-sex parenting, then, is to study not one phenomenon but many. As of this writing, indeed, the many same-sex couples whom researchers have studied share just one common trait: not one of them was legally married.[9] So—with suitable caveats about the diversity of same-sex family relationships and structures—what can we say about same-sex parenting and its impact on children? As it happens, the literature on same-sex parenting and its effects on children is significant and growing. For the present article, we reviewed most of it: more than fifty studies, many literature reviews, and accounts of a number of dissertations and conference papers dating back to the 1970s.

Why Same-Sex Parenting Is Hard to Study

This body of research grew partly out of court cases in which lesbian and gay parents (or co-parents) sought to defend or obtain custody of children.[10] Many researchers approached the subject with a sympathetic or protective attitude toward the children and families they studied. Critics have accused researchers of downplaying differences between children of gay and straight parents, especially if those differences could be interpreted unfavorably—a charge that has been debated in the field.[11] We will not enter that debate here, beyond noting that the best defense against bias is always to judge each study, whatever its author's motivation, critically and on its merits.

More significant, we believe, are the daunting methodological challenges that the researchers faced, especially at first.

Difficulty Finding Representative Samples

Perhaps the most important such challenge is that researchers have no complete listing of gay and lesbian parents from which to draw representative samples (probability samples, as researchers call them). To find study participants, they have often had to rely on word-of-mouth referrals, advertisements, and other recruiting tools that may produce samples not at all like the full population of gay and lesbian parents. All but one of the studies we examined employed samples composed of either totally or predominantly white participants. Almost all the participants were middle- to upper-middle-class, urban, well educated, and "out." Most were lesbians, not gay men. Participants were often clustered in a single place. It may be that most same-sex parents *are* white, relatively affluent lesbians, or it may be merely that these parents are the easiest for researchers to find and recruit, or both may be partly true. No one knows. Absent probability samples, generalizing findings is impossible.

Small Sample Sizes

Gay- and lesbian-headed families can be difficult to locate, and funding for this research has been sparse.[12] Those factors and others have forced researchers to deal with the challenge of small samples. Most studies describing the development of children raised in gay or lesbian homes report findings on fewer than twenty-five children, and most comparative studies compare fewer than thirty children in each of the groups studied. Other things being equal, the smaller the number of subjects in the groups studied, the harder it is to detect differences between those groups.[13]

Comparison Groups

The question is often not just how well same-sex parents and their children fare, but compared with whom? Should a single lesbian mother be compared with a single heterosexual mother? If so, divorced or never married? Should a two-mother family be compared with a two-biological-parent family, a mother-father family headed by one biological parent and one stepparent, or a single-parent family? It all depends on what the researcher wants to know. Identifying appropriate comparison groups has proved vexing, and no consistent or wholly convincing approach has emerged. Many studies mix family forms in both their homosexual and heterosexual groups, blurring the meaning of the comparison being made. Some studies do not use comparison groups at all and simply describe children or adults in same-sex households. Some, in fact, have argued that comparing gay and straight families, no matter how closely matched the groups, is inappropriate inasmuch as it assumes a "heterosexual norm" against which same-sex parents and their children should be judged.[14]

Subject-Group Heterogeneity

As we noted, families headed by same-sex parents are structurally very different from one another. That fact presents researchers with another challenge, because studies are most accurate when each of the groups being examined or compared is made up of similar individuals or families. When the pool of potential subjects is small, as it is for same-sex parents, assuring within-group homogeneity is often difficult. Thus some studies use "mixed" groups of lesbian-headed households, yielding results that are difficult to interpret. For example, partnered lesbians are often included with single lesbians, with all called "single" by the author; children who live both in and outside the home are discussed as a single group; children born into homes that originated both as heterosexual marriages and as lesbian households are included in the same sample; and separated and divorced women are mixed with never-married women and called "single." In at least one of the studies reviewed, children of transsexuals and lesbians, children who are both biological and adopted, and parents who are both biological and adopters are treated as a single group.

Measurement Issues

Another challenge is to gauge how well children are faring. Few studies collect data from the children directly, and even fewer observe the children's behavior—the gold standard for research of this kind, but more expensive and time-consuming than asking parents and children to evaluate themselves. Some studies use nonstandardized measures, while others use either measures with poor reliability and validity or measures whose reliability and validity were either not known or not reported.

Another measurement issue arises from the sometimes dated content of the measures used. In one 1986 study, for example, dressing in pants and wanting to be a doctor or lawyer were considered masculine for girls, and seeking leadership roles was considered a display of dominance.[15] Those classifications look rather quaint today.

Statistical Issues

To some extent, researchers can compensate for heterogeneous samples and nonequivalent comparison groups by using statistical methods that control for differences, particularly in studies with larger samples. Not all studies have done so, especially in the era before today's advanced software made statistical work considerably easier. Some studies thus did not perform appropriate statistical analyses when that was possible. Others did not report the direction of the significant relationships that they found, leaving unclear which group of children fared better. Most failed to control for potentially confounding factors, such as divorce stress or the status of a current relationship with a former partner.

Putting the Research Challenges in Perspective

This is an imposing catalog of challenges and shortcomings, and it needs to be seen in context. The challenges we describe are by no means unique to the research on same-sex parenting, and neither are the flaws that result.[16] Studying small, hard-to-locate populations is inherently difficult, especially if the subject pool is reticent. One of us, Meezan, has been conducting and reviewing field research on foster and adoptive families since the 1970s; he finds that the studies reviewed here are not under par by the standards of their discipline at the time they were conducted.

What the Evidence Shows— and Means

So what do the studies find? Summarizing the research, the American Psychological Association concluded in its July 2004 "Resolution on Sexual Orientation, Parents, and Children,"

There is no scientific basis for concluding that lesbian mothers or gay fathers are unfit parents on the basis of their sexual orientation. . . . On the contrary, results of research suggest that lesbian and gay parents are as likely as heterosexual parents to provide supportive and healthy environments for their children. . . . Overall, results of research suggest that the development, adjustment, and well-being of children with lesbian and gay parents do not differ markedly from that of children with heterosexual parents.[17]

Our own review of the evidence is consistent with that characterization. Specifically, the research supports four conclusions.

First, lesbian mothers, and gay fathers (about whom less is known), are much like other parents. Where differences are found, they sometimes favor same-sex parents. For instance, although one study finds that heterosexual fathers had greater emotional involvement with their children than did lesbian co-mothers, others find either no difference or that lesbian co-mothers seem to be more involved in the lives of their children than are heterosexual fathers.[18]

Second, there is no evidence that children of lesbian and gay parents are confused about their gender identity, either in childhood or adulthood, or that they are more likely to be homosexual. Evidence on gender behavior (as opposed to identification) is mixed; some studies find no differences, whereas others find that girls raised by lesbians may be more "masculine" in play and aspirations and that boys of lesbian parents are less aggressive.[19] Finally, some interesting differences have been noted in sexual behavior and attitudes (as opposed to orientation). Some studies report that children, particularly daughters, of lesbian parents adopt more accepting and open attitudes toward various sexual identities and are more willing to question their own sexuality. Others report that young women raised in lesbian-headed families are more likely to have homosexual friends and to disclose that they have had or would consider having same-sex sexual relationships.[20] (Just how to view such differences in behavior and attitude is a matter of disagreement. Where conservatives may see lax or immoral sexual standards, liberals may see commendably open-minded attitudes.)

Third, in general, children raised in same-sex environments show no differences in cognitive abilities, behavior, general emotional development, or such specific areas of emotional development as self-esteem, depression, or anxiety. In the few cases where differences in emotional development are found, they tend to favor children raised in

---

There is no evidence that children of lesbian and gay parents are confused about their gender identity, either in childhood or adulthood, or that they are more likely to be homosexual.

---

lesbian families. For example, one study reports that preschool children of lesbian mothers tend to be less aggressive, bossy, and domineering than children of heterosexual mothers. Another finds more psychiatric difficulties and a greater number of psychiatric referrals among children of heterosexual parents.[21] The only negative suggestion to have been uncovered about the emotional development of children of same-sex parents is a fear on the part of the children—which seems to dissipate during adolescence when sexual orientation is first expressed—that they might be homosexual.[22]

Finally, many gay and lesbian parents worry about their children being teased, and children often expend emotional energy hiding or otherwise controlling information about their parents, mainly to avoid ridicule. The evidence is mixed, however, on whether the children have heightened difficulty with peers, with more studies finding no particular problems.[23]

The significance of this body of evidence is a matter of contention, to say the least. Steven Nock, a prominent scholar reviewing the literature in 2001 as an expert witness in a Canadian court case, found it so flawed methodologically that the "only acceptable conclusion at this point is that the literature on this topic does not constitute a solid body of scientific evidence," and that "all of the articles I reviewed contained at least one fatal flaw of design or execution. . . . Not a single one was conducted according to generally accepted standards of scientific research."[24] Two equally prominent scholars, Judith Stacey and Timothy Biblarz, vigorously disputed the point: "He is simply wrong to say that all of the studies published to date are virtually worthless and unscientific. . . . If the Court were to accept Professor Nock's primary criticisms of these studies, it would have to dismiss virtually the entire discipline of psychology."[25]

We believe that both sides of that argument are right, at least partially. The evidence provides a great deal of information about the particular families and children studied, and the children now number more than a thousand.[26] They are doing about as well as children normally do. What the evidence does not provide, because of the methodological difficulties we outlined, is much knowledge about whether those studied are typical or atypical of the general population of children raised by gay and lesbian couples. We do not know how the *normative* child in a same-sex family compares with other children. To make the same point a little differently, those who say the evidence shows that many same-sex parents do an excellent job of parenting are right. Those who say the evidence falls short of showing that same-sex parenting is equivalent to opposite-sex parenting (or better, or worse) are also right.

Fortunately, the research situation is improving, so we may soon have clearer answers. Over the past several decades researchers have worked to improve their methods, and the population of gay and lesbian parents has become easier to study. Studies using larger samples are appearing in the literature, the first long-term study following the same group of people over time has been published, and studies using representative, population-based samples have appeared. More studies now use standardized instruments with acceptable reliability and validity. Recent studies are much more likely to match comparison groups closely and are also more likely to use statistical methods to control for differences both within and between the study groups.

We identified four studies—all comparatively recent (dating from 1997)—that we believe represent the state of the art, studies that are as rigorous as such research could today reasonably be expected to be (see box). Their conclusions do not differ from those of the main body of research.

It bears emphasizing that the issue of same-sex parenting is directly relevant to same-sex marriage only to the extent that the latter extends the scope of the former. Gay and lesbian couples make up only a small share of the population, not all of those couples have or want children, and many who do have or want children are likely to raise them whether or not same-sex marriage is legal. The number of additional children who might be raised by same-sex couples as a result of same-sex marriage is probably small. Moreover, an important question, where family arrangements are concerned, is al-

Four Strong Studies

How do children of lesbian or gay parents fare and compare? Following are summaries of four methodologically rigorous studies.

Wainwright, Russell, and Patterson (2004)

Methodology: Drawing on a nationally representative sample of more than 12,105 adolescents in the National Study of Adolescent Health, the authors compared forty-four adolescents being raised by female same-sex couples with forty-four raised by heterosexual couples. The comparison groups were matched child for child (not on group averages) on many traits, and the study samples did not differ on numerous demographic characteristics from the national sample of 12,105. Metrics were mostly standardized instruments with good reliability and validity, and many were the most commonly used measures in the field. Multivariate analysis was used to determine the impact of family type, controlling for other demographic and social factors.

Findings: "No differences in adolescents' psychosocial adjustment," including depressive symptoms, anxiety, and self-esteem; no differences in grade-point averages or problems in school. Adolescents with same-sex parents reported feeling more connected to school. The authors found that "it was the qualities of adolescent-parent relationships rather than the structural features of families (for example, same- versus opposite-sex parents) that were significantly associated with adolescent adjustment. . . . Across a diverse array of assessments, we found that the personal, family, and school adjustment of adolescents living with same-sex parents did not differ from that of adolescents living with opposite-sex parents."

Golombok and others (2003)

Methodology: In southwest England, researchers drew on a geographic population study of almost 14,000 mothers and their children to identify eighteen lesbian-mother families (headed both by lesbian couples and single mothers) and then added twenty-one lesbian mothers identified through personal referrals, a lesbian mothers' support organization, and advertisements. The twenty-one supplementary subjects were "closely comparable" to the eighteen drawn from the population study. The resulting sample of thirty-nine "cannot be deemed truly representative of the population of lesbian-mother families" but "constitutes the closest approximation achieved so far." Those families were compared with seventy-four families headed by heterosexual couples and sixty families headed by single heterosexual mothers. Standardized measures were administered and interview data were coded by personnel blind to the family's type and structure and were checked for reliability.

Findings: "Children reared by lesbian mothers appear to be functioning well and do not experience negative psychological consequences arising from the nature of their family environment." After the authors controlled for initial differences between groups (age of children, number of siblings) and the number of statistical comparisons made, "the only finding that remained significant . . . was greater smacking of children by fathers than by co-mothers." Also, "boys and girls in lesbian-mother families were not found to differ in gender-typed behavior from their counterparts from

continued on next page

Four Strong Studies *(continued)*

heterosexual homes." Children did better psychologically with two parents, regardless of whether the parents were same-sex or opposite-sex couples, than with a single mother.

Chan, Raboy, and Patterson (1998)

Methodology: Using a sample drawn from people who used the same sperm bank (in California), and thus controlling for the effects of biological relatedness, the researchers compared four family structures: lesbian couples (thirty-four), lesbian single mothers (twenty-one), heterosexual couples (sixteen), and single heterosexual mothers (nine). Participation rates were significantly higher for lesbian couples than for others. Though education and income levels were above average for all groups, lesbian parents had completed more education, and lesbian and coupled families had higher incomes; otherwise group demographics were similar. Information on children's adjustment was collected from parents and teachers, using standardized measures with good reliability and validity.

Findings: "Children's outcomes were unrelated to parental sexual orientation," for both single-parent and coupled families. "On the basis of assessments of children's social competence and behavior problems that we collected, it was impossible to distinguish children born to and brought up by lesbian versus heterosexual parents." Sample size was large enough to detect large or medium effects but not small ones, so family structure had either small or nonexistent effects.

Brewaeys and others (1997)

Methodology: Using a sample drawn from the fertility clinic at Brussels University Hospital, thirty lesbian-couple families who conceived through donor insemination (DI) were compared with thirty-eight heterosexual families who conceived through DI and thirty heterosexual families who conceived naturally. Response rates were generally good, but better for lesbian co-mothers than for heterosexual fathers. Statistical analysis controlled for demographic differences between comparison groups and for number of comparisons made, and good metrics were used.

Findings: Children's emotional and behavior adjustment "did not differ" between lesbian and opposite-sex families, and "boys and girls born in lesbian mother families showed similar gender-role behaviour compared to boys and girls born in heterosexual families." The quality of parents' relationship with each other did not differ across the two family types, nor did the quality of interaction between children and biological parents. "However, one striking difference was found between lesbian and heterosexual families: social mothers [that is, nonbiological lesbian parents] showed greater interaction with their children than did fathers."

Sources: Jennifer L. Wainwright, Stephen T. Russell, and Charlotte J. Patterson, "Psychosocial Adjustment, School Outcomes, and Romantic Relationships of Adolescents with Same-Sex Parents," *Child Development* 75, no. 6 (December 2004): 1886–98, quotes pp. 1892, 1895; Susan Golombok and others, "Children with Lesbian Parents: A Community Study," *Developmental Psychology* 39, no. 1 (January 2003): 20–33, quotes pp. 30, 31; Raymond Chan, Barbara Raboy, and Charlotte J. Patterson, "Psychosocial Adjustment among Children Conceived via Donor Insemination by Lesbian and Heterosexual Mothers," *Child Development* 69, no. 2 (April 1998): 443–57, quotes p. 453; A. Brewaeys and others, "Donor Insemination: Child Development and Family Functioning in Lesbian Mother Families," *Human Reproduction* 12, no. 6 (1997): 1349–59, quotes pp. 1356, 1357.

ways, "Compared with what?" We doubt that same-sex marriage would shift any significant number of children out of the homes of loving heterosexual parents and into same-sex households; and, to the extent that same-sex marriage helps move children out of foster care and into caring adoptive homes, the prospect should be welcomed. If the past several decades' research establishes anything, it is that the less time children spend in the public child welfare system, the better. Put simply, research shows that the state makes a poor parent for many of the children in its custody, particularly compared with stable, loving, developmentally appropriate environments.

Will Kids Benefit When Same-Sex Parents Marry?

We turn, finally, to a group of children to whom same-sex marriage, per se, is directly and immediately relevant—the children we mentioned early on and then set aside. These are children who are being raised, or who would be raised, by same-sex couples even without same-sex marriage. For them, the advent of legal same-sex marriage would mean that their parents could get married. Whether or not same-sex marriage would expand the scope of same-sex parenting, it clearly would expand the scope of same-sex *married* parenting. Marriage would also affect family dynamics. Some gay and lesbian cohabitants with children would become spouses; others might find that the prospect of marriage deepened their bond; still others might break up in disagreement over whether to tie the knot.

We know of no reputable scholar who believes that their parents' getting married would harm these children on average (though particular marriages may be bad for children). The pertinent question is: to what extent, and in what ways, might children benefit from the marriage of their lesbian and gay parents? This question turns out to be somewhat more difficult to answer than it may appear.

There is a vast literature on how marriage benefits children, and this is not the place to rehash it. Admirable discussions may be found in the articles by Paul Amato and by Adam Thomas and Isabel Sawhill elsewhere in this volume.[27] Of necessity, however, the literature pertains to heterosexual couples, not homosexual ones. Moreover, most such studies look at what happens when children's two biological parents marry. In same-sex families, of course, at least one parent is not the child's biological parent. Research on whether children of heterosexual couples do better in married than in cohabiting stepfamilies (where only one parent is the child's biological parent) is sparse and inconclusive.[28] Whether that research is pertinent to same-sex couples—who may be more likely than cohabiting straight couples to bring children into the home as a carefully considered joint decision—is at best unclear.

In other words, virtually no empirical evidence exists on how same-sex parents' marriage might affect their children. Nonetheless, we can do some theoretical probing, if only to understand how the introduction of marriage might affect the dynamics of same-sex families.

One benefit of traditional marriage—some would argue the central benefit—is that it helps tie fathers and mothers to their biological children. Obviously, that would not be the case with same-sex marriage, where one or both parents are, by definition, nonbiological. There are three other broad areas, however, where benefits to children of opposite-sex marriage might carry over to same-sex families.

The first is *material well-being*. In general, heterosexual marriage increases the economic capital available to children. Marriage conveys such public and private economic benefits as family leave from work and spousal health insurance eligibility (though it can also raise tax burdens; see the article by Adam Carasso and Eugene Steuerle in this volume). Marriage also entails a host of provisions that help ensure financial continuity if a spouse dies or is disabled. As Evan Wolfson

---

> *Another area where same-sex marriage might benefit children is in the durability and stability of the parental relationship.*

---

notes in *Why Marriage Matters*, "If one of the parents in a marriage dies, the law provides financial security not only for the surviving spouse, but for the children as well, by ensuring eligibility for all appropriate entitlements, such as Social Security survivor benefits, and inheritance rights."[29]

The family dynamics of marriage also seem to bring material benefits, partly because married couples are more likely to pool their resources, and partly because they engage in economic specialization, with one partner focusing primarily on work outside the home and the other primarily on work inside the home.

No doubt some of these advantages would carry over to homosexual marriages. Certainly the availability of various forms of spousal survivors' benefits, such as Social Security and tax-free inheritance of a home,

would benefit the child of a surviving same-sex spouse. The same would be true of disability and medical benefits, which cushion families—and thus children—from economic shocks. Resource pooling may also increase somewhat. On the other hand, to whatever extent same-sex couples have already compensated for the unavailability of marriage by arranging their affairs to mimic marriage, the transition from cohabitation to marriage may bring them less of an economic "bonus." Specialization gains might also be smaller for same-sex couples, to whatever extent the inside-outside division of labor is a function of gender roles rather than marriage as such.[30]

The second area where same-sex marriage might benefit children is in the *durability and stability of the parental relationship*. In the heterosexual world, a substantial body of research shows that, other things held equal, marriages are more durable and stable than cohabitation; and stability is, most scholars agree, of vital importance to children. To some extent, marriage may owe its greater durability to the simple fact that it is legally much harder to get out of than cohabitation. That may give couples an incentive to work out their problems. Yet there is reason to believe that the act of marriage, in particular its status as a solemn commitment in the eyes of the couple and their community (and, for many, their God), fortifies as well as deepens couples' bonds.

To what extent this would be true of same-sex couples is not as yet known in any rigorous way, but anecdotal evidence suggests that a similar dynamic may apply. Gay couples who have been formally married in Massachusetts, Canada, and San Francisco (the city briefly allowed such marriages, subsequently ruled invalid) have attested that the act of marriage has deepened their relationship—

often to no one's surprise more than their own.[31] Some people have predicted that married same-sex couples (especially male ones) will be less stable than married opposite-sex couples, but few if any have questioned that married same-sex couples will likely be more stable than unmarried same-sex couples.[32]

Finally, same-sex marriage might benefit children through *social investment*. Heterosexual marriage benefits children by bringing with it a host of social resources, some as tangible as legal and regulatory protections (spouses do not have to testify in court against each other, for example, and can permanently reside together in the United States even if one is not a citizen), others as intangible as social prestige and unquestioned parental authority. Explaining why she wished she could marry her lesbian partner, one woman said, "We're tired of having to explain our relationship. When you say you're married, everyone understands that."[33] The very fact that people routinely ask their friends and co-workers "How's your husband?" or "How's your wife?" tells couples—and their children—that they are perceived and treated as a family unit, with the autonomy and clear responsibility that this implies. Marriage also brings closer and more formal relationships with in-laws and grandparents, who are more likely to relate to a nonbiological child as a full-fledged grandchild or niece or nephew if the parents' union is formalized (and children who have more contact with grandparents tend to be better adjusted).[34] Though less stigma attaches to cohabitation today than in the past, married families still benefit from stronger community support and kinship networks, easing the burden on parents and children alike.

Some of these benefits would no doubt carry over to same-sex married couples. For instance, it seems reasonable to imagine that the formal, socially recognized bond of marriage may strengthen the emotional attachments between children and their nonbiological same-sex parents and grandparents. Marriage might also induce more jurisdictions to permit second-parent adoptions by gay and lesbian families. Such adoptions can be very meaningful, bringing the nonbiological parent closer to the child. As one parent put it, "I really didn't feel Jon was my son until I got that stupid piece of paper." Another couple felt that formal adoption put a "seal of legitimacy" on the parent-child relationship.[35]

Beyond the circle of kin, however, the social dynamics of same-sex marriage may be rather complicated. In communities that embrace the notion of same-sex marriage, marriage might bring added support and investment from neighbors, teachers, employers, peers, and others on whom children and parents rely. Indeed, the very existence of same-sex marriage may reduce the stigmatization or perceived peculiarity of same-sex families, which would presumably reduce the social pressure on the children. On the other hand, social acceptance of same-sex marriages as "real" marriages—marriages viewed as authentic by family, friends, and such institutions as churches and neighborhood groups—cannot be forced. In Massachusetts, for example, a labor union declared that its members' same-sex spouses would not be eligible for health and pension benefits.[36] If imposed legally over the resistance of a community, same-sex marriage might bring little additional social investment; indeed, it might become a new source of backlash against same-sex couples and their children. For children, same-sex marriage might in some places bring closer and warmer relationships with extended families and communities, but in other places it might relieve one form of stigma or hostility only to replace it with another.

Our own belief, on balance, is that society's time-honored preference for marriage over nonmarriage as a context for raising children would prove as justified for same-sex couples as for opposite-sex couples, for many of the same reasons. One piece of evidence is that many same-sex couples who are raising children *say* they need marriage. If it is true that parents are generally competent judges of what is good for their children, then their opinion deserves some weight.

An Opportunity to Learn

It is important, we think, to recognize that social science cannot settle the debate over same-sex marriage, even in principle. Some people believe the United States should have same-sex marriage as a matter of basic right even if the change proves deleterious for children; others believe the country should reject same-sex marriage as a matter of morality or faith even if the change would benefit kids. Consequential factors are but one piece of a larger puzzle; and, as is almost always the case, social research will for the most part follow rather than lead the national debate.

Both authors of this paper are openly gay and advocates of same-sex marriage, a fact that readers should weigh as they see fit. In any case, our personal judgments about the facts presented here are no better than anyone else's. Two points, however, seem to us to be both incontrovertible and important.

First, whether same-sex marriage would prove socially beneficial, socially harmful, or trivial is an empirical question that cannot be settled by any amount of armchair theorizing. There are plausible arguments on all sides of the issue, and as yet there is no evidence sufficient to settle them.

Second, the costs and benefits of same-sex marriage cannot be weighed if it cannot be tried—and, preferably, compared with other alternatives (such as civil unions). Either a national constitutional ban on same-sex marriage or a national judicial mandate would, for all practical purposes, throw away the chance to collect the information the country needs in order to make a properly informed decision.

As it happens, the United States is well situated, politically and legally, to try same-sex marriage on a limited scale—without, so to speak, betting the whole country. As of this writing, one state (Massachusetts) is marrying same-sex couples, two others (Vermont and Connecticut) offer civil unions, and several more (notably California) offer partner-benefit programs of one sort or another. Most other states have preemptively banned gay marriage, and some have banned civil unions as well. The upshot is that the nation is running exactly the sort of limited, localized experiment that can repay intensive study.

In particular, the clustering in four neighboring states of all three kinds of arrangement—same-sex marriage in Massachusetts, civil unions in Vermont and Connecticut, and neither in New Hampshire—offers a near-ideal natural laboratory. A rigorous study of how children fare when they are raised in these various arrangements and environments would not be easy to design and execute, and it would require a considerable amount of time and money; but the knowledge gained would make the debate over gay marriage better lit and perhaps less heated, to the benefit of all sides of the argument.

Endnotes

1. The thirteen were Arkansas, Georgia, Kentucky, Louisiana, Michigan, Mississippi, Missouri, Montana, North Dakota, Oklahoma, Ohio, Oregon, and Utah.

2. *Los Angeles Times* poll, March 27–30, 2004. Among respondents under age thirty, 44 percent supported same-sex marriage and 31 percent supported civil unions; 22 percent favored neither.

3. U.S. Census Bureau, *Married-Couple and Unmarried-Partner Households: 2000* (February 2003). See also Gary J. Gates and Jason Ost, *The Gay and Lesbian Atlas* (Washington: Urban Institute, 2004), p. 45.

4. Because same-sex couples, especially those with children, may be reluctant to identify themselves to census takers, and because small populations are inherently difficult to count, this number is likely to be an undercount. See Gates and Ost, *The Gay and Lesbian Atlas* (see note 3). Other estimates range much higher. See, for example, Frederick W. Bozett, "Gay Fathers: A Review of the Literature," in *Psychological Perspectives on Lesbian and Gay Male Experiences,* edited by Linda Garnets and Douglas Kimmel (Columbia University Press, 1993), pp. 437–57.

5. See, for example, Maggie Gallagher, "What Is Marriage For?" *Weekly Standard,* August 4–11, 2003; and Mitt Romney, testimony before the U.S. Senate Judiciary Committee, June 22, 2004.

6. Jonathan Rauch, *Gay Marriage: Why It Is Good for Gays, Good for Straights, and Good for America* (New York: Times Books, 2004).

7. As of this writing, the Netherlands, Belgium, and several Canadian provinces had adopted same-sex marriage, but only recently. The effects, if any, on the welfare of children and families are both unclear and disputed. See, for example, Stanley Kurtz, "The End of Marriage in Scandinavia," *Weekly Standard,* February 2, 2004; and in rebuttal, M. V. Lee Badgett, *Will Providing Marriage Rights to Same-Sex Couples Undermine Heterosexual Marriage? Evidence from Scandinavia and the Netherlands,* Discussion Paper (Council on Contemporary Families and Institute for Gay and Lesbian Strategic Studies, July 2004). Also in rebuttal, William N. Eskridge, Darren R. Spedale, and Hans Ytterberg, "Nordic Bliss? Scandinavian Registered Partnerships and the Same-Sex Marriage Debate," *Issues in Legal Scholarship,* Article 4, available at www.bepress.com/ils/iss5/art4/.

8. The authors are indebted to the Human Rights Campaign, the Lambda Legal Defense and Education Fund, and the National Adoption Information Clearinghouse for information on state adoption policies. Because adoption policies are often set by courts on a case-by-case basis, adoption rules are in flux and vary within as well as between states. The summary counts presented here are subject to interpretation and may have changed by the time of publication.

9. At this writing, same-sex marriage was too new in Massachusetts to have generated any research results.

10. "A third perspective from which [research] interest in lesbian and gay families with children has arisen is that of the law. . . . Because judicial and legislative bodies in some states have found lesbians and gay men unfit as parents because of their sexual orientation, lesbian mothers and gay fathers have often been denied custody or visitation with their children following divorce." Charlotte Patterson, "Lesbian Mothers, Gay Fathers, and Their Children," in *Lesbian, Gay and Bisexual Identities over the Lifespan: Psychological Perspectives,* edited by Anthony R. D'Augelli and Charlotte Patterson (Oxford University Press, 1995), p. 264.

11. Judith Stacey and Timothy J. Biblarz examine twenty-one studies and find that "researchers frequently downplay findings indicating difference regarding children's gender and sexual preferences and behavior." Judith Stacey and Timothy Biblarz, "(How) Does the Sexual Orientation of Parents Matter?" *American Sociological Review* 66 (April 2001): 159–83. Golombok and others reply that it is Stacey and Biblarz who "have overemphasized the differences that have been reported between children with lesbian and heterosexual parents." Susan Golombok and others, "Children with Lesbian Parents: A Community Study," *Developmental Psychology* 39, no. 1 (January 2003): 21.

12. For example, as best we can discern, none of the studies reviewed for this article was funded by the federal government, the major source of social science research funding in the United States.

13. For example, Tasker and Golombok note that there was only a 51 percent chance of detecting a moderate effect size in their sample, and an even lower possibility (if any at all) of detecting a small effect size. See Fiona Tasker and Susan Golombok, *Growing Up in a Lesbian Family* (New York: Guilford Press, 1997).

14. From the perspective of gay men, Gerald Mallon states, "Usually, explorations of gay parenting focus on the differences between gay and straight parents. [I] approach this topic through a gay-affirming lens, meaning that I do not take heterosexuality as the norm and then compare gay parenting to that model and discuss how it measures up. In most cases heterosexually oriented men become fathers for different reasons and in different ways than do gay men. Comparisons of gay fathers to heterosexual fathers are therefore inappropriate." Gerald Mallon, *Gay Men Choosing Parenthood* (Columbia University Press, 2004), p. xii. From a lesbian perspective, Victoria Clarke states, "In the rush to prove . . . our similarities to heterosexual families, oppressive norms of femininity, masculinity, and heterosexuality are reinforced. The use of sameness arguments suppresses feminist critiques of the family as a prime site of hetero-patriarchal oppression. . . . By taking mainstream concerns seriously, lesbian and gay psychologists inadvertently invest them with validity and reinforce the anti-lesbian agendas informing popular debates about lesbian parenting." Victoria Clarke, "Sameness and Differences in Lesbian Parenting," *Journal of Community and Applied Social Psychology* 12 (2002): 218.

15. Richard Green and others, "Lesbian Mothers and Their Children: A Comparison with Solo Parent Heterosexual Mothers and Their Children," *Archives of Sexual Behavior* 15, no. 2 (1986): 167–83.

16. For example, similar issues arise in the study of transracial adoption: "Study findings that support greater use of transracial adoption as a placement option . . . are fraught with conceptual and methodological limitations. . . . For instance, many have small sample sizes and no—or inappropriate—comparison groups. While they tend to be cross-sectional, those that are longitudinal are potentially biased from sample attrition." Devon Brooks and Richard P. Barth, "Adult Transracial and Inracial Adoptees: Effects of Race, Gender, Adoptive Family Structure, and Placement History on Adjustment Outcomes," *American Journal of Orthopsychiatry* 69 (January 1999): 88.

17. Available at www.apa.org/pi/lgbc/.

18. A. Brewaeys and others, "Donor Insemination: Child Development and Family Functioning in Lesbian Mother Families," *Human Reproduction* 12 (1997): 1349–59; David K. Flaks and others, "Lesbians Choosing Motherhood: A Comparative Study of Heterosexual Parents and Their Children," *Developmental Psychology* 31 (1995): 105–14; Golombok and others, "Children with Lesbian Parents" (see note 11), pp. 20–33; Katrien Vanfraussen, Ingrid Ponjaert-Kristoffersen, and Anne Brewaeys. "Family Functioning in Lesbian Families Created by Donor Insemination," *American Journal of Orthopsychiatry* 73, no. 1 (January 2003): 78–90.

19. Green and others, "Lesbian Mothers and Their Children" (see note 15); Beverly Hoeffer, "Children's Acquisition of Sex Role Behavior in Lesbian-Mother Families," *American Journal of Orthopsychiatry* 51, no. 3 (1981): 536–44; Ailsa Steckel, "Psychosocial Development of Children of Lesbian Mothers," in *Gay and Lesbian Parents*, edited by Frederick W. Bozett (New York: Praeger, 1987), pp. 75–85.

20. Lisa Saffron, *"What about the Children?" Sons and Daughters of Lesbian and Gay Parents Talk about Their Lives* (London: Cassell, 1996); Tasker and Golombok, *Growing Up in a Lesbian Family* (see note 13). It is unclear whether the young women are more likely to *engage* in same-sex relations, more likely to *disclose* them, or some combination of the two.

21. Steckel, "Psychosocial Development of Children of Lesbian Mothers" (see note 19); Susan Golombok, Ann Spencer, and Michael Rutter, "Children in Lesbian and Single-Parent Households: Psychosexual and Psychiatric Appraisal," *Journal of Child Psychology and Psychiatry* 24, no. 4 (1983): 551–72.

22. Karen G. Lewis, "Children of Lesbians: Their Point of View," *Social Work* 25 (May 1980): 198–203; Ann O'Connell, "Voices from the Heart: The Developmental Impact of Mother's Lesbianism on Her Adolescent Children," *Smith College Studies in Social Work* 63, no. 3 (June 1993): 281–99; S. J. Pennington, "Children of Lesbian Mothers," in *Gay and Lesbian Parents*, edited by Bozett (see note 19), pp. 58–74.

23. Phillip A. Belcastro and others, "A Review of Data Based Studies Addressing the Effects of Homosexual Parenting on Children's Sexual and Social Functioning," *Journal of Divorce and Remarriage* 20, nos. 1–2 (1993): 105–22; Frederick W. Bozett, "Children of Gay Fathers," *Gay and Lesbian Parents*, edited by Bozett (see note 19), pp. 39–57; Margaret Crosbie-Burnett and Lawrence Helmbrecht, "A Descriptive Empirical Study of Gay Male Stepfamilies," *Family Relations* 42 (1993): 256–62; Nanette Gatrell and others, "The National Lesbian Family Study: Interviews with Mothers of Five-Year-Olds," *American Journal of Orthopsychiatry* 70, no. 4 (October 2000): 542–48; Tamar D. Gershon, Jeanne M. Tschann, and John M. Jemerin, "Stigmatization, Self-Esteem, and Coping among the Adolescent Children of Lesbian Mothers," *Journal of Adolescent Health* 24, no. 6 (June 1999): 437–45; Golombok, Spencer, and Rutter, "Children in Lesbian and Single-Parent Households" (see note 21); Golombok and others, "Children with Lesbian Parents"(see note 11); Jan Hare, "Concerns and Issues Faced by Families Headed by a Lesbian Couple," *Families in Society* 75 (1994): 27–35; Ghazala Afzal Javaid, "The Children of Homosexual and Heterosexual Single Mothers," *Child Psychiatry and Human Development* 24 (1993): 235–48; Suzanne M. Johnson and Elizabeth O'Connor, *The Gay Baby Boom: The Psychology of Gay Parenthood* (New York University Press, 2002); Lewis, "Children of Lesbians" (see note 22); O'Connell, "Voices from the Heart" (see note 22); Pennington, "Children of Lesbian Mothers" (see note 22); Tasker and Golombok, *Growing Up in a Lesbian Family* (see note 13); Norman Wyers, "Homosexuality and the Family: Lesbian and Gay Spouses," *Social Work* 32 (1987): 143–48.

24. Steven L. Nock, affidavit in the superior court of Ontario, Canada, *Halpern et al.* v. *Canada* and *MCCT* v. *Canada* (2001), at items 141 (p. 47) and 115 (p. 39).

25. Judith Stacey and Timothy Biblarz, affidavit in the superior court of Ontario, Canada, *Halpern et al.* v. *Canada* and *MCCT* v. *Canada* (2001), at items 4 (p. 3) and 14 (p. 7).

26. Anderssen and others' review of the literature up until 2000, which did not cover all of the studies through that date, puts the number of children studied at 615. Norman Anderssen, Christine Amlie, and Erling Andre Ytteroy, "Outcomes for Children with Lesbian or Gay Parents: A Review of Studies from 1978 to 2000," *Scandinavian Journal of Psychology* 43 (2002): 335–51. Since that time, larger-scale studies, some

with samples larger than 200, have been undertaken. Stacey and Biblarz, in their affidavit (see note 25) at item 41 (p. 19), cite more than 1,000 children, and 500 observed in "22 of the best studies."

27. A useful compilation is *Why Marriage Matters: Twenty-One Conclusions from the Social Sciences,* by a consortium of thirteen family scholars; available at www.marriagemovement.org/WhyMarriageMatters. html.

28. See Susan L. Brown, "Family Structure and Child Well-Being: The Significance of Parental Cohabitation," *Journal of Marriage and the Family* 66 (May 2004): 351–67; Wendy D. Manning and Kathleen A. Lamb, "Adolescent Well-Being in Cohabiting, Married, and Single-Parent Families," *Journal of Marriage and the Family* 65 (November 2003): 876–93. According to Manning and Lamb, "The findings from empirical work suggest that teenagers and children in cohabiting parent step-families sometimes fare worse in terms of behavior problems and academic performance than children in married stepparent families. . . . Other research suggests that adolescents and children in cohabiting stepparent families share similar levels of behavior problems and academic achievement as children in married stepparent families. . . . The findings seem to depend on the gender and age of the child as well as the specific dependent or outcome variable" (p. 878).

29. Evan Wolfson, *Why Marriage Matters: America, Equality, and Gay People's Right to Marry* (New York: Simon and Schuster, 2004), pp. 95–96.

30. Research has shown that gay and lesbian couples are more equal in their division of labor than heterosexual couples. See Henny M. W. Bos, Frank van Balen, and Dymphna C. van den Boom, "Experience of Parenthood, Couple Relationship, Social Support, and Child-Rearing Goals in Planned Lesbian Mother Families," *Journal of Child Psychology and Psychiatry* 45, no. 4 (2004): 755–64; Raymond W. Chan and others, "Division of Labor among Lesbian and Heterosexual Parents: Associations with Children's Adjustment," *Journal of Family Psychology* 12, no. 3 (1998): 402–19; Claudia Ciano-Boyce and Lynn Shelley-Sireci, "Who Is Mommy Tonight? Lesbian Parenting Issues," *Journal of Homosexuality* 43 (2002): 1–13; Daniel W. McPherson, "Gay Parenting Couples: Parenting Arrangements, Arrangement Satisfaction, and Relationship Satisfaction," Ph.D. diss., Pacific Graduate School of Psychology, 1993; Charlotte J. Patterson, "Families of the Lesbian Baby Boom: Parents' Division of Labor and Children's Adjustment," *Developmental Psychology* 31 (1995): 115–23; Charlotte J. Patterson and Raymond W. Chan, "Families Headed by Gay and Lesbian Parents," in *Parenting and Child Development in "Nontraditional" Families,* edited by Michael Lamb (Mahwah, N.J.: Lawrence Erlbaum Associates, 1999), pp. 191–219.

31. See, for example, Shawn Hubler, "Nothing but 'I Do' Will Do Now for Many Gays," *Los Angeles Times,* March 21, 2004. One man who married his male partner in San Francisco said, "It has reconnected our relationship in ways I wasn't expecting, and to have a whole city reinforce it was amazing. I used to refer to Dave as my partner or boyfriend. Now I refer to him as my husband." One of the present authors (Rauch), while on a book tour last year, personally heard a number of such testimonials from gay couples.

32. For example, Stanley Kurtz has argued that male couples, if allowed to marry, would "help redefine marriage as a non-monogamous institution." "Beyond Gay Marriage: The Road to Polyamory," *Weekly Standard,* August 4–11, 2003.

33. Andrew Jacobs, "More than Mere Partners: By Example, Lesbian Couple Try to State Case for Marriage," *New York Times,* December 20, 2003.

34. See, for example, Charlotte J. Patterson, Susan Hurt, and Chandra D. Mason, "Families of the Lesbian Baby Boom: Children's Contact with Grandparents and Other Adults," *American Journal of Orthopsychiatry* 68, no. 3 (July 1998): 390–99.

35. Catherine Connolly, "The Voice of the Petitioner: The Experiences of Gay and Lesbian Parents in Successful Second-Parent Adoption Proceedings," *Law and Society Review* 36, no. 2 (2002): 325–46, quotes p. 337.

36. Donovan Slack, "Union Denies Benefits to Gay Couples," *Boston Globe*, May 11, 2004.

Why Don't They Just Get Married?
Barriers to Marriage among the Disadvantaged

Kathryn Edin and Joanna M. Reed

Summary

Kathryn Edin and Joanna Reed review recent research on social and economic barriers to marriage among the poor and discuss the efficacy of efforts by federal and state policymakers to promote marriage among poor unmarried couples, especially those with children, in light of these findings.

Social barriers include marital aspirations and expectations, norms about childbearing, financial standards for marriage, the quality of relationships, an aversion to divorce, and children by other partners. Edin and Reed note that disadvantaged men and women highly value marriage but believe they are currently unable to meet the high standards of relationship quality and financial stability they believe are necessary to sustain a marriage and avoid divorce. Despite their regard for marriage, however, poor Americans do not view it as a prerequisite for childbearing, and it is typical for either or both parents in an unmarried-couple family to have a child by another partner. Economic barriers include men's low earnings, women's earnings, and the marriage tax.

In view of these findings, Edin and Reed argue that public campaigns to convince poor Americans of the value of marriage are preaching to the choir. Instead, campaigns should emphasize the benefits for children of living with both biological parents and stress the harmful effects for children of high-conflict parental relationships. Programs to improve relationship quality must address head-on the significant problems many couple face. Because disadvantaged men and women view some degree of financial stability as a prerequisite for marriage, policymakers must address the instability and low pay of the jobs they typically hold as well as devise ways to promote homeownership and other asset development to encourage marriage. Moreover, programs need to help couples meet the challenges of parenting families where children are some combination of his, hers, and theirs. Encouraging more low-income couples to marry without giving them tools to help their marriages thrive may simply increase the divorce rate.

www.futureofchildren.org

Kathryn Edin is associate professor of sociology in the Department of Sociology and the Population Studies Center, University of Pennsylvania. Joanna M. Reed is a graduate student in sociology at Northwestern University. The authors wish to thank Kristen Harknett, Maria Kefalas, Timothy Nelson, and Sharon Sassler for their comments and suggestions.

Kathryn Edin and Joanna M. Reed

Half a century ago, Americans, whether poor or well-to-do, all married at roughly the same rate. But by the mid-1980s, poor women were only about three-quarters as likely to marry as women who were not poor. And marriage rates among the disadvantaged have continued to decline.[1] Today, poor men and women are only about half as likely to be married as those with incomes at three or more times the poverty level.[2]

For those concerned with child well-being, the most worrisome aspect of the decline in marriage among the poor is the increase in nonmarital childbearing. Though the share of first births within marriage has fallen dramatically for the nation as a whole—down from more than 90 percent in the 1940s to only about 60 percent today—nearly a third of poor women aged twenty-five or older have had a child outside marriage, compared with only 5 percent of women who are not poor.[3]

In an attempt to promote marriage among poor unmarried couples who are expecting a baby, federal and state policymakers are offering an extensive array of services around the time of the baby's birth—which many regard as a "magic moment" within these relationships. State and local agencies are recruiting expectant or new unmarried parents into innovative programs to improve their relationship skills, adapting curriculums traditionally used to improve the relationships of middle-class married couples. By teaching such skills to these unwed couples, most of whom are poor and minority, policymakers hope both to boost their marriage rates and to make their marriages last.

Many observers, however, are skeptical that these new programs, which have not been evaluated scientifically, will do much to restore marriage, especially healthy and enduring marriage, among the poor. They question whether these programs can effectively address the realities—both social and economic—that keep poor couples from getting married. Some on the political left have been sharply critical of such programs. One observer editorializes, "It's impossible to justify spending $1.5 billion on unproven marriage programs when there's not enough to pay for back-to-work *basics* like child care."[4]

We review findings from an emerging field of research that investigates the reasons why low-income couples, particularly those who share children, refrain from marriage. We begin by sorting the evidence into two types: economic and social. Social barriers to marriage include marital attitudes, childbearing attitudes, norms about the standard of living required for marriage, relationship quality, an aversion to divorce, and the tendency of both men and women to bring children from previous partners to the new relationship. The economic barriers that, at least in theory, affect the marriage rates of the poor include low earnings and employment among unskilled men, increasing employment among unskilled women, and the welfare state, which imposes a significant "tax" on marriage for low-income populations.

As we assess the evidence offered by this new research, we focus primarily on couples coping with economic disadvantage, rather than with other forms of disadvantage such as race or ethnicity. Whenever possible, we review qualitative as well as quantitative data.[5] While quantitative data show whether and under what conditions a belief is held or an event occurs, qualitative data can reveal the mechanisms and social processes that underlie these statistical relationships. Several new qualitative studies are especially valuable because they offer insight into how low-income couples, particularly those with shared children, view marriage. We begin with social factors because the financial barriers we review can be better understood in light of the social and cultural expectations that underlie them.

Social Barriers

In this section, we investigate six possible social barriers to marriage among disadvantaged Americans: their marital aspirations and expectations, their norms about childbearing, their financial standards for marriage, the quality of their relationships, their aversion to divorce, and their children by other partners.

Marital Aspirations and Expectations

If, as social psychologists have posited, one can predict an action based on an individual's intent to engage in it, then perhaps the poor are marrying at a low rate because they no longer aspire to matrimony.[6] Indeed, several survey analyses show that unmarried Americans who see marriage as important are more likely to wed than those who do not.[7] During the 1990s, a number of leading family researchers used national surveys to measure respondents' marital aspirations (whether they hope to marry) and expectations (whether they think they will get married) to see whether and how they vary. These studies uniformly show that marital aspirations are quite high among all Americans, including the economically disadvantaged. For example, Scott South, using the 1988–99 waves of the National Survey of Families and Households, finds little variation in marital aspirations by employment or earnings, relatively little by race, and only slightly more variation by education (better-educated respondents have only slightly higher aspirations to marry than their less well-educated counterparts).[8]

Richard and Kris Bulcroft analyze the same data and also find no significant differences in marital aspirations by income or employment, by education, or by the receipt of public assistance.[9] Sharon Sassler and Robert Schoen find an interesting difference by race, but not in the direction one might expect: single black women are substantially more likely than single white women to believe their lives would be better if they were married.[10]

More recently Daniel Lichter, Christine Batson, and J. Brian Brown analyzed data on noncohabiting unmarried individuals from the 1995 wave of the National Longitudinal Survey of Youth. They focus specifically on the marital aspirations of a variety of disadvantaged respondents, including those with low incomes, those from poor backgrounds, members of racial and ethnic minorities, recipients of public assistance, and women with children born outside marriage.[11] Although unmarried mothers are the least likely to aspire to marriage, nearly 70 percent report that they would like to marry eventually. And similar studies show that single mothers, welfare recipients, and black Americans have the same marital aspirations as other women (though education boosts these aspirations somewhat).[12]

Marital aspirations—the overall desire to marry "someday"—are less concrete, and therefore presumably less useful in predicting behavior, than are marital expectations. Two nationally representative surveys have measured marital expectations, although in somewhat different ways. In the National Survey of Family Growth, noncohabiting unmarried women were asked, "Do you expect to marry (again) at some time in the future?" A large majority of those surveyed across a variety of disadvantaged groups reported that they do expect to marry, though women who were not single mothers reported higher expectations of marriage than did single mothers. In addition, women from disadvantaged family backgrounds, those with little education, and those on welfare have lower expectations for marriage.[13] The survey also asked cohabiting women if they expected to marry their current boyfriend. Here, the results show that men's economic disadvantage does deter their partner's marital expectations.[14] Nonetheless, both sets of survey findings

---

The notion that marriage profoundly changes the meaning of a relationship and is suitable only for those who can meet these high standards speaks to its strong symbolic value.

---

show that marital expectations among the disadvantaged are still very high.

The Fragile Families and Child Wellbeing Study, a large nationally representative study of an urban birth cohort of just under 3,800 children of unmarried parents, documented that the vast majority (83 percent) of all out-of-wedlock births to adult women are to romantically involved couples, about half of whom are living together at the time the child is born.[15] When these couples were asked, "How would you rate your chances of marrying your baby's mother/father?" in the hours immediately following their child's birth, nearly three-quarters of the mothers rated their chances as at least 50-50, and almost six in ten believed their chances were good or almost certain.[16] Fathers are even more optimistic: a stunning 90 percent felt

their chances were at least 50-50, and 75 percent felt they were good or almost certain.[17]

Some researchers doubt the validity of these findings because the couples were interviewed just hours after their child's birth. However, the Time, Love, and Cash in Couples with Children study (TLC3) conducted intensive qualitative interviews with a subsample of forty-nine unmarried couples from the Fragile Families Study two to three months after the births.[18] At this point, the euphoria of the new birth had presumably succumbed to sleepless nights and other strains of parenting a newborn, but interviewers found that these couples were nearly as optimistic about marriage as they had been just hours after their babies were born.[19]

There are several conclusions to be drawn. The first is that although marital aspirations do not vary much along most dimensions of disadvantage, marital expectations do. One possible reason for this discrepancy is that questions about marital aspirations are value laden and thus subject to what methodologists call "social desirability bias," the tendency for respondents to answer survey questions according to prevailing societal norms. Questions about marital expectations are more concrete and reflect specific situations and potential partners rather than overall values and attitudes. Another interpretation is that although disadvantaged men and women want to marry, they face more formidable barriers than do members of the middle class. Recognizing these barriers may, in turn, lower expectations of marriage in spite of high aspirations. Whichever interpretation one chooses, the second conclusion we draw from these findings is that both marital aspirations and expectations are still quite high among disadvantaged groups, including unmarried parents.

Yet these high hopes and expectations are hard to square with the findings on marital behavior. For example, Lichter, Batson, and Brown find that only 20 percent of all women who aspire to marriage realize that goal within four years.[20] Among unwed new parents in the Fragile Families Study, only about 15 percent marry by the time their child turns three.[21] Lichter, Batson, and Brown pose the obvious question, "Why is the transition to marriage so low among single women who want to marry?"[22]

Recent research suggests that Americans, rich and poor alike, have adopted a new definition of marriage and that new notions of what marriage means may be part of the answer.[23] In particular, marriage seems to have lost much of its instrumental value. That is, society has become much more accepting of premarital sexual activity, cohabitation, and nonmarital childbearing than it once was.[24] When a wedding is no longer a prerequisite for open sexual activity, cohabitation, and childbearing; when abortion and birth control are widely available; and when a gold wedding band is no longer necessary for American women to claim social personhood, the practical value of marriage is severely diminished. In the TLC3 qualitative study, unmarried parents were asked how they felt their lives would change if they were to marry. Not surprisingly, both mothers and fathers, most of whom were already living together, typically said that marriage would not change their day-to-day lives at all.[25]

Yet this same research also suggests that the symbolic value of marriage may still be quite high. In fact, it may even have increased, precisely because of marriage's diminishing instrumental value.[26] Marriage has become a luxury rather than a necessity, a status symbol in the true meaning of the phrase.[27] Kathryn

Edin and Maria Kefalas argue that as a result of this transformation in the meaning of marriage, both poor and more advantaged Americans now have strikingly similar expectations regarding a marriage partner and an ideal marital relationship.[28] The same couples in the TLC3 study who believed their day-to-day lives would not change at all if they married went on to say that getting married would profoundly transform the meaning of their relationship, in no small part because they believe that marriage carries with it much higher expectations about relationship quality and financial stability than does cohabitation—a point to which we will return. The notion that marriage profoundly changes the meaning of a relationship and is suitable only for those who can meet these high standards speaks to its strong symbolic value. If this interpretation is correct, the poor may marry at a lower rate simply because they are not able to meet this higher marital standard.

Attitudes about Childbearing

Policymakers care most about promoting marriage as a setting for raising children. Yet despite their high regard for marriage, poor Americans do not view it as a prerequisite for childbearing.[29] Indeed, qualitative studies of low-income unmarried parents suggest that for the disadvantaged, childbearing and marriage no longer necessarily "go together."[30] The TLC3 study asked new unmarried parents an extensive set of open-ended questions about their beliefs about marriage and their marriage aspirations and plans. Though most couples reported having had many conversations about marriage and were eager to share their marital views and plans with interviewers, the subject of children almost never came up in these conversations, except for the frequent assertion that merely having a child together is *not* a sufficient reason to marry.[31] In stark contrast, in-depth interviews with a college-based sample of twenty-five cohabiting women and men living in New York City revealed that most saw marriage as a crucial prerequisite for childbearing. In fact, many could not imagine having children outside marriage.[32]

Ethnographic research by Edin and Kefalas in eight low-income Philadelphia-area neighborhoods between 1995 and 2001, along with repeated in-depth interviews with a racially diverse group of 162 single mothers in these neighborhoods, uncovered complex attitudes toward children and marriage.[33] Though these mothers generally believe that having children before marriage is not the ideal way of doing things, they must calculate the risks and rewards of the partnerships available to them and balance their marital aspirations with their strong moral views about the conditions under which it is right and proper to marry, a theme that recurs throughout this review.

Economic Standards for Marriage

We discuss the importance of men's employment and earnings later. Here, we focus on a related topic: norms and values about the standard of living required for marriage. Theories about the connection between marriage rates and men's earnings assume the existence of a financial "floor" below which marriage is not viewed as practical. One survey analysis shows that men and women who believe that it is necessary to be financially established before marriage are less likely to marry than those who do not.[34]

Qualitative evidence supports the notion that poor couples' beliefs about what constitutes the proper financial position for marriage may pose a barrier to marriage. Edin and Kefalas's work with single mothers in Philadelphia (noted above) shows that "getting the finances together" is a crucial prerequisite for marriage.[35] But marriageability is not merely about having funds to set up a common household. Indeed, many couples are already cohabiting. Rather, these mothers believe that marriage ought to be reserved for couples who can support what some of them term a "white picket fence" lifestyle—a standard of living that generally includes two or more of the following: a mortgage on a modest row home, a car and some furniture, some savings in the bank, and enough money left over to pay for a "decent" wedding.[36]

During the early to mid-1990s, Edin carried out in-depth interviews with a racially diverse group of 292 low-income single mothers in Chicago; Camden, New Jersey; and Charleston, South Carolina. She found that most believed a poor but happy marriage has virtually no chance of survival and that the daily stress of living "paycheck to paycheck" would put undue pressure on a marital relationship. These mothers believed that couples who wish to marry must demonstrate to the community—their family, friends, and neighbors—that they have "arrived" financially.[37] To meet this goal, they said, couples must accumulate the common assets that visibly demonstrate their fiscal responsibility and long-term planning skills.

Interviewers for the TLC3 study of unmarried couples asked those who aspired to marriage to identify barriers to marriage. In 74 percent of the couples, either the father or the mother, or both, saw their financial situation as standing in the way, even though 77 percent of the couples were living together at the time, almost all in independent households.[38] Joanna Reed analyzed the TLC3 study's fourteen-, twenty-six-, and fifty-month waves and found that almost all the couples who stayed together over the whole four-year period were unwavering in their commitment to these economic goals, nor did they lower their standards to fit their current circumstances.[39] Those who broke up and formed new partnerships almost universally adopted a similar set of goals in their new relationships, as did their new partners. If these high economic standards were merely paying lip service to middle-class ideals—a socially acceptable way to mask a reluctance to marry for other reasons—couples who achieved the goals would have still held off on marriage. But most couples who met their economic goals and did not have serious relationship problems did indeed marry one another during the four-year window of the study.[40]

Relationship Quality

Recent federal and state marriage initiatives have focused on teaching low-income unmarried couples how to build relationship skills that will lead to healthy marriage relationships, and several quantitative studies lend credence to the idea that low relationship quality is a barrier to marriage.[41] One such study uses two waves of the National Survey of Families and Households and finds that among cohabiting couples, higher relationship quality does increase the odds of a transition to marriage.[42] Marcia Carlson, Sara McLanahan, and Paula England's analysis of the baseline and twelve-month waves of the Fragile Families Survey also finds that perceived relationship quality—specifically, partner's supportiveness—and mothers' trust of men are both significant predictors of marriage. In a simulation, they show that higher relationship quality would boost marriage rates more than would a significant increase in fathers' earnings.[43]

Psychologists have long held that stressful events may interfere with couples' ability to

relate positively to one another, and the Fragile Families Survey shows that unmarried parents face many challenging circumstances around the time of their child's birth.[44] Beyond their typically low levels of education, employment, and financial stability (roughly 40 percent of both mothers and fathers had not graduated from high school, and 20 percent of fathers were jobless when the child was born), an alarmingly high share of new fathers had already spent time in jail or

---

Several quantitative studies lend credence to the idea that low relationship quality is a barrier to marriage.

---

prison, indicating a high rate of past criminal involvement.[45] In addition, their family situations posed unusual challenges: in more than 60 percent of these couples, one or both partners already had at least one child from a previous relationship.[46]

Edin and Kefalas asked each of the Philadelphia-area single mothers they interviewed to chronicle their most recent breakup. They asked them to identify why their relationship had failed, allowing them to cite problems on their own rather than prompting them with a list of potential difficulties. Nearly half the mothers cited a chronic pattern of domestic violence, while four in ten blamed repeated and often flagrant infidelities of their partner. About a third named their partner's ongoing involvement with crime and the imprisonment that so often followed. More than a third cited drug and alcohol abuse.[47] These problems are also rife in the relationships of the unmarried couples in the TLC3 study, and though both mothers and fathers report such problems with their partners, women are far more likely to do so than men.[48]

Many disadvantaged women, it appears, have children in the context of romantic relationships of perilously low quality.[49] Yet these same women hold a marriage relationship to high standards. What may be tolerable behavior in a boyfriend, at least for a time, is completely unacceptable in a husband. Further, it is foolish even to consider marriage until a man has shown that he is ready and able to meet these higher standards.[50] The TLC3 study finds that in 57 percent of unmarried couples with a newborn, either he or she, or both, point to problems in their relationship that they would have to resolve before they could marry. The TLC3 study also shows that most unmarried couples believe they are not close to meeting these higher relationship standards at the time their child is born.[51]

Why are these couples so insistent that marriage requires a much higher level of relationship quality than living together while sharing parenting tasks for their mutual children? First, their relationships are usually relatively new. The typical TLC3 couple had been together less than a year before conceiving their first child together (very similar to what Edin and Kefalas's Philadelphia-area single mothers reported).[52] Second, few of these conceptions were the result of a clearly articulated plan.[53] The emphasis that these new unmarried parents place on relationship quality (and on the need to test the relationship for several more years) is thus quite understandable: the couples do not know each other well and did not typically plan to have a child together when they did.

When the TLC3 interviewers asked respondents to describe the qualities most important

for a good marriage, most men and women responded with an almost identical litany: "Communication, honesty, and trust."[54] The issue of trust is particularly salient for relationships frequently threatened by episodes of domestic violence and rampant infidelity. Indeed, Frank Furstenberg's qualitative interviews among a group of low-income Baltimore residents uncovered a "culture of distrust" between men and women. This pervasive lack of trust keeps couples continually vigilant for signs of relational trouble and makes them quick to exit the relationship as soon as such signs appear.[55] The theme of distrust is also evident in Edin and Kefalas's ethnographic work in Philadelphia, as well as in Edin's interviews with mothers from Chicago, Camden, and Charleston.[56]

Aversion to Divorce

Although Americans as a whole have grown much more accepting of divorce over the past half-century, poorly educated men and women have been slower to shed their negative views than their better-educated counterparts.[57] This divergence of opinion is ironic, because marriages among college-educated adults have grown more stable since 1980: the divorce rate of this group has been falling as the divorce rate for the least educated has increased.[58]

We know of no analysis that directly assesses whether fear of divorce is affecting marriage rates. But one analysis using two waves of the Fragile Families Survey finds that couples with characteristics that make them more likely to divorce (being younger or less educated, reporting serious relational conflict or abuse) are less likely to marry, even if they have other characteristics that are strongly associated with entry into marriage. Christina Gibson-Davis, Kathryn Edin, and Sara McLanahan write, "Based on this evidence, we conclude that unmarried parents delay marriage when they perceive a high risk of divorce."[59] Data from several qualitative studies support the hypothesis that the poor may be reluctant to marry precisely because of a perception that the risk of divorce is high. The single mothers in Philadelphia studied by Edin and Kefalas reported that the stigma of a failed marriage was far worse than that of an out-of-wedlock birth.[60] Edin's interviews in Chicago, Camden, and Charleston show that most low-income single mothers believe marriage is "sacred" and that divorce makes a mockery of the institution they revere.[61]

In 53 percent of the unmarried TLC3 couples, one or both partners say their fear of divorce is part of what is keeping them from getting married. In one memorable interview, a mother quipped, "I don't believe in divorce. That's why none of the women in my family are married!" One analysis of these data concludes that "at the heart of marital hesitancy is a deep respect for the institution of marriage."[62] On a practical level, these couples fear subjecting a relationship that does not meet these standards to the normative expectations of marriage prematurely, as doing so might put the relationship in jeopardy. In the meantime, cohabitation allows enough flexibility for the couple to stay together even in the face of financial trouble and relationship problems.

Children by Other Partners

The typical nonmarital birth is to a couple in which the father, the mother, or both already have a child by another partner. Because multiple partner fertility is more common among disadvantaged groups, and poor women and men who marry are much more likely to do so after already having a child, children by other partners may pose a special barrier to marriage among these groups.[63]

Men may be less willing to marry a woman who must care for another man's child, and women may hesitate to marry a man with child support obligations. Only one study, an analysis of the baseline and twelve-month waves of the Fragile Families Survey, has looked at the effect of children by other partners on marriage transitions. It finds that a father's children by other partners do affect

One analysis of these data concludes that "at the heart of marital hesitancy is a deep respect for the institution of marriage."

transitions to marriage somewhat, while a mother's children by other partners do not.[64]

Qualitative evidence of the baseline wave of the TLC3 study offers one reason why this may be so. Unmarried fathers typically live with the mother and her other children, whereas unmarried mothers almost never live with the children from their partner's past relationships; these children generally live with their biological mother. Although fathers in this situation are obligated to provide child support, potentially a source of financial strain for the couple, mothers in this study seldom complained about the flow of economic resources out of the household and toward the care of a partner's other children. In part they viewed fathers who paid support as acting responsibly—a quality they much admired. Their approval may also contain an element of self-interest, as they may be eager to ensure that they can count on such contributions if their own relationship with him dissolves.

Mothers are not so sanguine about the time fathers spend with their other children: complaints in this area were more frequent than complaints about child support. Mothers generally feel that time spent with other children detracts from the time spent with the new baby, and they express some unease about the circumstances under which fathers spent time with these children—usually in the home of the children's own mother.[65] At the root of some of these complaints is the fear that the father will become reinvolved sexually with her. That fear is not unreasonable, given Heather Hill's finding that by the study's end, more than one-third of the couples experienced at least one spell of infidelity, sometimes with a former boyfriend or girlfriend.[66]

Fathers, too, presumably weigh the costs and benefits of marriage differently when the woman has a custodial child by another partner, but no male respondent in the TLC3 study cited his partner's other children as a barrier, a finding consistent with the survey results.

Economic Barriers

We now turn to economic barriers to marriage. In this section, we consider the effect of men's low earnings, women's comparatively high earnings, and the marriage tax.

Low Male Earnings

Declines in men's employment and earnings have long been regarded as a primary explanation for the falling marriage rate among the poor. William Julius Wilson argues that lower wages and higher unemployment among unskilled urban minority men translates into fewer marriageable males for women seeking husbands.[67] Valerie Oppenheimer blames marital delay among the poor on the uncertainty engendered by the substantial slowing

of disadvantaged men's entry into full-time stable employment.[68] Because our task is to identify current barriers to marriage, we ignore the debate about the causes of the decline in marriage over time, beyond noting that changes in men's economic position do not explain much of the trend.[69] Instead, we focus on research examining the current effects of men's economic position on entry into marriage.

In nearly all analyses of surveys, stable male employment and earnings boost marriage rates for the population as a whole, though there is some debate over their effect on cohabiters.[70] Stable male employment and earnings also increase marriage rates among new, unmarried parents.[71] Conversely, employment instability and low educational attainment usually discourage marriage.[72] In all these analyses, however, the effect of men's employment and earnings on marital transitions is surprisingly small. To assess the role of employment and earnings among unmarried parents with children—the target population of the new marriage initiatives—Carlson, McLanahan, and England conducted a simulation to predict the share of unmarried parents who would have gotten married if men's earnings increased by 1 standard deviation. In this model, marriage rates increase only about 1.9 percentage points—an 18 percent increase—within one year of the child's birth (from 9 to 10.6 percent).[73]

In sum, the quantitative data show that men's education, employment, job stability, and income do make a difference in transitions to marriage, but not as much as one might expect. Edin's qualitative study of single mothers in Chicago, Camden, and Charleston shows that men's income matters enormously in mothers' calculations about whether their male partners are worth marrying or even worth staying with. But the study also shows that mothers are not entirely mercenary in their attitudes toward men. Rather, they place nearly equal emphasis on the regularity of his contributions, the effort he expends getting and keeping a job, and the source of the earnings (drug dealing is not viewed as a viable long-term employment strategy). Furthermore, though stable earnings seem to be a necessary precondition for marriage among this group, they are not sufficient to prompt marriage—men's earnings are only one of many barriers.

Women's Earnings

The past thirty years have seen sharp growth in the employment and earnings of American women. Beginning in the mid-1990s the combination of a strong economy, an expanded earned income tax credit (EITC), and welfare reform lured or pushed an unprecedented number of low-income single mothers into the workforce.[74] Researchers often cite the growth in women's employment as a primary reason for the declining marriage rate among disadvantaged Americans. Gary Becker, for example, argues that women's employment and their wages relative to men's reduce the gains from marriage that come from specialization (he in the breadwinner role and she as the homemaker), and thus lead to lower marriage rates.[75] Similarly, Sara McLanahan and Lynn Casper claim that couples may be delaying marriage because women are more economically independent and less reliant on a male wage.[76]

Here, the empirical results are somewhat murky. Among the population as a whole, some studies find that women's employment, hours of work, earnings, or potential earnings do delay marriage.[77] But others find no such effect, and still others find a *positive* effect of women's earnings on marriage transitions.[78]

Megan Sweeney offers a possible clarification of these contradictory findings, showing that the role of women's economic position might be changing over time. She finds that while women's earnings might have reduced marriage rates among earlier cohorts—women now in their early to mid-fifties—they have increased marriage rates among a more recent cohort, those now in their early to mid-forties.

Fortunately, studies that focus on disadvantaged women's economic situations and likelihood of marriage are quite consistent and straightforward in their findings: for those at the bottom of the educational distribution, women's employment increases marital transitions. That relationship is further confirmed by recent analyses of the Fragile Families Survey, which find that more education and a higher hourly wage for women increased marriage rates among couples in the year following their child's birth.[79]

Qualitative research offers some clues as to why greater employment and earnings among women may promote their marriage rates. Edin and Kefalas's interviews with single mothers in Philadelphia and Edin's interviews with single mothers in Chicago, Camden, and Charleston find that most insist that they will not marry if it means they must rely on a man's earnings.[80] Rather, they feel it is crucial to become economically self-sufficient before taking marriage vows, partly because they want a partnership of equals and believe that money buys power in a marital relationship, but also because money of one's own can provide insurance in case of divorce.[81]

The Marriage Tax

The American welfare state, which has grown dramatically from its inception in 1935 to the present, has also been named by some as a prime suspect in the mystery of declining marriage rates. Most notably, two decades ago Charles Murray posited that a generous social safety net is responsible for low marriage rates among the poor.[82] Murray claimed that the large "tax" imposed on single mothers who marry their children's father—that is, the potential loss of her benefits—makes it economically rational for many single mothers to

---

The EITC may play a positive role by boosting single mothers' incomes, thus helping them to reach the standard of living they believe is necessary for marriage.

---

remain unmarried. Robert Moffitt's review of the literature on the disincentive effects of the U.S. welfare system shows a significant, yet surprisingly small, dampening effect of welfare benefits on marriage. Moffitt concludes that "the welfare system does not appear to be capable of explaining most of the long-term trend of increasing numbers of female-headed families in the United States."[83]

The high economic standard to which disadvantaged Americans hold marriage is probably the main reason why the welfare system's marriage penalty has such a small effect on marriage rates. In addition, as three qualitative studies of unmarried parents find, women on welfare believe they are simply too far below the economic bar even to contemplate marriage.[84] Furthermore, hardly any of the mothers or fathers in these studies named welfare or the potential loss of the

EITC (which poor unmarried parents typically refer to as their "tax return") as a barrier to marriage. In fact, the EITC may play a positive role by boosting single mothers' incomes, thus helping them to reach the standard of living they believe is necessary for marriage. It also provides a strong incentive for single mothers who do not wish to rely either on work or on welfare (which is now time limited and mandates work for most recipients) to marry an employed man.

Are Policymakers' Marriage-Promotion Plans on Target?

Given what researchers are discovering about the barriers to marriage that low-income couples face, or believe they face, how well are the marriage-promotion plans of federal and state policymakers likely to fare?

Attitudes and Beliefs about Marriage

Disadvantaged women and men aspire to marriage and expect to marry some day. But they do not necessarily regard childbearing and marriage as life events that go together. They do often believe what the articles in this volume by Adam Thomas and Isabel Sawhill and by Paul Amato demonstrate: that, on average, children are better off when raised within marriage. For most poor couples, however, that ideal remains largely unrealized because of the complexities of their lives. For these reasons, public campaigns to convince poor Americans of the value of marriage are probably preaching to the choir. Instead, they should be aimed at informing them about the benefits to children of being raised in a household with both biological parents as well as about the harmful effects of violent or high-conflict relationships on child well-being.

Relationship Problems

Although federal and state marriage programs have evoked sharp criticism from many observers, particularly from political liberals, the findings we have cited suggest that programs aimed at improving relational quality are sorely needed. But marriage programs must address the reality of the lives that disadvantaged men and women lead. Often they face serious problems in their relationships. These issues must be directly addressed in any relationship skills curriculum, as it is hard to see how any relationship could, or even should, survive in the face of these very serious problems. Policymakers should also strongly consider whether it might be wise to address these issues much earlier, perhaps in high school or even sooner, before such serious difficulties have had a chance to develop.

Fear of Divorce

Policymakers must realize that one reason why poor men and women may hold the economic and relationship bar to marriage so high is that they are strongly averse to divorce and are convinced that divorce makes a mockery of an institution they revere. As this review shows, research is just beginning to illuminate what might be needed to encourage more low-income couples to marry. Doing so without also offering the tools necessary to make their marriages thrive may have serious unintended consequences, including more divorce. Oklahoma, which leads the nation in programs to promote and strengthen marriage, was spurred to act by the realization that its divorce rate was the second highest in the nation.[85] Divorce among low-income couples is already high. Presumably, the last thing federal and state policymakers want to do is to destabilize low-income marriage even more.

His, Her, or Their Kids?

Policymakers must recognize that encouraging marriage among the poor will lead to precious few "traditional" family arrangements. Rather, the children in these families will likely be some combination of his, hers, and theirs. As Marcia Carlson and Frank Furstenberg warn, parental resources must be spread across such relationships and may result in lower overall parenting quality than is typically observed in married-couple families today.[86] Therefore, within these blended families the children from other partners may not reap the same benefits as the children the couple share in common.[87] Relationship skills curriculums should be organized around helping parents meet these challenges. It is also worth noting that one of the strongest predictors of multiple partner fertility other than the race or educational level of the parents is a teen first birth, so public and private efforts to further decrease the teen childbearing rate should continue to receive support.[88]

Economic Situation of Low-Income Couples

Disadvantaged men and women hold marriage to an economic standard that demands a fairly high level of financial stability—enough to accumulate significant common assets. Therefore, policymakers who want to help couples with their relationship problems must also find ways to address the instability, low pay, and low premium on experience of the jobs they typically hold. They should also devise ways to promote homeownership and other asset development. Notions about the standard of living that couples must achieve before they can marry reflect strong moral views about the durability of marriage. Edin and Kefalas write, "Conservatives are acting upon the premise that not being married is what makes so many women and children poor. But poor women insist that their poverty is part of what makes marriage so difficult to sustain. Their keen observations of middle-class behavior tell them that given all the expectations Americans now place on it, modern-day marriage is hard enough without the added burden of financial worries. How, they ask, can an economically strained marriage hope to survive?"[89] To date, policymakers have devoted far more attention to enhancing relationship skills than to helping couples reach their economic goals.

Making welfare less generous is not likely to lead to large increases in marriage. Rather, policymakers must address both men's and women's employment and earnings, since mothers feel it is vital that they be on an economically sound footing before contemplating marriage. This makes practical sense, as the standard of living these couples aspire to, and insist on reaching before they marry, will require two incomes.

Endnotes

1. These figures represent the likelihood of marriage within a given year. See Diane K. McLaughlin and Daniel T. Lichter, "Poverty and the Marital Behavior of Young Women," *Journal of Marriage and the Family* 59 (1997): 589.

2. Forty percent of poor men and 30 percent of poor women are married, compared with about two-thirds of men and women with incomes at three or more times the poverty level. Between 1999 and 2001 the figures for the poor declined from 48 percent to 41 percent for men and from 37 percent to 33 percent for women. See Tamara Halle, "Charting Parenthood: A Statistical Portrait of Fathers and Mothers in America" (Washington: Child Trends, 2002).

3. Amara Bachu, "Trends in Marital Status of U.S. Women at First Birth: 1930–1994," Population Division Working Paper 20 (U.S. Bureau of the Census, 2003). This analysis excludes births to adolescents, almost all of which are nonmarital. Twenty-three percent of poor women aged twenty-five and older have had an adolescent birth, as against only 4 percent of nonpoor women. See Saul D. Hoffman and E. Michael Foster, "Economic Correlates of Nonmarital Childbearing among Adult Women," *Family Planning Perspectives* 29, no. 3 (1997): 137–40, table 2.

4. "Quick Hit," Editorial, *San Jose Mercury News*, September 19, 2003.

5. Because the marriage behaviors of the poor have changed significantly over the past several decades, we exclude any study published before 1990. For example, Carol Stack's 1972 account of the coping strategies of the welfare poor is excluded, though it does include a discussion of marital views. See Carol B. Stack, *All Our Kin: Strategies for Survival in a Black Community* (New York: Harper and Row, 1974). We also exclude ethnographic studies in which marriage is a peripheral, not a central, focus, such as Elijah Anderson's discussion of sex codes among inner-city African American teens. See Elijah Anderson, *The Code of the Street: Decency, Violence, and the Moral Life of the Inner City* (New York: Norton, 1999).

6. Martin Fishbein and Icek Ajzen, *Belief, Attitude, Intention, and Behavior* (Reading, Mass.: Addison-Wesley, 1975).

7. Marcia J. Carlson, Sara S. McLanahan, and Paula England, "Union Formation in Fragile Families," *Demography* 41 (2004): 237–61; Daniel T. Lichter, Christine Batson, and J. Brian Brown, "Marriage Promotion: The Marital Expectations and Desires of Single and Cohabiting Mothers," *Social Service Review* 78, no. 1 (2004): 2–25. An analysis of data from the National Survey of Families and Households (NSFH) finds that African Americans' higher valuation of marriage relative to that of whites narrows the racial gap in marriage. See Sharon Sassler and Robert Schoen, "The Effect of Attitudes and Economic Activity on Marriage," *Journal of Marriage and the Family* 61 (1999): 147–59. An analysis of new, unmarried parents confirms this as well. See Kristen Harknett and Sara McLanahan, "Explaining Racial and Ethnic Differences in Marriage among New, Unwed Parents," *American Sociological Review* 69, no. 9 (2004): 790–811.

8. Scott J. South, "Racial and Ethnic Differences in the Desire to Marry," *Journal of Marriage and the Family* 55 (1993): 357–70.

9. Richard A. Bulcroft and Kris A. Bulcroft, "Race Differences in Attitudinal and Motivational Factors in the Decision to Marry," *Journal of Marriage and the Family* 55 (1993): 338–55.

10. Sassler and Schoen, "The Effect of Attitudes" (see note 7). This could be due to selection, as black women with positive attitudes toward marriage may have fewer partners to marry.

11. Lichter, Batson, and Brown, "Marriage Promotion" (see note 7).

12. See also Jane G. Mauldon and others, "What Do They Think? Welfare Recipients' Attitudes toward Marriage and Childbearing," Research Brief 2, Welfare Reform and Family Formation Project (Bethesda, Md.: Abt Associates, 2002).

13. Lichter, Batson, and Brown, "Marriage Promotion" (see note 7).

14. Wendy D. Manning and Pamela J. Smock, "First Comes Cohabitation and Then Comes Marriage? A Research Note," *Journal of Family Issues* 23, no. 8 (2002): 1065–87.

15. Carlson, McLanahan, and England, "Union Formation in Fragile Families" (see note 7). Figures from 1994 showed that 40 percent of nonmarital births were to cohabiters, though the rate could be higher now. See Larry L. Bumpass and Hsien-Hen Lu, "Trends in Cohabitation and Implications for Children's Family Contexts," *Population Studies* 54 (2000): 29–41.

16. The response rate for fathers was somewhat lower than for mothers, but for mothers with a father interviewed, 85 percent said their chances for marriage were at least 50-50. Sara S. McLanahan and others, *The Fragile Families and Child Wellbeing Study: Baseline National Report* (Princeton: Center for Research on Child Wellbeing, Princeton University, 2003).

17. Ibid.

18. These couples are a subsample of respondents in the Fragile Families Survey. The respondents are a stratified random sample of parents of new babies delivered in three of the seventy-five hospitals the Fragile Families Survey used to construct its sample—one hospital in each of three major U.S. cities (Chicago, Milwaukee, and New York). See Christina Gibson-Davis, Kathryn Edin, and Sara McLanahan, "High Hopes, But Even Higher Expectations: The Retreat from Marriage among Low-Income Couples," *Journal of Marriage and the Family* (forthcoming).

19. Ibid.

20. Lichter, Batson, and Brown, "Marriage Promotion" (see note 7). The likelihood of marriage is unaffected by family background, education, employment, and the receipt of public assistance, but is reduced among stigmatized racial and ethnic minority groups and among single mothers.

21. Author calculation using Fragile Family data.

22. Lichter, Batson, and Brown, "Marriage Promotion" (see note 7), pp. 17–18.

23. Larry L. Bumpass and James A. Sweet, "Marriage, Divorce, and Intergenerational Relationships," in *The Well-Being of Children and Families: Research and Data Needs*, edited by Arland Thorton (University of Michigan Press, 2001): 295–313; Andrew J. Cherlin, "The Deinstitutionalization of American Marriage," *Journal of Marriage and the Family* 66 (2004): 848–61; Kathryn Edin and Maria J. Kefalas, *Promises I Can Keep: Why Poor Women Put Motherhood before Marriage* (University of California Press, 2005); Judith A. Seltzer, "Families Formed outside of Marriage," *Journal of Marriage and the Family* 55 (2000): 408–14; Megan M. Sweeney, "Two Decades of Family Change: The Shifting Economic Foundations of Marriage," *American Sociological Review* 67 (2002): 132–47; Arland Thorton and Linda Young-DeMarco, "Four Decades of Trends in Attitudes toward Family Issues in the United States: The 1960s through the 1990s," *Journal of Marriage and the Family* 63 (2001): 1009–37.

24. William G. Axinn and Arland Thorton, "The Transformation in the Meaning of Marriage," in *The Ties That Bind: Perspectives on Marriage and Cohabitation*, edited by Linda J. Waite (New York: Aldine de Gruyter, 2000): 147–65; Thorton and Young-Demarco, "Four Decades of Trends" (see note 23).

25. Joanna Reed, "The Meanings of Marriage and Cohabitation for Unmarried Couples with Children," paper presented at the annual meeting of the American Sociological Association, Atlanta, 2003.

26. Cherlin, "The Deinstitutionalization of American Marriage" (see note 23); Edin and Kefalas, *Promises I Can Keep* (see note 23); Kathryn Edin, Maria J. Kefalas, and Joanna M. Reed, "A Peek inside the Black Box: What Marriage Means for Poor Unmarried Parents," *Journal of Marriage and the Family* 67 (2004): 1007–14.

27. Edin and Kefalas, *Promises I Can Keep* (see note 23).

28. Ibid.

29. Sayer, Wright, and Edin find no educational differences in women's general acceptance of nonmarital childbearing or in their odds of disapproving of women who have children outside marriage. There are also no educational differences in men's general acceptance, though less educated men have greater odds of disapproving of women who bear children outside marriage. See Liana Sayer, Nathan Wright, and Kathryn Edin, "Class Differences in Family Values: A 30-Year Exploration of Americans' Attitudes toward the Family," paper presented at the annual meeting of the Population Association of America, Minneapolis, May 2003. For trends in such attitudes over time and for racial-ethic differences in these attitudes, see Axinn and Thorton, "The Transformation" (see note 24); Thorton and Young-DeMarco, "Four Decades" (see note 23).

30. Edin and Kefalas, *Promises I Can Keep* (see note 23); Frank F. Furstenberg Jr., "Fading Dream: Prospects for Marriage in the Inner City," in *Problem of the Century*, edited by Douglas Massey and Elijah Anderson (New York: Russell Sage Foundation, 2001); Gibson-Davis, Edin, and McLanahan, "High Hopes" (see note 18); Maureen J. Waller, "Meaning and Motives in New Family Stories: The Separation of Reproduction and Marriage among Low Income Black and White Parents," in *The Cultural Territories of Race: Black and White Boundaries*, edited by Michelle Lamont (New York: Russell Sage Foundation, 1999): 182–218.

31. Joanna M. Reed, "A Closer Look at the Relationships of Unmarried Parents: Relationship Trajectories, Meanings and Implications for Processes of Cultural Change," unpublished, Northwestern University, 2005.

32. Whether the difference is due to their socioeconomic status or their parental status cannot be assessed.

33. Edin and Kefalas, *Promises I Can Keep* (see note 23).

34. Sassler and Schoen, "The Effect of Attitudes" (see note 7). Bulcroft and Bulcroft ("Race Differences in Attitudinal and Motivational Factors in the Decision to Marry" [see note 9]) show that African Americans place the most emphasis on economic prerequisites for marriage. They argue that this emphasis exacerbates the effects of poor economic circumstances.

35. Edin and Kefalas, *Promises I Can Keep* (see note 23).

36. In fact, they bear striking similarity to the standards held by their working- and lower-middle-class counterparts. For a description of working- and middle-class conceptions of marriage, see Pamela J. Smock,

Wendy K. Manning, and Meredith Porter, "Everything's There Except Money: How Money Shapes Decisions to Marry among Cohabiters," *Journal of Marriage and the Family* (forthcoming).

37. Kathryn Edin, "How Low-Income Single Mothers Talk about Marriage," *Social Problems* 47 (2000): 112–33.

38. Gibson-Davis, Edin, and McLanahan, "High Hopes" (see note 18). Though TLC3 did not select couples based on their cohabitation status, this is a higher rate of cohabitation than for the romantically involved portion of the Fragile Families Survey.

39. Reed, "A Closer Look" (see note 31).

40. Because the numbers are small—nine of the forty-nine couples both met their economic goals and married—these results should be interpreted with caution. However, demographers project that 72 percent of all women with a nonmarital birth can still expect to marry eventually. See Deborah R. Graefe and Daniel T. Lichter, "Marriage among Unwed Mothers: Whites, Blacks and Hispanics Compared," *Perspectives on Sexual and Reproductive Health* 34, no. 6 (2002): 286–93.

41. Theodora T. Ooms, "Strengthening Couples and Marriage in Low-Income Communities," in *Revitalizing the Institution of Marriage for the Twenty-First Century: An Agenda for Strengthening Marriage*, edited by Alan J. Hawkins, Lynn D. Wardle, and David O. Coolidge (Westport, Conn.: Praeger, 2002): 79–99.

42. Susan Brown, "Union Transitions among Cohabiters: The Significance of Relationship Assessments and Expectations," *Journal of Marriage and the Family* 62 (2000): 833–46.

43. Carlson, McLanahan, and England, "Union Formation" (see note 7).

44. Lisa A. Neff and Benjamin R. Karney, "The Dynamic Structure of Relationship Perceptions: Differential Importance as a Strategy of Relationship Maintenance," *Personal Social Psychology Bulletin* 29 (2003): 1433–46; Abraham Tesser and Steven R. H. Beach, "Life Events, Relationship Quality, and Depression: An Investigation of Judgment Discontinuity in Vivo," *Journal of Personality and Social Psychology* 74, no. 1 (1998): 36–52.

45. McLanahan and others, *The Fragile Families and Child Wellbeing Study* (see note 16); Center for Research on Child Wellbeing, "Incarceration and the Bonds among Fragile Families," Research Brief 12 (Princeton University, 2002).

46. Marcia J. Carlson and Frank F. Furstenberg Jr., "Complex Families: Documenting the Prevalence and Correlates of Multiple Partnered Fertility in the United States," Working Paper 03-14-FF (Center for Research on Child Wellbeing, Princeton University, 2004).

47. Edin and Kefalas, *Promises I Can Keep* (see note 23), p. 81.

48. Paula England, Kathryn Edin, and Kathryn Linnenberg, "Love and Distrust among Unmarried Partners," paper presented at the National Poverty Center conference "Marriage and Family Formation among Low-Income Couples: What Do We Know from Research," Georgetown University, September 2003; Heather Hill, "Steppin' Out: Sexual Jealousy and Infidelity among Unmarried Parents," paper presented at the annual meeting of the Population Association of America, Philadelphia, March 2005.

49. See also Andrew J. Cherlin and others, "The Influence of Child Sexual Abuse on Marriage and Cohabitation," *American Journal of Sociology* (forthcoming). Violence, infidelity, and drug and alcohol use within

marriage are associated with low marital quality and with divorce. See Paul R. Amato and Stacy J. Rogers, "Do Attitudes toward Divorce Affect Marital Quality?" *Journal of Family Issues* 20 (1999): 69–86; Demie Kurz, *For Richer, for Poorer: Mothers Confront Divorce* (New York: Routledge, 1995); Liana C. Sayer and Suzanne M. Bianchi, "Women's Economic Independence and the Probability of Divorce," *Journal of Family Issues* 21 (2000): 906–43.

50. Edin and Kefalas, *Promises I Can Keep* (see note 23); Edin, "How Low-Income Single Mothers Talk about Marriage" (see note 37).

51. Gibson-Davis, Edin, and McLanahan, "High Hopes" (see note 18).

52. England, Edin, and Linnenberg, "Love and Distrust" (see note 48).

53. Kathryn Edin, Paula England, and Joanna M. Reed, "Planned, Accidental, or Somewhere in Between: Pregnancy Intentionality among Unmarried Couples," in *Unmarried Couples with Children*, edited by Paula England and Kathryn Edin (New York: Russell Sage Foundation, forthcoming).

54. Gibson-Davis, Edin, and McLanahan, "High Hopes" (see note 18).

55. Furstenberg, "Fading Dream" (see note 30).

56. Edin and Kefalas, *Promises I Can Keep* (see note 23); Edin, "How Low-Income Single Mothers Talk" (see note 37).

57. Sayer, Wright, and Edin, "Class Differences" (see note 29).

58. Steven P. Martin, "Delayed Marriage and Childbearing: Implications and Measurement of Diverging Trends in Family Timing," Russell Sage Foundation Discussion Paper (New York, 2002).

59. Maureen R. Waller and H. Elizabeth Peters, "The Risk of Divorce as a Barrier to Marriage," Working Paper 2005-03-FF (Center for Research on Child Wellbeing, Princeton University, 2005), p. 2.

60. Edin and Kefalas, *Promises I Can Keep* (see note 23).

61. Edin, "How Low-Income Single Mothers Talk" (see note 37).

62. Gibson-Davis, Edin, and McLanahan, "High Hopes" (see note 18).

63. Carlson and Furstenberg, "Complex Families" (see note 46).

64. Carlson, McLanahan, and England, "Union Formation in Fragile Families" (see note 7).

65. Erin Metz, "Making Child Support Meaning-Full: The Social Meaning of Child Support Arrangements for Low Income Parents," unpublished, Northwestern University, 2004; England, Edin, and Linnenberg, "Love and Distrust" (see note 48).

66. Hill, "Steppin' Out" (see note 48).

67. William J. Wilson, *The Truly Disadvantaged* (University of Chicago Press, 1987).

68. Valerie K. Oppenheimer, "Cohabiting and Marriage during Young Men's Career Development Process," *Demography* 40, no. 1 (2003): 127–49; Valerie K. Oppenheimer, Matthijs Kalmijn, and Nelson Lim, "Men's Career Development and Marriage Timing during a Period of Rising Inequality," *Demography* 34, no. 3

(1997): 311–30. A variant of this argument is that for subgroups with high male incarceration and death rates, imbalanced sex ratios create a dearth of marriageable men.

69. David Ellwood and Christopher Jencks, "The Spread of Single-Parent Families in the United States since 1960," Working Paper RWP04-008 (Kennedy School of Government, Harvard University, 2004).

70. Marin Clarkberg, "The Price of Partnering: The Role of Economic Well-Being in Young Adults' First Union Experiences," *Social Forces* 77 (1999): 609–34; Heather Koball, "Have African American Men Become Less Committed to Marriage? Explaining the Twentieth Century Racial Cross-Over in Men's Marriage Timing," *Demography* 35, no. 2 (1998): 251–58; Steven L. Nock, "The Consequences of Premarital Fatherhood," *American Sociological Review* 62, no. 2 (1998): 250–63; Oppenheimer, Kalmijn, and Lim, "Men's Career Development" (see note 68); Brown, "Union Transitions" (see note 42). Smock and Manning find that cohabiting men's earnings are positively associated with marriage, though Sassler and Mc-Nally, Oppenheimer, and Brines and Joyner find that cohabiting men's earnings have a negative or insignificant effect on transitions to marriage. See Pamela J. Smock and Wendy K. Manning, "Cohabiting Partners' Economic Circumstances and Marriage," *Demography* 34 (1997): 331–41; Sharon Sassler and James Mc-Nally, "Cohabiting Couples' Economic Circumstances and Union Transitions: A Re-Examination Using Multiple Imputation Techniques," *Social Science Research* (forthcoming); Oppenheimer, "Cohabiting and Marriage" (see note 68); Julie Brines and Kara Joyner, "The Ties That Bind: Principles of Cohesion in Cohabitation and Marriage," *American Sociological Review* 64, no. 3 (1999): 333–56.

71. Carlson, McLanahan, and England, "Union Formation" (see note 7).

72. Oppenheimer, "Cohabiting and Marriage" (see note 68).

73. Carlson, McLanahan, and England, "Union Formation" (see note 7). After adjusting income upward, men were then reassigned to the appropriate dichotomous category, more than $25,000 for 73 percent of cases and $10,000–$24,999 for the remaining 27 percent.

74. Daniel Lichter and Rukmalie Jayakody, "Welfare Reform: How Do We Measure Success?" *Annual Review of Sociology* 28 (2002): 117–41.

75. Gary S. Becker, *A Treatise on the Family* (Harvard University Press, 1991).

76. Sara McLanahan and Lynn Casper, "Growing Diversity and Inequality in the American Family," in *State of the Union, America in the 1990s*, vol. 2, *Social Trends*, edited by Reynolds J. Farley (New York: Russell Sage Foundation, 1995): 1–43.

77. Francine D. Blau, Lawrence M. Kahn, and Jane Waldfogel, "Understanding Young Women's Marriage Decisions: The Role of Labor and Marriage Market Conditions," *Industrial and Labor Relations Review* 53, no. 4 (2000): 624–47; Cynthia Cready, Mark A. Fossett, and Jill K. Kiecolt, "Mate Availability and African American Family Structure in the U.S. Nonmetropolitan South, 1960–1990," *Journal of Marriage and the Family* 59 (1997): 192–203; Kim M. Lloyd and Scott J. South, "Contextual Influences on Young Men's Transition to First Marriage," *Social Forces* 74 (1996): 1097–2119.

78. Wendy D. Manning and Pamela J. Smock, "Why Marry: Race and the Transition to Marriage among Cohabiters," *Demography* 32 (1995): 509–20; McLaughlin and Lichter, "Poverty and the Marital Behavior" (see note 1); R. Kelly Raley, "A Shortage of Marriageable Men: A Note on the Role of Cohabitation in

Black-White Differences in Marriage Rates," *American Sociological Review* 61 (1996): 973–83; Sweeney, "Two Decades of Family Change" (see note 23).

79. McLaughlin and Lichter, "Poverty and Marital Behavior" (see note 1); Daniel T. Lichter and others, "Race and the Retreat from Marriage: A Shortage of Marriageable Men?" *American Sociological Review* 57 (1992): 781–99; Carlson, McLanahan, and England, "Union Formation" (see note 7). The hourly wage results are restricted to those women who were employed.

80. Edin and Kefalas, *Promises I Can Keep* (see note 23).

81. This reflects the findings of qualitative interviews with a group of 292 racially and ethnically diverse single mothers in three cities; see Edin, "How Low-Income Single Mothers Talk" (see note 37). The theme of financial independence is much less evident among a qualitative study of working and lower-middle class Toledo respondents; see Smock, Manning, and Porter, "Everything's There Except Money" (see note 36). South finds that men prefer wives with strong economic prospects. See Scott J. South, "Sociodemographic Differentials in Mate Selection Preferences," *Journal of Marriage and the Family* 53 (1991): 928–40.

82. Charles Murray, *Losing Ground* (New York: Basic Books, 1984).

83. Robert Moffitt, "Incentive Effects in the U.S. Welfare System," *Journal of Economic Literature* 30, no. 1 (2002): 56–57. The studies Moffitt reviewed were conducted before welfare benefits became time limited and work conditioned. These changes reduced the value of welfare, which presumably means that transfers play an even smaller role in reducing marriage rates now.

84. Edin, "How Low-Income Single Mothers Talk" (see note 37); Edin and Kefalas, *Promises I Can Keep* (see note 23); Gibson-Davis, Edin, and McLanahan, "High Hopes" (see note 18).

85. This figure is by state of residence. Nevada is the state that grants the most divorces. Jerry Regier, Cabinet Secretary, Oklahoma Health and Human Services, and Acting Director, Oklahoma Department of Health, Testimony before the Subcommittee on Human Resources of the House Committee on Ways and Means, Hearing on Welfare and Marriage Issues, May 22, 2001.

86. Carlson and Furstenberg, "Complex Families" (see note 46).

87. Sara S. McLanahan and Gary Sandefur, *Growing Up with a Single Parent: What Helps, What Hurts* (Harvard University Press, 1994).

88. Carlson and Furstenberg, "Complex Families" (see note 46).

89. Edin and Kefalas, *Promises I Can Keep* (see note 23), p. 218.

Healthy Marriage Programs: Learning What Works

M. Robin Dion

Summary

Evidence of public and private interest in programs designed to strengthen the institution of marriage and reduce the number of children growing up without both their parents is growing. Robin Dion addresses the question of whether such programs can be effective, especially among disadvantaged populations.

She begins by describing a variety of marriage education programs. Although new to the social welfare umbrella, such programs have existed for several decades. Social scientists have evaluated a number of these programs and found them effective in improving relationship satisfaction and communication among romantically involved couples. All the programs tested so far, however, have served primarily white, middle-class, well-educated couples who were engaged or already married.

Because these programs were neither designed for nor tested with disadvantaged populations, Dion observes, there is some question whether they can respond to the unique needs and circumstances of low-income couples, many of whom have multiple stressors and life challenges that can make stable relationships and marriages especially difficult. New research suggests that low-income families often face specific relationship issues that are rarely addressed in the standard programs, such as lingering effects of prior sexual abuse, lower levels of trust and commitment, and lack of exposure to positive role models for marriage. Dion describes the recent efforts of several groups to adapt research-supported marriage education programs or create entirely new curriculums so they are more responsive to and respectful of the needs of low-income families.

Finally, Dion describes ongoing efforts by the Administration for Children and Families to evaluate rigorously the effectiveness of several healthy marriage initiative models being implemented on a large scale across the country. These evaluations will determine whether such programs can work with less advantaged and more culturally diverse families, including whether the impacts on couples' relationships will translate into positive effects on the well-being of their children.

www.futureofchildren.org

M. Robin Dion is a senior researcher at Mathematica Policy Research.

Federal and state legislation enacted over the past decade clearly reflects a growing national interest in reducing the number of children growing up without both parents. In 1996, Congress passed a law allowing states to use part of their welfare block grants to promote the formation of two-parent families and marriage. The Administration for Children and Families (ACF) at the U.S. Department of Health and Human Services announced a Healthy Marriage Initiative in 2001, prompted in part by research showing that children fare best when raised by their married parents.[1] As of fall 2004, more than forty states had launched government-sponsored efforts to support marriage and couple relationships.[2] Congress is now considering legislation to provide $200 million annually in competitive grants to states and organizations to advance marriage-related activities, including demonstration programs to help couples form and sustain healthy marriages and research to determine the effectiveness of those programs.[3]

These policies and programs take a range of approaches to promoting the benefits of stable marriage—from changes in divorce laws to services that teach relationship skills, to media campaigns. The central policy question is whether it is possible to implement programs that can increase the number of children who are raised by both parents in healthy and stable marriages, especially within disadvantaged populations known to be at higher risk for family instability. This article describes such marriage programs, discusses the main challenges and opportunities in implementing them in low-income populations, and explains how researchers, policymakers, and practitioners are beginning to learn whether they work.

What Is a Marriage Program?

Broadly speaking, marriage programs provide support, information, and education about healthy relationships and marriage. Also called healthy marriage initiatives, they are often led by public or private organizations or agencies seeking to support marriage in a certain geographic area or target population. These state, federal, and community-sponsored efforts take many forms.[4] Some are grassroots coalitions to promote marriage. Others aim to educate high school or college students about what it takes to have a successful relationship and marriage. Some seek to make marriage-related services (such as marital counseling) more widely available, while still others have created web-based resources for couples in a given community. A few states offer marriage licenses at reduced rates to couples who participate in brief premarital education courses; others have developed marriage handbooks or similar materials for people applying for a marriage license. Programs are being developed to provide marriage-related services for specific populations, including refugees, parents receiving child welfare services, and low-income unmarried parents at risk for child support.[5] Other, more general efforts simply publicize and promote the benefits of marriage.[6] Although some of these strategies seem to have merit, few have been scientifically evaluated for their effect on the stability or quality of marriages.

Marriage Education

Increasingly, the heart of many marriage programs is what is known as marriage education—a curriculum-guided approach to giving couples the skills and information needed to develop or maintain successful relationships and marriage. Marriage education is typically delivered in a group session led by one or more trained facilitators. Although a new element of the social welfare umbrella, it has existed in a variety of forms for several decades, and several curriculums have been scientifically evaluated. Some curriculums arose out of observations of couple interaction by scientists who, over the years, have identified the behaviors leading to relationship success or failure.[7] Others were developed as part of religious efforts to strengthen marriage within specific congregations or faiths. Still others were created on the basis of clinical or personal experience. The vast majority were developed for a mainstream audience and have thus been used primarily with white, middle- to upper-class married or engaged couples.

More than 100 marriage education curriculums exist today, and they vary widely in content, target population, teaching method, and service delivery approach.[8] Curriculum developers typically disseminate their programs by training interested people or agencies to teach the curriculum and by selling their books, leader's guides, and participant materials. After being trained, individual therapists, counselors, clergy, and other professionals independently apply the curriculums in various ways and contexts.

Most marriage education curriculums address communication (such as listening and expressing oneself effectively), conflict management, and problem-solving skills—at least to some extent. Other topics may include intimacy and friendship, family-of-origin issues, empathy, commitment, forgiveness, negotiation and compromise, power and control, expectations, finances, anger and stress management, self-care, identifying destructive behaviors and patterns, self-awareness, emotional literacy, trust, mutual respect and responsibility, and roles, values, and beliefs.

Some marriage curriculums have been tested for effectiveness many times, while others have never been evaluated at all. The evaluations vary in their degree of scientific rigor. In a recent systematic and quantitative review of evaluations of marital interventions, policy researchers identified studies that met strict criteria and assessed how these programs af-

---

Most marriage education curriculums address communication (such as listening and expressing oneself effectively), conflict management, and problem-solving skills—at least to some extent.

---

fected couples' relationships.[9] This rigorous review confirms that marriage interventions, broadly speaking, can improve relationship satisfaction and communication among romantically involved couples. Many of the marriage education curriculums in use today, however, did not meet the criteria for inclusion in this review of program effectiveness.

In what follows I briefly survey a sample of popular contemporary programs and present information about their effectiveness.[10] In general, research on program effectiveness seeks to answer a basic question: does the program make a difference? The degree of confidence that can be claimed for findings of positive impacts in any given study depends in large part on the study's methodology, particularly the degree to which its design can rule out alternative explanations for

Common Evaluation Designs and Claims for Causality

Nonexperimental: The researcher observes and documents naturally occurring phenomena or analyzes effects without systematically varying exposure to the treatment of interest. Generally a weak design for inferring causality.

Quasi-experimental: The researcher identifies a no-treatment condition against which outcomes for the treatment group can be compared—but does not randomly assign participants to the comparison and treatment groups. By definition, the two groups are nonequivalent at the outset, reducing the confidence with which one can make causal inferences.

Experimental: Often called the gold standard of evaluation research, experimental designs control for preexisting differences by randomly assigning participants to the intervention or a no-treatment control group. A randomized design has the advantage of controlling for most factors that are known to jeopardize the ability to make strong causal inferences.

observed outcomes. While any evaluation research can be methodologically flawed in a number of ways, randomized experimental designs are generally considered the most scientifically rigorous because any differences in outcomes between intervention and control groups can be unequivocally attributed to the program (see box).[11]

One limitation of evaluation research is that the results cannot be generalized beyond the population from which the study sample is drawn. It is important to note that nearly all of the evaluations of marriage education programs were conducted with primarily middle- to upper-middle-class white engaged or married couples.

Bringing Baby Home is a structured curriculum for use in strengthening the marriages of couples who are expecting a child, a time of great vulnerability in most relationships. It addresses relationship skills and prepares couples to deal with the inevitable stresses and life changes that come with a new baby and to be involved and effective parents. Ad-

ministered by hospital personnel in a two-day workshop and six-month support group, the program teaches couples how to avoid marital meltdown and increase marital satisfaction, deal with stress, keep fathers involved in infant care, and improve parent-infant interaction. It also provides instruction on early child development. An initial randomized evaluation of the workshop showed that one year after participating, both husbands and wives reported significantly higher marital quality, lower postpartum depression, and lower hostile affect than couples assigned to a control group. A second randomized and long-term evaluation of the workshop and support group, as taught by staff at Swedish Hospital in Seattle, is under way and showing promising results for both parents and their children.[12]

Marriage Savers is a community-level intervention that aims to reduce divorce rates by establishing a shared public commitment among clergy to support and strengthen marriage. It focuses primarily on the adoption of community marriage policies, in which local clergy pledge to revitalize marriage in their congregations. One strategy is to require four months of marriage preparation, during which engaged couples complete a premarital "inventory" to identify relationship issues and then discuss these issues with mentor couples. Another is to train mentor couples whose own marriages have almost failed how to help other couples in crisis. Marriage Savers was designed on the basis of its developer's personal experience and insights rather than social science research. A nonexperimental evaluation recently found that the decline in divorce rates was 2 percentage points greater in communities where it had been adopted.[13]

Practical Application of Intimate Relationship Skills (PAIRS) is a psychoeducational program to promote self-understanding and the ability to sustain satisfying intimate relationships. It is based on its developer's personal and clinical experience and borrows techniques from experiential, behavioral, and family systems approaches. It focuses on communication, conflict, and commitment and on helping individuals experience pleasure, healing, and personal growth within an intimate relationship. The curriculum is available in several different formats, from a semester-long course to an intensive one-day seminar. In a quasi-experimental one-group pre-test–post-test research design, couples who attended the semester-long format showed greater marital satisfaction and less conflict and unhappiness six to eight months following the intervention.[14] To my knowledge, no randomized trial of the program has been conducted.

Relationship Enhancement (RE) is a thirteen- to fourteen-hour program that stresses the development of empathy and mutual understanding to enhance intimacy, manage conflict, and deal effectively with the inevitable difficulties that arise from differences in partners' beliefs, feelings, needs, and desires. Instead of addressing specific topics, it teaches a set of ten communication and problem-solving skills with which couples can address most relationship issues. Both professionals and paraprofessionals have been trained to deliver this program to groups of couples. Created more than forty years ago, Relationship Enhancement has been evaluated many times with random-assignment research designs. Although the samples are typically small and follow-ups are limited to no more than twelve months, several studies demonstrate positive effects on marital adjustment and communication in comparison to other types of marital treatment programs or a control group.[15]

Premarital Relationship Enhancement Program (PREP) emphasizes speaking and listening skills to equip couples to resolve conflicts and prevent harmful fights. Besides basic communication skills, topics include clarifying expectations, enhancing friendship and fun, and understanding commitment. Couples are most often taught in a group setting over a weekend or in another format covering about fifteen hours of material. A randomized evaluation of PREP conducted by the developers used a small number of middle-income, nondistressed, engaged couples. Five-year follow-up data showed that couples in the program had higher levels of positive and lower levels of negative communication skills and less marital violence than couples assigned to the control group. About half of the couples assigned to the program group participated in the program, leaving open the possibility that those who participated were more highly motivated to improve their relationships and thus would have had more positive outcomes than control group couples even in the absence of the intervention.[16]

PREPARE is used by clergy and counselors to help premarital couples identify relationship strengths and weaknesses. Each partner privately indicates his or her level of agreement with 125 statements about a range of areas thought to affect relationships, including expectations, personality, communication, conflict resolution, financial management, leisure activity, sexuality, children and parenting, family and friends, gender roles, and religion. The partners' responses are then compared and a score indicating the couple's level of agreement is computed. PREPARE is most often used to help couples address their differences and decide whether a marriage is likely to be successful. The predictive validity of the inventory has been studied and found to distinguish between couples who got divorced and those who stayed together over a three-year period. Its use as a strategy for helping couples identify their issues and effectively address them has not been rigorously evaluated.[17]

Creating Marriage Programs for Low-Income Couples

Many of the publicly sponsored healthy marriage initiatives try to reach across various population groups and across socioeconomic status. But the problems associated with forming and sustaining healthy and stable marriages are particularly acute in poor communities, where rates of nonmarital births, divorce, and single parenting are especially high. Despite the greater family instability in low-income populations, marriage programs designed to serve these groups are extremely rare.[18]

This situation is especially surprising given that many low-income men and women

would welcome the chance to participate in classes or sessions to help them with their relationships.[19] Between 86 and 90 percent of low-income men and women surveyed in Florida, Oklahoma, and Utah considered it a "good or very good idea" for government to develop programs to strengthen marriage and reduce divorce. More telling, 72 to 87 percent indicated that they would consider using workshops or classes to strengthen their own relationships if such were available.

As noted, the vast majority of marriage interventions in use today were primarily designed for and tested with white, middle-class, well-educated couples who were engaged or already married. Thus, although the foundation supporting marriage education programs may be promising, there is some question whether these standard programs can meet the needs, interests, and circumstances of low-income couples.[20]

Responding to the Needs of Low-Income Couples

New research on the relationship dynamics of low-income couples suggests that certain issues may stand in the way of a healthy marriage. For example, some unmarried parents set an "economic bar" as a prerequisite to marriage that is perhaps unrealistically high, and many struggle with issues of trust, fidelity, and commitment.[21] The prevalence of traumatic experiences such as childhood sexual abuse may be higher among disadvantaged individuals and may make it harder to form healthy adult relationships.[22] Couples who conceive a child soon after beginning to date may be romantically involved but need more time to get to know one another better.[23] Research has documented that whether or not they are married, low-income couples often struggle with issues related to having children by multiple partners.[24] Compared with the general population, lower-income couples tend to be less well educated, to have lower levels of literacy, to have had less success in school, and to be members of minorities and come from diverse cultural backgrounds.[25] All of these differences have implications for both the content and the presentation of marriage and relationship skills education for lower-income couples.

Most marriage experts believe that the basic concepts and skills taught in conventional programs (such as communication skills) are likely to be universally important. Many practitioners who serve low-income men and women also agree that such skills are likely to be useful, but they consider the standard materials inadequate because they do not deal with the issues unique to low-income couples. Experts who work with low-income families tend to find conventional teaching methods, such as lectures and didactic instruction, inappropriate for the literacy levels and learning styles prevalent among lower-income populations. In light of these concerns, several developers and practitioners have begun to adapt conventional programs or create new curriculums that are specifically responsive to the needs and circumstances of low-income couples. In preparation, some developers have conducted focus groups, curriculum field tests, and pilot programs.[26]

These "next generation" curriculums often take a more experiential, hands-on, and engaging teaching approach. Abstract concepts are made more concrete, the level of language fluency and literacy is adjusted, and materials are revised to rely less on written exercises, reading, and homework and more on discussion, dialogue, role playing, and skills practice. In addition, curriculums are often made more culturally appropriate, particularly in terms of illustrative stories, examples, references, and activities.

New curriculum materials tend to supplement traditional topics and skills to help couples work on such issues as trust, fidelity, and commitment; deal with problems related to multiple-partner fertility; learn how to set

---

Developers and practitioners have begun to adapt conventional programs or create new curriculums that are specifically responsive to the needs and circumstances of low-income couples.

---

and achieve economic goals as a team; heal from past psychological injuries, such as physical or sexual abuse; avoid violence; and understand the characteristics of healthy relationships and marriage. Several of these next generation programs for low-income families will be tested as part of large-scale national evaluations of healthy marriage initiatives; a sampling follows.[27]

Loving Couples Loving Children (LCLC) is a curriculum developed by John and Julie Gottman especially for low-income couples who are expecting a child. John Gottman is world-renowned for his scientific work identifying the predictors of relationship success and failure, while Julie Gottman is a master clinician who provides advanced training in marriage education and couples therapy. The Gottmans based Loving Couples Loving Children on the concepts and skills taught in Bringing Baby Home, their curriculum for new parents that has recently shown positive impacts on couples and their children. To engage and retain the interest of low-income couples, they substantially modified the presentation of the material by developing a series of video "talk shows" in which racially and ethnically diverse low-income couples discuss relationship issues. Each of the forty-two sessions in LCLC begins with such a talk show, which leads to a lively discussion among group participants. In these unscripted shows real couples, not actors, describe the challenges they have faced in their relationship and how they overcame them. The second half of each group session is devoted to activities that teach specific skills and techniques that couples can use to address the issues raised in the video. Participants practice skills with their partners during the session, with individual attention from the male and female co-facilitators, as needed.

In addition to building intimacy, dealing with conflict, and developing shared meaning, which are addressed in Bringing Baby Home, Loving Couples Loving Children includes topics that are important for low-income couples—trust and fidelity, dealing with ex-partners, healing old wounds, avoiding relationship violence, understanding the importance of the father's role, dealing with incarceration and addiction, and learning what it means to be happily married, to name a few. The curriculum was field-tested with numerous low-income couples in several cities and is now being piloted and evaluated in the Building Strong Families (BSF) project, a large-scale national demonstration.

Love's Cradle is based on the well-established Relationship Enhancement program, adapted and supplemented by new material developed especially to address issues identified by researchers as crucial barriers to positive family formation in fragile families. Created by Mary Ortwein, a marriage and family therapist with experience serving low-income families, and Bernard Guerney, the original developer of RE, Love's Cradle relies on a simplified and more culturally sensitive version of Relationship Enhancement taught at the fifth-grade level, and adds content to the standard RE skills. The simplified version avoids psychological jargon and teaches skills at a slower pace, with greater access to individual skills coaching. Love's Cradle consists of twenty-one two-hour group sessions. Ten sessions, most at the beginning of the program, are devoted to the simplified RE skills. Eleven additional sessions adapted from Supplementary Marriage Education Modules for Low-Income Couples (see below) allow couples to use their new skills to address the issues indicated by research to be common to low-income couples, including how to build, rebuild, and maintain trust; deal with multiple-partner fertility; manage emotions; work as a team on money matters; and reframe their understanding of marriage. Love's Cradle was field-tested with low-income couples and will be part of the Building Strong Families national evaluation.

Exploring Relationships and Marriage with Fragile Families is a new curriculum to help low-income single parents, especially African Americans, learn about relationships and marriage. With support from the state of Louisiana, it was developed by staff at the Center for Fathers, Families, and Workforce Development, a nonprofit organization serving low-income African American men and women. The curriculum includes three stand-alone components—for mothers, for fathers, and for couples—consisting of eight two-hour sessions. Each single-gender component is for parents in the early stages of deciding whether to make a relationship commitment; the couples component is designed for men and women in a relationship that they want to last. The material borrows concepts from a range of marriage education programs, but rather than telling participants what to do, it offers various activities that set up experiences from which parents can draw their own conclusions. The curriculum is especially tailored for an African American audience, drawing on African symbols, rituals, and proverbs, and including notes for facilitators on cultural issues. Several organizations are being trained in the curriculum, though it has not yet been field-tested or evaluated.

Supplementary Marriage Education Modules for Low-Income Couples was developed to fill gaps in conventional marriage education curriculums regarding the needs of low-income families. It is not a stand-alone curriculum, but rather a supplement to traditional programs; for example, most of the modules have been integrated into the simplified version of the Relationship Enhancement program to create Love's Cradle. It was developed in direct response to work by fragile family researchers to address the issues that low-income, especially unmarried, couples have reported as obstacles to achieving happy and satisfying relationships and marriage. These include multiple-partner fertility, gender distrust, the high economic bar placed on marriage, and the lack of accurate information on and positive role models for marriage. The modules were developed by a multidisciplinary and multicultural group led by Pamela Wilson, a highly regarded expert in curriculum development for low-income families. The group also included a marriage and family therapist, the director of a home-visiting program for at-risk families, a specialist working with low-income African American fathers, a public health practitioner who

works with unwed pregnant African American women, and a professional counselor. The material in this curriculum will be included in the national evaluation of the Building Strong Families program.

Better Together is an eight-session curriculum for low-income unmarried, cohabiting parents who are living with their children. Created by a team led by Judy Charlick and Sandra Bender of the Cleveland Marriage Coalition, the curriculum was developed with the assistance of a committee composed of African American and white educators and a couple from the target population, who identified topics likely to be important to low-income unmarried parents. The curriculum borrows some content and teaching methods from a program called Survival Skills for Healthy Families but adds other topics to fit the needs of unmarried, low-income couples and to make it more culturally sensitive to African American families.[28] It takes a down-to-earth, concrete approach to teaching basic skills for parenting, speaking and listening, problem solving, managing money, and coping with stress and change. The sessions also provide information on the stages of relationships, the traits of a healthy family and a healthy marriage, the advantages of being sexually faithful, and the role of paternity and child support. The curriculum has not been evaluated but was recently piloted in a small program in Cleveland, Ohio.

Learning What Works

Social scientists know that marriage education can generally be effective in terms of improving relationship communication and satisfaction among couples who are at the higher end of the educational and economic spectrum. They are discovering what types of issues stand in the way of low-income couples' attainment of strong and lasting rela-

Table 1. Major Healthy Marriage Demonstration and Evaluation Projects

Characteristic	Building Strong Families	Supporting Healthy Marriage	Community Healthy Marriage Initiative
Target population	Unmarried romantically involved couples expecting a child, or with an infant less than three months old	Low-income married couples with at least one child under 18 years (or expecting a child)	Individuals within a specified geographic area
Primary objective	Strengthen unwed couple relationships and support the marital aspirations of those who choose marriage	Prevent unnecessary divorce by helping couples prepare for and strengthen their marriages and repair troubled marriages	Restore cultural norms and values for the institution of marriage through community support. Increase paternity establishment and child support payments
Intervention strategy	Group sessions focused on skills associated with healthy marriage	Group sessions focused on skills associated with healthy marriage	Media campaigns on value of marriage
	Additional family support services as needed	Extended curricular activities	Multisector coalitions to support marriage
	One-on-one support by a family coordinator	Family support services, as needed	Some direct services (scope and population group vary)
Scope	6,000 couples Up to six sites	8,000 couples Up to eight sites	Varies Up to twelve sites
Evaluation	Experimental	Experimental	Nonexperimental
Primary outcomes expected	Increased number of healthy marriages, improved relationship quality and child well-being	Decreased number of divorces, improved marital quality and child well-being	Reduced community divorce rate and community nonmarital childbearing
Follow-up	18, 36, possibly 60 months	12, 36, 60 months	12, 36, 60 months

tionships and marriage. What they do not yet know is whether marriage education, including programs that have been carefully adapted, will work with more diverse and less advantaged individuals. Nor can they be certain whether improving couples' relationships will enhance the well-being of their children. To answer these questions, the Office of Planning, Research, and Evaluation (OPRE) at ACF commissioned three large-scale, multisite, long-term evaluations of marriage programs. As shown in table 1, each of these projects is stimulating the development of marriage initiatives and measuring the effects of these programs on both parents and their children over several years.

The Building Strong Families Project

Building Strong Families is an evaluation of programs to help expectant unwed couples strengthen their relationships and, for those who are interested, consider marriage.[29] The nine-year project, which was initiated by

ACF in late 2002, will provide information on whether supporting the marital aspirations of unwed couples can enhance the well-being of their children. Led by Mathematica Policy Research, the BSF evaluation is the first major investigation of a healthy marriage initiative involving a rigorous research design. Participation in BSF is entirely voluntary—families are not mandated or ordered to attend, nor is participation tied to any public benefits. The concept of the program was motivated by findings from the Fragile Families and Child Wellbeing Survey, which showed that more than 80 percent of unwed couples are romantically involved at the time of their child's birth. Although many of these couples expect to marry, very few do so, and many break up quickly.[30]

The project has two major goals. The first is to stimulate and support the development of well-conceived local programs that will nurture the relationships of unmarried couples, starting around the time of their child's birth. The second is to rigorously test the effectiveness of these programs on couples and children. All BSF programs must conform to a model that was carefully developed over several years through collaboration between ACF, the research team, and a diverse group of experts and practitioners.[31] The model has three required components: a structured series of group sessions led by trained facilitators who teach the skills and knowledge shown through research to be associated with healthy marriage; access to family support services, such as parenting education, employment services, and mental health treatment, as needed; and ongoing, one-on-one family support over a sustained period.

Although BSF targets unmarried couples, its goal is not to persuade them to marry but to improve the quality and stability of their relationships, and also to support couples who do wish to marry. Programs that aspire to be part of BSF adopt a marriage education curriculum that meets the criteria outlined in the program model guidelines. Two such curriculums have so far been adopted by local BSF sites: Loving Couples Loving Children and Love's Cradle.[32] As noted, both are based on curriculums that have been shown to be effective in the general population, and both have been adapted in content and presentation to be suitable for low-income, unmarried, new parents. Despite differences in approach, both cover the same broad topics, including communication and conflict management skills, affection and intimacy, trust and commitment, adjusting to a new baby, parent-infant interactions, learning about marriage, co-parenting and managing complex family relationships, emotion regulation, and communicating about money. In BSF, eligible couples expecting a child (or with a child younger than three months old) attend

group sessions with six to nine other couples, usually once a week for several months. Specially trained family coordinators assess and link couples to additional services as needed, and provide ongoing support to individual couples over a year or more.

The BSF evaluation, to be conducted at up to six sites nationwide, includes an implementation study and an impact analysis in which thousands of couples will be randomly assigned to an intervention or a control group. Couples and their children are assessed at baseline and then again eighteen months and three years after they enroll in the program. Compared with the control group, the intervention group is expected to show an increase in the number of children being raised by both parents in a healthy and stable marriage; more stable, higher-quality couple relationships; and improved child well-being. Lessons from the pilot phase and findings from the implementation and impact studies will be disseminated through a series of reports over the coming years.

Several programs aiming to be selected as evaluation sites are beginning to implement the BSF model. After a pilot period up to six sites will be chosen, based on criteria such as the ability to enroll a sample of adequate size. Brief descriptions of the pilot sites under consideration for the national evaluation follow.

Florida: Orange and Broward Counties. In Florida, the BSF model is being integrated into an existing home-visiting program to promote positive parent-child interaction and healthy child development, with the goal of preventing child abuse and neglect in vulnerable families. Healthy Families Florida is a statewide program serving at-risk mothers for up to five years, beginning with their child's birth. During home visits, family social workers teach parents about child development and parenting and link them to other needed social services. In the BSF program (called Healthy Families Plus in Florida), fathers join mothers for the home visits, and both parents participate in the marriage and relationship curriculum workshops. Healthy

---

In the BSF program (called Healthy Families Plus in Florida), fathers join mothers for the home visits, and both parents participate in the marriage and relationship curriculum workshops.

Families Plus selected Loving Couples Loving Children as its curriculum and began enrolling couples in two counties in February 2005 for its pilot. Depending on its progress and the availability of funding, the program will expand to several additional Florida counties for full-scale implementation.

Georgia: Greater Atlanta. In the greater Atlanta area, BSF will be provided by two local nonprofit organizations: the Latin American Association and Families First. The Latin American Association provides transitional services for Latinos and operates the Latino Fatherhood Initiative to help fathers become more responsible and sensitive to the needs of their children. The Latin American Association will provide BSF services in Spanish. English-speaking couples will be served by Families First, which has a more than 100-year history in Georgia, with centers and facilities serving at-risk, mostly minority families. Its services include adolescent pregnancy prevention, domestic violence treatment, adoption and foster care, substance abuse and mental health treatment, after-school programs, and individual counseling. BSF couples will be recruited through the neighborhood public health clinics in Fulton, DeKalb, Clayton, Gwinnett, and Cobb counties, and through Grady Memorial Hospital. Couples will be recruited when their pregnancy tests are done as part of their Medicaid application. Enrollment of BSF couples for a pilot study began in May 2005.

Indiana: Marion, Lake, Allen, and Miami Counties. As in Florida, in Indiana BSF is embedded within local Healthy Families programs in several counties. Like similar programs, Healthy Families Indiana is a voluntary home-visiting program designed to promote healthy children and families by offering such services as access to health care, parenting education, and information about child development for up to five years after the birth of the child. The program systematically identifies at-risk families around the time of their child's birth, often in hospital maternity wards. Healthy Families Indiana chose Loving Couples Loving Children for its relationship and marriage education curriculum, and enrollment for its pilot began in eight locations in February 2005. Once the full demonstration is under way, enrollment will be expanded in these sites.

Louisiana: Greater Baton Rouge. A community-based nonprofit organization called Family Road of Greater Baton Rouge is leading the BSF effort in Louisiana. Family Road offers a comprehensive set of social services to expecting and new parents. The award-winning "one-stop" center provides mostly African American unmarried parents with services and referrals, including parenting education, birth preparation classes, prenatal care, Medicaid and WIC, Healthy Start, money management, substance abuse and domestic violence treatment, employment services, a fatherhood program, and individual counseling. The addition of BSF to this array will fill a gap by serving low-income couples—rather than only mothers or fathers—and helping them with their relationships for the first time, using Loving Couples Loving Children as its curriculum. Baton Rouge BSF began enrolling couples for the pilot study in April 2005. Depending on the availability of funds, services will be expanded to two additional community-based organizations in the area.

Maryland: Baltimore. The Center for Fathers, Families, and Workforce Development has been funded to implement the BSF model in Baltimore. The center has worked for many years to strengthen families by reaching out to young, low-income, mostly African American men in Baltimore to help them become better fathers by developing life skills and removing barriers to parental involvement and employment. In its 50/50 Parenting Program, the center works with both unwed mothers and fathers, teaching co-parenting skills and helping each family develop a parenting plan. For BSF, the program will collaborate with several area birthing hospitals to recruit unwed couples who are romantically involved and interested in participating. The center has selected Loving Couples Loving Children as its curriculum for BSF services. Program enrollment was expected to begin in late summer 2005.

Oklahoma: Oklahoma City. The Oklahoma Marriage Initiative (OMI) is planning a BSF program that would first conduct pilot operations in Oklahoma City and County and then expand to other counties throughout the

state. During the pilot operation of the Transition to Parenthood Program, a large women's health center run by a community-based organization and serving a population with a substantial Hispanic component will recruit couples as part of its delivery of prenatal services. The OMI will provide BSF group workshops following an adaptation of the Becoming Parents Program (now being developed) and offer a variety of family support services through a newly created "one-stop" service center adjacent to the health center. Program enrollment was scheduled to start in late summer 2005.

Texas: Houston and San Angelo. The BSF program model is being implemented in two Healthy Families sites in Texas: Houston and San Angelo. The Houston location has a bilingual staff and provides home-visiting services in Spanish to its primarily Hispanic population. BSF services will also be offered in English. Unlike other Healthy Families programs, the San Angelo site has been serving couples as well as mothers for several years through a monthly couples support group. The two sites plan to use Love's Cradle as their relationship skills and marriage education curriculum. Program staff at both locations have been trained in the BSF model and began recruiting couples at local birthing hospitals in February 2005.

The Supporting Healthy Marriage Project

ACF launched the Supporting Healthy Marriage (SHM) initiative in fall 2003 in response to two important research findings: low-income married couples tend to be at higher risk for divorce than couples in the general population; and children fare better on a range of outcomes when they grow up with married parents. The initiative targets low-income couples because once married, they tend to be less stable than couples with higher incomes and they are likely to face more obstacles to maintaining healthy marriages.[33] SHM will test whether instruction in relationship skills and support for low-income married couples can enhance marital quality,

Supporting Healthy Marriages targets low-income couples because once married, they tend to be less stable than couples with higher incomes and they are likely to face more obstacles to maintaining healthy marriages.

reduce divorce rates, and improve child well-being.[34]

SHM differs from BSF primarily in its target population. While BSF serves unmarried couples, SHM will serve economically disadvantaged couples who are already married and have at least one child under age 18 or are expecting a child. More than 8 million married couples live at below 200 percent of the federal poverty line in the United States. Compared with more affluent married couples, they are more likely to have had children before they were married, to have children by multiple partners, and to use various types of public assistance. Low-income married couples are mostly Latino (35 percent) or white (47 percent); few are African American.[35]

Like BSF, SHM will involve extensive program development and a rigorous evaluation of impacts. The project team has developed a program model in collaboration with a range of experts and will work with state and local organizations to design and implement SHM programs that follow the model. Programs will be expected to include three major components: delivery of a marriage education curriculum that covers a specified set of topics; extended marriage education activities, which could include booster sessions, social events, or peer mentoring; and supplemental services that support other family needs, such as referrals for job assistance.[36] The research team is now seeking groups that would be interested in implementing the SHM program model. Curriculum selection and program operations have not yet begun. To further inform the program model, a series of focus groups with members of the target population will be conducted over the next two years to better identify the needs and interests of low-income married couples with children.

The evaluation, led by MDRC and Abt Associates, is expected to include eight sites, each of which must be able to randomly assign many couples to program or control groups. Both implementation and impact will be analyzed. Families will be assessed at baseline and at twelve, thirty-six, and sixty months after the intervention. Expected effects include improved marital quality, lower rate of divorce, and improved well-being of children.

Evaluation of the Community Healthy Marriage Initiative

The third major OPRE project, the evaluation of the Community Healthy Marriage Initiative (CHMI), is designed to assess whether community-level initiatives to promote healthy marriage, parental responsibility, and the financial well-being of children can be effective. These initiatives are primarily intended to improve family well-being by reducing a community's divorce rate and number of nonmarital births and by ensuring that paternity is established and child support payments are made. Through its Office of Child Support Enforcement, ACF has contributed to community healthy marriage initiatives in Idaho, Illinois, Louisiana, Massachusetts, Michigan, Minnesota, and Virginia. More grants are expected.[37]

In providing funding for these programs, ACF has encouraged a community saturation model, in which community coalitions work together to find ways to promote healthy marriage.[38] These coalitions may include faith-based organizations, government agencies, and nonprofits. Most CHMIs attempt to improve the well-being of all families by changing societal norms related to marriage. Some provide marriage education services, although the scope, target population, and intervention approach vary widely from program to program. Of those that will provide marriage education services, most are considering the use of conventional programs, such as PREP, PAIRS, RE, or Survival Skills for Healthy Families.

The seven-year evaluation, which will include up to twelve sites, is being led by a team of researchers at RTI International and the Urban Institute. Because CHMIs seek change at the community level, it is not possible to conduct a random-assignment evaluation of their effects, so a nonexperimental or quasi-experimental design is being considered instead. Changes in outcomes related to marriage, child well-being, and child support will be assessed at twelve, thirty-six, and sixty months after program inception and compared across similar communities. The evaluation will also include an analysis of program development and implementation.

Conclusions

The documented ill effects on children of growing up without the benefit of two parents in a loving and stable marriage have increased interest in learning whether a new kind of policy and new types of programs can help strengthen the institution of marriage. Many different strategies are being tried, but most have not been examined for their effectiveness. One of the more promising approaches relies on marriage education to teach interested couples the skills shown through research to be instrumental in building and maintaining strong and stable marriages. Such programs are known to be effective in increasing relationship satisfaction and communication among groups composed mostly of white, middle-class, married or engaged couples, but they have rarely been provided to low-income, culturally diverse, married and unmarried couples. Recent research has identified many barriers faced by low-income men and women in developing and maintaining healthy long-term relationships and marriage. Marriage education experts therefore are now creating curriculums based on the core research-supported skills and principles but adapted to be more accessible and appealing to low-income couples and supplemented with material to help couples address barriers to healthy relationships and stable marriage. Three large-scale rigorous evaluations will provide insight into whether and how healthy marriage programs for low-income populations can be effective.

Endnotes

1. Administration for Children and Families, "The Healthy Marriage Initiative," U.S. Department of Health and Human Services (www.acf.hhs.gov/healthymarriage/index.html [March 2, 2005]).

2   Theodora Ooms, Stacey Bouchet, and Mary Parke, *Beyond Marriage Licenses: Efforts in States to Strengthen Marriage and Two-Parent Families* (Washington: Center for Law and Social Policy, 2004).

3. For a description of allowable activities under the pending legislation, see Mary Parke, *Marriage-Related Provisions in Recent Welfare Reauthorization Proposals: A Summary* (Washington: Center for Law and Social Policy, 2003).

4. Ooms, Bouchet, and Parke, *Beyond Marriage Licenses* (see note 2).

5. Administration for Children and Families, "Healthy Marriage Initiative Activities and Accomplishments 2002–2004," U.S. Department of Health and Human Services (www.acf.hhs.gov/healthymarriage [June 16, 2005]).

6. Administration for Children and Families, "Currently Funded Healthy Marriage Programs," U.S. Department of Health and Human Services (www.acf.hhs.gov/healthymarriage/funding [March 2, 2005]).

7. For example, see John Gottman and Robert Levenson, "Marital Processes Predictive of Later Dissolution: Behavior, Physiology, and Health," *Journal of Personality and Social Psychology* 63 (1992): 221–50; John Gottman and Lowell Krokoff, "Marital Interaction and Marital Satisfaction: A Longitudinal View," *Journal of Consulting and Clinical Psychology* 57 (1989): 47–52; and John Gottman, *Why Marriages Succeed or Fail* (New York: Simon and Schuster, 1994).

8. The many resources describing conventional marriage education curriculums include a website maintained by the Coalition for Marriage, Family, and Couples Education in Washington, D.C. (www.smartmarriages.com [March 2, 2005]); Administration for Children and Families, U.S. Department of Health and Human Services, *Strengthening Healthy Marriages: A Compendium of Approaches to Help Couples Who Choose Marriage for Themselves, Develop the Skills and Knowledge to Form and Sustain Healthy Marriages* (Government Printing Office, 2004); and "Summary Descriptions of Marriage Education Programs," a technical assistance tool developed by the Lewin Group (www.lewin.com/Spotlight_Feature_CHMI.htm [March 2, 2005]).

9. Jane Reardon-Anderson and others, *Systematic Review of the Impact of Marriage and Relationship Programs* (Washington: Urban Institute, 2005).

10. The curriculum programs described in this chapter were selected as illustrative of the range of programs available and in use. Inclusion in this article does not imply endorsement by the author, the editors of this journal, Mathematica Policy Research, or the Administration for Children and Families.

11. Donald Campbell and Julian Stanley, *Experimental and Quasi-Experimental Designs for Research* (Chicago: Rand-McNally, 1966).

12. Alyson F. Shapiro and John M. Gottman, "Effects on Marriage of a Psycho-Communicative-Educational Intervention with Couples Undergoing the Transition to Parenthood, Evaluation at 1-Year Post Intervention," *Journal of Family Communication* 5, no. 1 (2005): 1–24.

13. Paul James Birch, Stan E. Wood, and Joseph Olsen, "Assessing the Impact of Community Marriage Policies on County Divorce Rates," *Family Relations* 53 (2004): 495–503.

14. Carlos Durana, "A Longitudinal Evaluation of the Effectiveness of the PAIRS Psychoeducational Program for Couples," *Family Therapy* 23 (1994): 11–36.

15. Michael Accordino and Bernard Guerney Jr., "The Empirical Validation of Relationship Enhancement Couple/Family Therapies," in *Handbook of Research and Practice in Humanistic Psychotherapies*, edited by David Cain and Jules Seeman (Washington: American Psychological Association, 2001), chapter 13.

16. Howard Markman and others, "Preventing Marital Distress through Communication and Conflict Management Training: A 4- and 5-Year Follow-Up," *Journal of Consulting and Clinical Psychology* 61 (1993): 70–77.

17. Andrea S. Larsen and David H. Olson, "Predicting Marital Satisfaction Using PREPARE: A Replication Study," *Journal of Marital and Family Therapy* 15, no. 3 (1989): 311–22.

18. Robin Dion and others, *Helping Unwed Parents Build Strong and Healthy Marriages: A Conceptual Framework for Interventions* (Washington: Mathematica Policy Research, 2003); Jennifer Ehrle Macomber, Julie Murray, and Matthew Stagner, *Service Delivery and Evaluation Design Options for Strengthening and Promoting Healthy Marriages* (Washington: Urban Institute, 2005).

19. Robin Dion, Heather Hesketh, and Courtney Harrison, "Marriage and Family Formation in Four State Surveys," presentation for the National Governors' Association, Center for Best Practices (Washington: Mathematica Policy Research, 2004).

20. For example, see Marta McClintock-Comeaux, Elaine Anderson, and Kate Kuvalanka, "TANF and Marriage Education: Utilizing Marriage Legislation to Design a New Educational Curriculum That Meets the Needs of Low-Income Families," in *Vision 2004: What Is the Future of Marriage?* edited by Paul Amato and others (Minneapolis: National Council on Family Relations, 2004).

21. Christine Gibson, Kathryn Edin, and Sara McLanahan, "High Hopes but Even Higher Expectations: The Retreat from Marriage among Low-Income Couples," Working Paper 2003-06 (Center for Reseach on Child Wellbeing, Princeton University, 2003). See also Kathryn Edin and Maria Kefalas, *Promises I Can Keep* (University of California Press, 2005).

22. Andrew Cherlin and others, "Domestic Abuse and Patterns of Marriage and Cohabitation: Evidence from a Multi-Method Study," presented at the conference "Marriage and Family Formation among Low-Income Couples: What Do We Know from Research?" sponsored by the National Poverty Center (Washington, September 2003).

23. Ronald Mincy and others, "Fragile Families in Focus: A Look at How Never-Married, Low-Income Parents Perceive Marriage and Relationships," paper presented at the conference "Let's Get Married," sponsored by State of Louisiana, TANF Executive Office, Division of Administration (New Orleans, December 2003).

24. Ronald Mincy, "Who Should Marry Whom? The Incidence of Multiple-Partner Fertility among New Unmarried Parents," Working Paper 02-03-FF (Center for Research on Child Wellbeing, Princeton University, 2002).

25. David Fein, *Married and Poor: Basic Characteristics of Economically Disadvantaged Couples in the U.S.* (Washington: Abt Associates, 2004). Also see the comparisons between middle-income and low-income families in Benjamin Karney, Cynthia Wilson Garvan, and Michael S. Thomas, *Family Formation in Florida: 2003 Baseline Survey of Attitudes, Beliefs, and Demographics Relating to Marriage and Family Formation* (University of Florida Press, 2004). See also Kathryn Edin and Joanna M. Reed, "Why Don't They Just Get Married?" in this volume.

26. For example, focus groups were conducted in various program development efforts by the Center for Fathers and Workforce Development (CFWD); Dennis Orthner and Anne Jones at the University of North

Carolina; John and Julie Gottman; and Decision Information Resources for the Building Strong Families project. Curriculum field tests have been conducted by Pamela Jordan, Mary Ortwein, John Gottman, and Joseph Jones. The experiences of one pilot program for low-income families are documented in Robin Dion and Debra Strong, *Implementing Programs to Strengthen the Relationships of Unwed Parents: Lessons from Family Connections of Alabama* (Washington: Mathematica Policy Research, 2004). Additional information is available from reports delivered at a meeting of ACF marriage initiative grantees at the Healthy Marriage Best Practices Meeting, Washington, January 5–6, 2005.

27. See note 10. No endorsement of any curriculum is implied.

28. George Doub and Florence Creighton, *Survival Skills for Healthy Families* (Scotts Valley, Calif.: Family Wellness Associates, 1999).

29. For more information, see the Building Strong Families website at www.buildingstrongfamilies.info. Also see Administration for Children and Families, Office of Planning Research and Evaluation, "Programs to Strengthen Marriages and Families," U.S. Department of Health and Human Services (www.acf.hhs.gov/healthymarriage/funding/opre_projects.html [March 2, 2005]).

30. Marcia Carlson, Sara McLanahan, and Paula England, "Union Formation and Dissolution in Fragile Families," *Demography* 41, no. 2 (2004): 237–62.

31. Alan Hershey and others, *Building Strong Families: Guidelines for Developing Programs* (Washington: Mathematica Policy Research, 2004). Also see Robin Dion and others, *Helping Unwed Parents* (see note 18).

32. Although these curriculums may be used in the Building Strong Families evaluation sponsored by the U.S. Department of Health and Human Services, no endorsement by the government nor by Mathematica Policy Research is implied. Building Strong Families sites are free to select other curriculums, as long as they meet the requirements of the national program model.

33. David Fein, *Married and Poor: Basic Characteristics of Economically Disadvantaged Married Couples in the U.S.*, Working Paper SHM-04-0 for Supporting Healthy Marriage Demonstration (Bethesda, Md.: Abt Associates, 2004).

34. For more information, see "Supporting Healthy Marriage" at www.mdrc.org; and Administration for Children and Families, Office of Planning, Research and Evaluation, "Programs to Strengthen Marriages and Families," U.S. Department of Health and Human Services (www.acf.hhs.gov/healthymarriage/funding/opre_projects.html [March 2, 2005]).

35. See "The Supporting Healthy Marriage Evaluation," a presentation available at www.supportinghealthymarriage.org/resources/4/resource_4.html [March 2, 2005].

36. MDRC, *Guidelines for Supporting Healthy Marriage Demonstration Programs* (www.mdrc.org/project_12_64.html [June 16, 2005]).

37. For a description of each of these programs, see *Office of Child Support Enforcement (OCSE) Healthy Marriage Profile* at ACF's Healthy Marriage Initiative website (www.acf.hhs.gov/healthymarriage/funding/child_support.html [March 2, 2005]).

38. Chris Gersten, "The Community Healthy Marriage Initiative," presentation by the principal deputy assistant secretary for children and families, Administration for Children and Families, U.S. Department of Health and Human Services, in Chattanooga, Tenn., June 10, 2003.

The Hefty Penalty on Marriage Facing Many Households with Children

Adam Carasso and C. Eugene Steuerle

Summary

Over the past seventy years Congress has enacted dozens of tax and transfer programs, giving little if any attention to the marriage subsidies and penalties that they inadvertently impose. Although the programs affect both rich and poor Americans, the penalties fall most heavily on low- or moderate-income households with children. In this article, Adam Carasso and Eugene Steuerle review important penalties and subsidies, explain how they work, and help fill a big research gap by beginning to provide comprehensive data on the size of the penalties and subsidies arising from all public programs considered together.

Marriage penalties arise because of the combination of variable U.S. tax rates and joint, rather than individual, filing by married couples for benefits and taxes. If graduated taxes were accompanied by individual filing or if all income and transfers were taxed at a flat rate, there would be no marriage penalties. Specifically, the penalties are a result of policymakers' efforts to achieve the goal of progressivity—giving greater tax and welfare benefits to those with lower income—while trying to keep down program costs. Thus benefits in transfer programs fall, sometimes steeply, as households earn more income. Combining the direct tax rate in the tax code and the benefit reduction rates in the transfer system can result in extremely high effective marginal tax rates for many low- to moderate-income families—rates far higher than those of families earning over $90,000. These high rates lead to the marriage penalties because additional income brought into a household by marriage thus causes other benefits to be reduced or lost altogether. In extreme cases, households can lose a dollar or more for every dollar earned.

In recent years lawmakers have begun to try to reduce marriage penalties, primarily by reforming welfare and cutting taxes, but huge penalties remain. The authors offer several options for reducing or eliminating the marriage penalty and recommend two in particular. The first is to set a maximum marginal tax rate for lower-income individuals, similar to the maximum rate set for highest-income individuals. The second is to provide individual wage subsidies to lower-income earners, so that such workers who marry can combine their income with that of their spouse without incurring penalties.

www.futureofchildren.org

Adam Carasso is a research associate at the Urban Institute. C. Eugene Steuerle is a senior fellow at the Urban Institute and a co-director of the Urban-Brookings Tax Policy Center. A version of this paper was presented at the 26th Annual APPAM Research Conference in Atlanta, Georgia.

Adam Carasso and C. Eugene Steuerle

Public controversy over whether it is appropriate for state and federal governments to promote marriage overlooks a simple truth: government is already heavily entrenched in the institution of marriage. While debates swirl over whether to spend a few hundred million public dollars on marriage promotion and counseling, hundreds of billions of dollars in government tax and social welfare programs are at stake for tens of millions of couples, depending on whether they are married.[1]

The primary focus of this article is marriage penalties in tax and social welfare programs for low- to moderate-income households with working parents and children. But the penalties and subsidies within government tax and transfer programs affect all Americans. When two very-low-earning parents marry and receive more in earned income tax credit (EITC) than they did before they were married, they are receiving a marriage subsidy. When, at retirement, the nonworking spouse in a well-to-do couple receives Social Security spousal and survivors benefits just because she is married (while the working single mother does not), she too is receiving a marriage subsidy. When a single parent earning the minimum wage marries another worker at minimum wage and loses several thousand dollars of food stamp benefits, he incurs a marriage penalty. When, say, a police officer marries a nurse making similar income, placing both in a higher tax bracket, where they owe several thousand dollars more in taxes, he too incurs a marriage penalty. Often couples face simultaneous subsidies and penalties. For instance, the couple that sees their EITC benefit double because they marry might simultaneously see their welfare or food stamp benefits diminish or disappear. This article steers readers

through this policy maze, although its emphasis is on low-income men and women when they are younger, have children, and participate in programs likely to bring about penalties, rather than when they are older, their children have left home, and Social Security often provides bonuses.[2]

How the Penalties and Subsidies Work

Various tax and transfer programs act singly and in concert to penalize or subsidize marriage, depending on the mix of income and the number of eligible children two people bring to a marriage. On the tax front, particularly important provisions that can result in marriage penalties or subsidies are the earned income tax credit and the child tax credit.

To see how a marriage tax subsidy might work, consider the child tax credit. Working parents must earn more than $10,750 to receive any credit. The credit pays 10 cents for each dollar more that a working parent earns, up to a maximum of $1,000 for each child. A single mother with one child who earns $10,750 receives no child credit. But if she marries a childless man who earns $6,250, so that together they earn $17,000, the couple receives $625 as a subsidy for getting married—10 cents for each dollar more than $10,750.

The EITC can provide both subsidies and penalties. A single parent with two children who earns $15,000 enjoys an EITC benefit of about $4,100. The credit decreases by 21.06 cents for every dollar a married couple earns above $15,040. Based on that phase-out rate, if the single parent marries someone earning $10,000, for a combined income of $25,000, the EITC benefit will drop to about $2,200. The couple faces a marriage tax penalty of $4,100 minus $2,200, or $1,900.

On the transfer front, important programs with marriage penalties (but fewer bonuses) include Temporary Assistance for Needy Families (TANF), food stamps, housing assistance, child care, and Medicaid—all means-tested programs for which citizens cannot qualify unless their income (and resources and assets) is below a certain level. How much transfer program benefits are worth and the rate at which their value falls as family income rises vary by state, by family size, by the age of the children, by additional factors like the cost of rent and child care, and by what other transfer programs the family may be enrolled in. As a simple example, consider a mother of two children in Pennsylvania who earns $20,000 and qualifies for Medicaid (with an insurance value estimated at $3,424).[3] If she marries someone making just $6,000, resulting in a combined income of $26,000, her children lose their Medicaid.[4] Unlike the child credit and EITC, most transfer programs for low-income families with children contain mainly marriage penalties—the additional income introduced by a spouse generally reduces or even ends benefits received before the marriage. Only later in life, as noted, does Social Security often provide marriage subsidies through spousal or survivor benefits that are triggered merely by marriage and require no additional contribution by the worker.

Citizens pay an overall marriage penalty when their combined social welfare benefits less taxes are lower as a married couple than as two single individuals. As a simple example, a single parent with two children earning $16,000 marries someone earning $10,000, thereby losing more in food stamps, Medicaid, and EITC than she gains in child tax credits. A marriage subsidy is the reverse—the couple receives more from the government (or pays less) if they marry than if they remain single. Consider, for example, a non-working mother with two children in Pennsylvania on TANF who marries someone without children who earns $5,000.[5] Their marriage bonus derives mainly from an increase in EITC of about $2,000 and no loss of TANF or Medicaid benefits.

Penalties and Subsidies: A Policy Accident

Today, most households with children who earn low or moderate incomes (say, under $40,000) are significantly penalized for getting married. The issue is seldom engaged consistently or rigorously by elected officials, primarily because they typically enact programs piecemeal, with little coordination or thought to how they affect married couples. Congress enacted Social Security, Aid to Families with Dependent Children (AFDC), and various housing programs in 1935; the Food Stamp Act in 1964; Medicare and Medicaid in 1965; the EITC in 1975 (and subsequent expansions of the credit in 1987, 1990, 1993, and 2001); the Child Care Development Block Grant in 1990; welfare reform in 1996 (which replaced AFDC with TANF); the State Children's Health Insurance Program (SCHIP) in 1997; and the child tax credit in 1997 (expanded and made refundable in 2001). The list could go on and on. Each program, as well as its subsequent reforms, was the product of unique social forces and was designed to address a specific social need. Had they all been enacted as one comprehensive program, lawmakers might have been more inclined to coordinate and focus on the marriage penalties, subsidies, and incentives. But because the programs were put in place one by one, over many years, lawmakers who now wish to rationalize the way government treats marriage must radically restructure much of the modern social welfare state.

Marriage penalties or subsidies are assessed primarily for taking wedding vows, not for living together with another adult. Those who do not feel morally compelled to swear fidelity in religious or public ceremonies for the most part do not suffer the penalties. For instance, for the EITC, the tax system's con-

---

Under the tax system, married and cohabiting couples are treated differently, whereas under the transfer system, the distinction is less clear.

---

cern is whoever financially maintains the house in which the child stays for more than half the year. The IRS does not generally go to the household to determine how many days some other adult (who may contribute to the household's income) is living there if there is no marriage certificate.

In the transfer system, many program benefits are determined by household size. By law, these programs would treat a couple who admits to cohabiting (for an appreciable period of time) just as they treat a couple who marries.[6] In practice, however, administrators seldom go knocking to check on cohabitation, often cannot find proof of round-the-clock cohabitation, as opposed to several days or nights a week, and are unlikely to require joint filing unless the couple has been together a long time.[7] There are some exceptions, as when welfare officials attempt to assess whether someone is living in a home on a regular or fairly permanent basis to determine household status or when a state attempts to establish a child support order against the noncustodial parent and requires he provide an address. But we know of no study that has examined in depth the extent of such checks across EITC, food stamps, Medicaid, TANF, and so on. For our purposes, the distinction between marriage and acknowledged cohabiting often makes little difference with respect to how families are treated under federal social welfare programs. When officials determine that a couple is cohabiting, what we describe as "marriage penalties" become "marriage and admitted cohabitation penalties." Under the tax system, married and cohabiting couples are treated differently, whereas under the transfer system, the distinction is less clear and may depend, in some cases, on the biological relationship between the father and child and whether the couple is candid about their relationship. Regardless of the rules of the program and the legal status of the cohabiting couple in the transfer system, in practice, cohabiting parents can avoid the marriage penalty more easily than can married parents.

What Research Has— and Hasn't—Found

Although there is a steadily growing body of research on how marriage affects the economic well-being of households with children, few studies attempt to measure the size of penalties and subsidies for marriage arising from all public programs considered together. The topic is admittedly complex, but in our view researchers have not fully come to grips with the long-term implications for the nation of policies that place large penalties on marriage for a considerable share of its poorer households. A first step is to measure how large the penalties are. This study provides the most comprehensive picture to date.

Why should we care about marriage in the first place? Two articles in this volume, one by Adam Thomas and Isabel Sawhill and the other by Paul Amato, survey research on the numerous benefits, both economic and noneconomic, that marriage provides. Many findings imply that "intrinsic" benefits accrue to the spouses and children in a marriage regardless of a couple's employment and education.[8] Some researchers follow changes in families' economic well-being resulting from transitions into and out of marriage,[9] although few try to measure formally the financial incentives to exchange or keep marriage vows for families participating in the patchwork of U.S. tax and transfer programs.[10]

Other researchers address separately the effects of the welfare system and the tax system on a couple's decision to marry or divorce. But they rarely consider taxes along with welfare benefits. On the welfare side, Robert Moffitt reviews sixty-eight studies on the effect of AFDC on marriage and fertility.[11] Most, he notes, show that the old AFDC program discouraged marriage to some degree, but a sizable minority find no effect at all. Marianne Bitler and her colleagues examine vital statistics data on marriage and divorce and find that the 1996 welfare reform law, which compelled most single heads of households to work and therefore earn some income, reduced the incentives for these single mothers to marry by giving them greater financial independence.[12]

Research on taxes, meanwhile, has paid increasing attention to the situation of single parents who file as head of household. These parents owe less tax than they would filing as singles because of the special tax-advantaged nature of this filing status, but they may forfeit this advantage if they marry.[13] Although the "married, filing jointly" status is even

more favorable than the head-of-household status at the same level of income, households with only one earner can lose any gains made from moving to the married status if the two incomes pooled together put the couple in a higher tax bracket. Researchers have also studied how marriage tax penalties have changed over the years and whether these changes have influenced people's decisions to marry or divorce. James Alm and Leslie Whittington find that tax penalties slightly discourage marriage, while David Sjodquist and Mary Beth Walker find no significant effect.[14] That the findings are inconclusive is not surprising, because the tax penalty or subsidy is very sensitive to the mix of income two spouses bring to a marriage.

Measuring empirically the behavioral effects of specific marriage penalties or subsidies is equally daunting. Some quantitative and ethnographic research suggests that people's decisions to marry or divorce are governed much more by such considerations as a potential spouse's suitability as a partner and as a parent, the desire for a fulfilling relationship, and the risk of infidelity, than by the tax and transfer program consequences.[15] Understanding how the raft of benefits a family might apply for responds to changes in family income or marital status is anything but straightforward.[16] Furthermore, researchers have great difficulty examining group effects that may unfold over time. For example, if incentives change the behavior of a few households, and other households follow suit, then a group effect like "copycat" behavior may wind up playing a bigger role than the actual incentives.

Finally, examining whether couples figure out marriage penalties before they marry offers only limited evidence about the effect of the penalties on the decision to marry. People may react to incentives even when they do not calculate them, as when partners choose to cohabit or people remain single because they simply observe that unmarried couples have a higher standard of living than those who marry—without necessarily understanding how rules in public programs create this result.

Reducing Marriage Penalties: A Beginning

In recent years lawmakers have tried to reduce marriage penalties in various ways, primarily by reforming welfare and cutting taxes. Although the penalties and subsidies that remain are huge, at least policymakers have taken note of the problem and taken steps to address it.

In 1996 Congress replaced AFDC with TANF, directly linking a family's continued receipt of cash assistance to greater work effort by parents. The new law set time limits on how long enrolled families could receive cash assistance. It also strengthened work requirements, increased the income a family can earn without losing cash assistance, and established financial sanctions for families failing to meet work requirements. Many analysts have written about the modest tendency of both AFDC and TANF to discourage marriage, and the jury is still out on whether welfare reform has reduced the marriage penalty. To the extent that fewer families are on welfare, fewer face its marriage penalties. For former welfare recipients who are now working and receiving the EITC, however, marriage penalties may be linked with the EITC, rather than TANF.

Marriage penalties and subsidies have been part of the U.S. tax code since 1948, when the nation moved from a system of taxation based on individuals to one based on marital status. The "married, filing jointly" filing status—which effectively splits a couple's income evenly between spouses for tax purposes—was added to hold marriage harmless relative to being single and to comport with a growing number of states that had passed community property laws.[17] Because few households at that time had two working parents, however, the new filing status usually resulted in bonuses for married couples. In 1969 Congress put in place standard deductions and tax brackets for married couples that were no longer twice as wide as those for singles, thus creating marriage penalties for two-earner couples whose incomes tended to be evenly split. This practice, and the marriage penalties it produced, continued, although penalties were sharply reduced by the 1986 tax reform.[18]

A 1998 report by the Congressional Budget Office estimated that in 1999, 52 percent of married couples would enjoy marriage bonuses under the tax system, while 43 percent would incur penalties. The report went on to say that bonuses would total about $43 billion in 1999, while penalties would sum to $32 billion.[19]

The enactment of President George W. Bush's requested tax cuts in 2001 significantly reduced marriage penalties (or increased marriage subsidies) for most middle-income families that filed taxes.[20] A suite of provisions, including a small increase in the income level at which a couple would begin to lose EITC benefits, was advertised as marriage penalty relief. Yet the most relief for lower- to middle-income families came from raising the child credit's value from $500 to $1,000 per child and making it partially refundable.[21] For higher-income families, marriage bonuses were increased by reverting back toward "income splitting" in the bracket structure, as in the 1948 tax law.

The succeeding 2003 and 2004 tax bills largely accelerated the implementation of the 2001 tax cut. They put most of the marriage penalty relief provisions into effect more quickly, accelerated the increase in the child credit from $600 to $1,000 to 2003, and raised its refundability rate from 10 percent to 15 percent for 2004. For many middle- and upper-income households, whether or not they had children, the bill also reduced marriage penalties by adjusting the brackets in which different tax rates began. The Joint Committee on Taxation (JTC) has forecast the cumulative cost of marriage-penalty-directed tax cuts in these three tax bills over the period 2001–11 to be $114 billion.[22] But in 2004, 81 percent of this marriage penalty relief was concentrated on couples earning above $75,000 (and most of this on households earning just between $100,000 and $200,000), who are not our primary focus—and much also went to increase marriage bonuses rather than simply reduce penalties.[23] Of more interest here, the expansion of the child tax credit lowered penalties or boosted bonuses, even though this was not its primary intent—and is not captured in the JCT $114 billion cost estimate of marriage penalty relief. Still, the bill shows that elected officials at times are willing to spend substantial sums to reduce marriage penalties.

How Marriage Penalties and Subsidies Arise

Lawmakers rarely intend to create marriage penalties; even subsidies are often accidental. Two conditions are necessary to cause marriage penalties and subsidies, and neither is sufficient by itself.[24] The first condition is tax rates that vary based on income. The second is joint filing by married couples for benefits or taxes. Both characterize the U.S. tax code.

The effect of the first condition, variable tax rates, is often exacerbated by government transfer programs that are also based on joint filing. During the past several decades, policymakers have pursued the dual objectives of progressivity—giving greater tax and welfare benefits to those with lower incomes—and cost containment. As a result, programs like the earned income tax credit or food stamps restrict benefits to lower-income citizens by

In 2004, 81 percent of the marriage penalty relief was concentrated on couples earning above $75,000 (and most of this on households earning just between $100,000 and $200,000).

reducing or "phasing out" the benefits at steep rates as households earn more income (see box on page 164 for an example).

Combining the direct tax rates in the tax code and the benefit reduction rates in the transfer system can result in extremely high tax rates, as an example will illustrate.[25] Suppose a single tax filer earns $18,000, placing her in the 10 percent income tax bracket, which means that she faces a *marginal* tax rate of 10 percent on each additional dollar earned above $18,000.[26] (The *average* tax rate applying to all her income might be well below 10 percent because most of her income below $18,000 may not be taxable at all.)[27] Suppose, further, that she has two children and is also receiving the EITC, which decreases by 21.06 cents for every dollar earned above $14,040. Her *effective marginal* tax rate includes this loss of benefits and amounts to the sum of the 10 percent marginal income tax rate and the

What Happens When Transfer Benefits Phase In and Out

The earned income tax credit "phases in" at 40 cents for each dollar of earned income up to $10,750, for a maximum benefit of $4,300 in tax year 2004. If Martha has two children and earns $5,000, she receives 40 percent of her earnings (or $2,000) in EITC. Suppose she marries Robert, who also earns $5,000 and has no children of his own, and they file a joint tax return. Together, they would have $10,000 in earned income, so they receive an EITC of $4,000, for a marriage subsidy of $2,000.

For incomes between $10,750 and $14,040 ($15,040 if a couple are married), a single parent (or married couple) neither receives additional EITC benefits for additional dollars of earnings nor loses any benefit. But as soon as earnings rise above that higher level, the EITC decreases, or "phases out," by 21.06 cents for every extra dollar earned by the household unit. The credit disappears completely when incomes exceed $34,458 ($35,458 for married couples).

Suppose Martha earns $14,040 and enjoys the full EITC benefit of $4,300. Now, suppose she marries Robert, who has no children. If Robert earns $1,000, they have a combined income of $15,040; they lose no EITC benefits, because they are right at the "phase-out threshold" for married couples. But if Robert earns $10,000, boosting the couple's earned income total to $24,040, their EITC benefit drops by $1,895, from $4,300 to $2,405. Martha and Robert are being penalized 21.06 cents for every dollar they earn over $15,040.

Now suppose Robert earns $22,000, putting him and Martha at $36,000 in total earned income. Because the EITC has phased out completely by $35,458 for married couples, Martha and Robert now receive no EITC for Martha's children. By marrying, they have been penalized $4,300 in EITC benefits—money they would have enjoyed had they simply cohabited or lived separately.

Note that the levels and rates given above apply to all households with two or more children. For households with just one child, the benefit amount and the phase-in and phase-out rates are less.

21.06 percent EITC phase-out rate, for a total rate of 31.06 percent.[28] (For this example, we are ignoring many other taxes and benefit reductions, such as Social Security tax or food stamps.) Thus, for the income range over which a given benefit phases out, the *effective marginal* tax rate bumps up by the phase-out rate until the benefit has fallen to zero. When our single tax filer's income (or if she marries, her and her husband's combined income) exceeds about $35,000, her EITC benefit is gone and the 21.06 percent phase-out rate no

longer applies, so her *effective marginal* rate then drops by 21.06 percentage points.

Although one may not typically think of it in this light, the loss of means-tested transfer benefits as earnings increase affects a household in much the same way as higher direct tax rates do—both are losses of income. Indeed, economists commonly apply the term "tax rates" to transfer programs to identify how much benefit is lost (effectively taxed away) as a family's income rises. This, by the way, is not a comment on the fairness of benefit phase-outs. Some observers believe that there is no entitlement to such benefits, and therefore that benefit reductions are different on equity grounds from direct taxes, which take away what one has earned rather than what one has received as a transfer. But in terms of incentives and size of penalties the issue remains, regardless of the fairness of benefit phase-outs.

Benefits from some programs, like Medicaid and the State Children's Health Insurance Program (SCHIP), do not phase out gradually but instead fall swiftly or end altogether as soon as a household's income exceeds some dollar threshold. In these cases, receiving one more dollar of earnings can strip a household of several thousand dollars of benefits.

The effective marginal tax rate—the rate created by steep benefit phase-out rates combined with graduated income tax rates—moves up and down a lot as income increases, as evidenced by the example above, but it is usually highest for low- to moderate-income families. This reality runs counter to the notion that marginal rates rise progressively with income, as one would be led to believe by looking only at the statutory rate schedule in the income tax.

Note that these variable tax rates do not by themselves penalize marriage. A second, simultaneous condition is necessary to create marriage penalties and bonuses—joint filing by married couples for taxes or benefits. Policymakers often look to the household unit, or joint tax return income, rather than to each individual's income separately to measure the need for transfer benefits or the ability to pay taxes. Their aim is to treat households with equal incomes equally, but in a system with variable rates, individuals with

equal incomes will then not be treated equally. If graduated or variable tax rates were accompanied by individual filing, there would be no marriage penalties. Marriage would have no effect on any benefit received or tax paid by the individual. Alternatively, if everything were taxed at a flat rate (including zero, as in the case of a universal grant that did not phase out) there would also be no marriage penalties.

Mapping the High Effective Marginal Tax Rates

Although our ultimate focus remains on penalties and subsidies related to marriage, it is best to begin by examining the tax situation of selected single parents before moving on, in the next section, to see in detail how the high tax rates contribute to marriage penalties when a single parent marries. Figure 1 tracks select tax and transfer benefits for a single head of household with two children, showing how these benefits generally decline as household income increases. The exact size of benefits and the rate at which they decline depend on the mix of programs in which the family is enrolled and the way these programs interact with one another.

Panel 1 includes federal income taxes, exemptions, and credits, employer and employee portions of the Social Security tax, and state taxes, plus food stamps, Medicaid, and SCHIP.[29] A focus on this set of programs is important because, in theory, every household with children is eligible for these programs if its income is low enough. The benefits are generally not restricted by waiting lists and are universally available as long as recipients meet certain eligibility criteria, which can vary by state. In a sense, then, the high tax rates levied by these programs apply to all households except those with annual earned incomes higher than $40,000, which

Figure 1. Select Tax and Transfer Benefits for a Head of Household with Two Children in Tax Year 2004

Panel 1. Tax system plus food stamps, Medicaid, and SCHIP

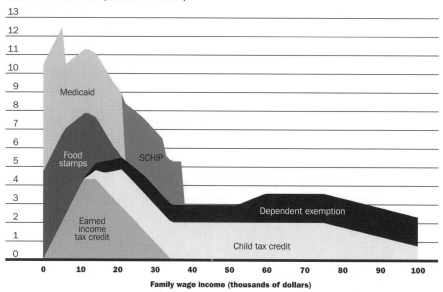

Tax and transfer benefits (thousands of dollars)

Panel 2. Plus federal public housing, TANF, child care subsidies, and WIC

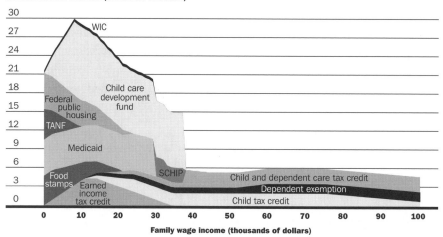

Tax and transfer benefits (thousands of dollars)

Source: Authors' calculations, Urban Institute (2005).

Note: SCHIP is the State Children's Health Insurance Program; TANF is Temporary Assistance to Needy Families; EITC is the earned income tax credit; WIC is the Special Supplemental Nutrition Program for Women, Infants, and Children. The children are assumed to be aged two and five. Tax calculations include the alternative minimum tax and assumptions on itemized deductions. Transfer programs apply rules for Pennsylvania, which is the median TANF benefit state. Maximum annual child care costs are assumed to be $5,000. Note that in panel 2, the adults in a family previously on TANF remain eligible for Medicaid up to 185 percent of poverty (for up to twelve months after leaving TANF).

Figure 2. Average Effective Marginal Tax Rates Confronting Low- to Moderate-Income Families and Well-Off Families

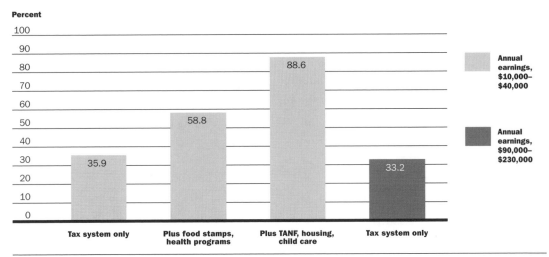

Source: See figure 1.

Note: Calculations assume two children and filing as head of household in tax year 2004. From left to right, the first bar includes rates in federal income taxes, Social Security taxes, the alternative minimum tax, and state taxes; the second adds in rates from the food stamp, Medicaid, and SCHIP programs; the third further adds in rates from TANF, public housing assistance, WIC, and child care subsidies; and the fourth bar includes the same rates as the first bar.

have moved beyond the income cutoffs for all or most transfer programs. Put in terms of panel 1, these latter households have moved to the right along the horizontal axis beyond, first, the high-benefit regime (which applies to earnings of roughly $0 to $10,000), and then, the high-tax-rate regime (which applies to incomes of roughly $10,000 to $40,000).

Panel 2 includes the same programs as panel 1 but also assumes the single-parent family of three is receiving welfare cash assistance (TANF),[30] housing assistance, and child care benefits (direct expenditures for child care from the Child Care and Development Fund or deductions through the tax system from the Child and Dependent Care Tax Credit).[31] As a general rule, these additional programs are not universal, in contrast to those in panel 1. Rather, they are parceled out either through time limits for years of eligibility or through queues as to who may participate (the modest child and dependent care tax

credit is not queued, but those claiming it must have tax liability to offset). Households are much less likely to benefit from the programs in panel 2 than those in panel 1.[32]

In both panels, the single-parent family receives the most benefits between about $5,000 and $10,000 of earnings—mostly because the EITC is fully phased in by that earnings level, while most other benefits are either still phasing in or have not yet phased out.[33] Benefits drop off steeply as earnings exceed $20,000.

Figure 2 compares the average effective marginal tax rates of various low- to middle-income (averaging between $10,000 and $40,000, including benefits) single-parent families with two young children with the rate of more well-to-do families.[34] The marginal tax rate in the first bar—35.9 percent—is based simply on federal and state direct taxes, including Social Security and the

EITC. The rate rises appreciably as the family enrolls in additional transfer programs in bars 2 and 3. For a family enrolled in more universal, non-wait-listed programs like food stamps, Medicaid, and SCHIP, the average effective marginal tax rate would be 58.8 percent. Enrolling the family in additional wait-listed programs, like housing assistance and child care, ratchets up that rate to 88.6 percent.[35] The fourth bar, by way of comparison, shows that the average effective marginal rate affecting families (lumping one- and two-parent families together) earning $90,000 or more is 33.2 percent—lower than that applying to all the other groupings of lower-earning families.

From High Tax Rates to Marriage Penalties

The extremely high effective marginal tax rates faced by low- to moderate-income adults with children, combined with the current U.S. practice of assessing taxes and benefits on the basis of household rather than individual income, lead directly to the marriage penalties. What triggers the penalty is that the earnings of one spouse are taxed at a different rate simply because of marriage. In a very common example, a man facing combined income and Social Security tax rates of about 30 cents for every additional dollar earned discovers that upon marrying a woman with EITC and food stamp benefits, the introduction of his income into the household reduces those benefits, and also causes her to lose eligibility for Medicaid.

Figure 3 graphs the dollar amounts of penalties and subsidies that a single earner and a single-parent head of household with two children would face if they were to marry. (The penalties are much higher in the less common example when two single people, both with children, marry.) Three scenarios

are presented, showing families with household earnings of $10,000, $20,000, and $30,000 a year. To take into account the various ways in which those earnings can be distributed between the couple, each scenario shows the single parent, as the secondary earner, earning between 0 percent and 100 percent (in 10 percent increments) of the couple's total income.[36] Generally, as the figure shows, when spouses have similar earnings, penalties are higher (subsidies are lower). When one spouse earns significantly more than the other, penalties are lower (subsidies are higher).[37] In the figure, the darker curve shows the marriage penalties in the tax system alone; the lighter curve shows combined penalties in the tax system and in the transfer system programs of food stamps, Medicaid, and SCHIP. Because these three programs, as noted, are almost universally available, effectively these penalties are faced by all families in these income ranges unless they fail to apply for the benefits. We have not included an even wider set of programs such as housing and TANF, where the penalties become very large.

As the figure shows, in the tax system by itself low-income families generally enjoy marriage subsidies, regardless of how earnings are divided, thanks largely to the generous phase-in of the EITC, which pays 40 cents for every dollar earned up to $10,750 for households with two children.[38] At modest earnings of $20,000 and above, however, both tax and transfer marriage penalties loom large, primarily because of the high phase-out of the EITC and the decline of food stamps, which fall several hundred dollars for every additional thousand dollars of earnings. For families not on TANF, as in this example, Medicaid becomes unavailable to parents after around $5,000 of income, though children are covered as long as parental income is rel-

Figure 3. Marriage Penalties and Subsidies in Select Federal Tax and Transfer Programs for a Married Couple with Two Children, Tax Year 2004

Panel 1. Household income of $10,000

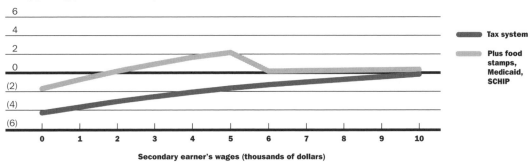

Panel 2. Household income of $20,000

Panel 3. Household income of $30,000

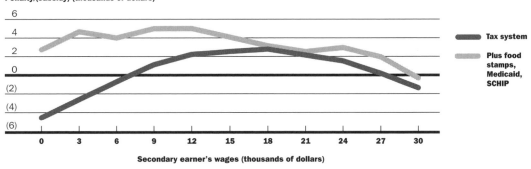

Source: See figure 1.

Note: Calculations assume that a single earner (the primary earner) marries a head of household with two children (the secondary earner). The earnings of the secondary earner range from 0 to 100 percent of household income in each example. The primary earner earns the balance and was a single filer without children before marriage. Marriage penalties and subsidies include the effects of Social Security taxes (both employer and employee portions) and state income taxes.

atively low. SCHIP, meanwhile, replaces Medicaid's coverage of children at incomes between 185 and 235 percent of poverty (that is, between $36,000 and $45,000 for a family of four) in Pennsylvania. In other words, in Pennsylvania, these health programs contribute substantially to marriage penalties, first, at very low incomes (below $10,000), and then again, at moderate incomes (above $36,000).[39]

Possibilities for Reform

Given the hundreds of billions of dollars in marriage penalties and subsidies processed each year through the nation's social welfare system, the prospects for reform may seem remote. But as recent tax legislation makes clear, elected officials are occasionally prepared to take sweeping action—even if their attention so far has focused mainly on those with incomes above the median.

We offer four options for reform. The first two, in our opinion, deserve special consideration as newer, although untried, approaches. The other two options have been applied in specific circumstances, but both would require major adjustments in benefit and tax structures if they were to be carried out on a wider scale. A combination of these approaches, nonetheless, could be used to lessen—and for many, remove—current marriage penalties.

A Maximum Tax Rate for Low- and Moderate-Income Families

A primary focus of self-labeled "supply-side" economists for the past thirty years has been to set a maximum marginal tax rate for higher-income individuals. That maximum rate, ranging from about 28 percent to 39 percent (and down from 70 percent in 1980) was incorporated into tax reform during both the early 1980s and the early 2000s, although pro-

ponents had pushed for rates as low as 20 to 25 percent. Yet the maximum effective marginal tax rate for lower- to moderate-income households is often far higher. As noted, single people typically may find their 30 percent marginal tax rate jumping to 50, 60, 80, or even 100 percent when they marry someone with children. To implement a maximum rate would require coordination and one-stop shopping for many of the nation's social welfare programs—but this action would go far toward reducing marriage penalties.

Individual Wage Subsidies

Although the EITC is sometimes considered so, it is not a true wage subsidy. Many workers with very low wages become ineligible for the EITC when their income is combined with that of a spouse. A wage subsidy based on individual wages, whether hourly or annual, would avoid this problem. Recent comments by First Lady Laura Bush, among others, have focused renewed attention on the plight of many men who can receive costly "public support" only if they break the law and enter the corrections system. Otherwise, most of the contact these men have with the social welfare system involves facing huge marriage penalties. Rather than being family breadwinners, many find themselves able to help their children financially only by moving out or never marrying. Individual wage subsidies would help make it possible for a low-wage man or woman to marry someone with children without losing substantial income and welfare.

Universal Programs

A universal program or tax credit—one that goes to households with children without diminution of benefits regardless of marital status or income—clearly would not create a marriage penalty. Many government spending programs, such as public education and

Medicare, fall into this category because they are not means tested. The recent adoption of a more universal child credit in the tax code reduced marriage penalties in exactly this manner.[40]

Mandatory Individual Filing or Choice of Filing

If married individuals were either required or given the option to file as single individuals, they could avoid marriage penalties. Many other nations, such as Canada, Australia, Italy, and Japan, allow or require individual filing for married couples for income tax purposes.[41]

Conclusion

For several decades now, policymakers have created public tax and transfer programs with little if any attention to the sometimes severe marriage penalties that they inadvertently impose. The expanded public subsidies thus put in place by lawmakers came at the expense of higher effective marginal tax rates, as program benefits often had to be phased out beginning at fairly low incomes to keep overall program costs in check. The combined effective marginal tax rates from these phase-outs and from regular taxes are very high—sometimes causing households to lose a dollar or more for every dollar earned and severely penalizing marriage. In aggregate, couples today face hundreds of billions of dollars in increased taxes or reduced benefits if they marry. Cohabitating—that is, not getting married—has become the tax shelter of the poor.

These developments are in no small part the consequence of a half-century of social policy enactments of roughly similar design. Liberals wishing to keep programs very progressive and conservatives wishing to keep budget costs low have together put a substantial portion of household subsidies and assistance onto this platform.

These penalties can be reduced in various ways. Most promising, in our view, is to establish a combined maximum marginal tax rate for low- and moderate-income households similar to the rates applying to the richest individuals in society. Another innovative strategy would be to provide a wage subsidy on an individual rather than a family basis for low-wage workers. Two other approaches, both of which have already been tried successfully on a smaller scale, would be to make some programs more universal, as with the child credit and public education, and to move toward mandatory or optional individual filing for benefits and taxes.

In recent years, couples in the United States have increasingly regarded marriage as optional, one among many ways of creating a household. This declining regard for marriage calls into question government's continued use of marriage vows as the primary mechanism by which to enforce household filing for benefits and to raise taxes or lower benefits. Whether Americans' changing views on marriage eventually lead to the radical restructuring required to reduce the very high level of marriage penalties facing most low- and moderate-income individuals remains to be seen.

Notes

1. That there could be hundreds of billions of dollars each year in marriage penalties and bonuses should not be surprising. Given that there were more than 112 million households in the United States in 2003, according to the Census Bureau, and that most ways a couple could divide up their income would result in hundreds and usually thousands of dollars of marriage penalties or bonuses (often in multiple tax and transfer programs), federal programs entail hundreds of billions of dollars in penalties and bonuses.

2. We will refer to marriage *subsidies* or *bonuses*; the two words are interchangeable.

3. Because transfer program eligibility and benefit rules are often state specific, we must choose one state as an example on which to run our simulations. We choose Pennsylvania, because the monthly TANF (welfare) benefits it provides are near or at the national median and also because its transfer programs' rules tend to be less complex than those of other states.

4. If he earned just $5,000, the couple would still be eligible, but would be at the very edge of Medicaid's income cutoff. In transfer programs like Medicaid, the benefit reduction schedule compensates somewhat for larger families—as a new person (the husband) joins the family, the income cutoffs for Medicaid benefit eligibility increase, but only slightly.

5. We will refer to TANF also as welfare.

6. See, for example, Wendell Primus and Jennifer Beeson, "Safety Net Programs, Marriage, and Cohabitation," paper presented at "Just Living Together: Implications for Children, Families, and Social Policy," Pennsylvania State University, October 30–31, 2000.

7. Robert A. Moffit, R. Reville, and A. E. Winkler, "Beyond Single Mothers: Cohabitation, Marriage, and the U.S. Welfare System," *Demography* 35, no. 3 (1998): 259–78.

8. See, for example, Gregory Acs and Sandi Nelson, "Should We Get Married in the Morning? A Profile of Cohabiting Couples with Children" (Washington: Urban Institute, March 2004); Paul R. Amato's article in this volume; and Robert I. Lerman, "Impacts of Marital Status and Parental Presence on the Material Hardship of Families with Children," paper prepared for the U.S. Department of Health and Human Services, Office of the Assistant Secretary for Planning and Evaluation (July 2002).

9. Robert I. Lerman, "Marriage and the Economic Well-Being of Families with Children: A Review of the Literature," paper prepared for the U.S. Department of Health and Human Services' Office of the Assistant Secretary for Planning and Evaluation (July 2002); and Robert I. Lerman, "Married and Unmarried Parenthood and Economic Well-Being: A Dynamic Analysis of a Recent Cohort," paper prepared for the U.S. Department of Health and Human Services' Office of the Assistant Secretary for Planning and Evaluation (July 2002).

10. For an attempt to quantify the returns to work for married households across all tax and welfare programs and across cohorts, see Jagadeesh Gokhale, Lawrence J. Kotlikoff, and Alexi Sluchynsky, "Does It Pay to Work?" Working Paper 9096 (Cambridge, Mass.: National Bureau of Economic Research, August 2002).

11. Robert A. Moffitt, "The Effect of Welfare on Marriage and Fertility: What Do We Know and What Do We Need to Know?" Discussion Paper 1153-97 (Institute for Research on Poverty, December 1997).

12. Marianne P. Bitler and others, "The Impact of Welfare Reform on Marriage and Divorce," *Demography* 41, no. 2 (May 2004): 213–36.

13. Those parents filing as head of household can claim a larger standard deduction and also benefit from a wider tax bracket than those who file as single.

14. James Alm and Leslie A. Whittington, "Marriage and the Marriage Tax," in *Proceedings of the Eighty-Fifth Annual Conference on Taxation* (Columbus, Ohio: National Tax Association–Tax Institute of America, 1993); James Alm and Leslie A. Whittington, "Income Taxes and the Marriage Decision," *Applied Economics* 27, no. 1 (1995): 25–31; James Alm and Leslie A. Whittington, "Does the Income Tax Affect Marital Decisions?" *National Tax Journal* 48, no. 4 (1995): 562–72; James Alm and Leslie A. Whittington, "Income Taxes and the Timing of Marital Decisions," *National Tax Journal* 49, no. 4 (1997): 571–89; and David Sjoquist and Mary Beth Walker, "The Marriage Tax and the Rate and Timing of Marriage," *National Tax Journal* 48, no. 4 (1995): 547–58.

15. See the article by Kathryn Edin and Joanna Reed in this volume.

16. Edin's ethnographic research seems to show that low-income households are fairly familiar with marriage penalties and their ramifications in the EITC. More moderate income households also display knowledge about penalties in education programs like the Pell Grant. However, the general understanding of marriage penalties in other transfer programs has not been widely examined.

17. See Joseph A. Pechman, *Federal Tax Policy*, 5th ed. (Brookings, 1987).

18. For a detailed history of marriage tax penalties, as well as family-related tax provisions, see Michael J. McIntyre and C. Eugene Steuerle, "Federal Tax Reform: A Family Perspective," prepared for the Finance Project (Washington: The Finance Project, July 1996); and James Alm and Mikhail I. Melnik, "Taxing the 'Family' in the Individual Income Tax" (Andrew Young School of Policy Studies, Georgia State University, July 2004). Alm and Melnik also compare, in detail, how family taxation is treated in the United States with its treatment in other developed countries.

19. See Congressional Budget Office, "Update of Marriage Penalties and Bonuses" (September 1998); and Congressional Budget Office, "For Better or for Worse: Marriage and the Federal Income Tax" (June 1997). Note, though, that aggregate estimates of bonuses and penalties fluctuate a lot from year to year, for a variety of reasons. As of the writing of this article, CBO has not published an update of the paper.

20. Adam Carasso and C. Eugene Steuerle, "How Marriage Penalties Change under the 2001 Tax Bill," Policy Discussion Paper 3 (Washington: Urban-Brookings Tax Policy Center, May 2002).

21. Where increases in penalties or decreases in subsidies do occur, they are fairly small. That is, the winners tend to win a lot, while the losers lose little.

22. Joint Committee on Taxation, "Estimated Budget Effects of the Conference Agreement for H.R. 1836" (U.S. Congress, May 26, 2001); Joint Committee on Taxation, "Estimated Revenue Effects of H.R. 2896, the 'American Jobs Creation Act of 2003'" (U.S. Congress, August 1, 2003); and Joint Committee on Taxation, "Estimated Revenue Effects of the Conference Agreement for H.R. 1308, the 'Working Families Tax Relief Act of 2004'" (U.S. Congress, September 23, 2004).

23. About 35 million married couples were affected by the legislation. Estimates from the Urban-Brookings Tax Microsimulation Model (version 0305-1).

24. C. Eugene Steuerle, "Valuing Marital Commitment: Radical Restructuring of Our Tax and Transfer Systems," *Responsive Community* 9, no. 2 (1999): 35–45. As many have noted, a tax system by itself cannot simultaneously be progressive in terms of rate structure, tax all households the same when they have the same income, and tax all individuals the same when they have the same income. See Steuerle, "Valuing Marital Commitment," this note; V. Joseph Hotz and John Karl Scholz, "The Earned Income Tax Credit," Working Paper 8078 (Cambridge, Mass.: National Bureau of Economic Research, January 2002); and Robert A. Moffit, "The Temporary Assistance for Needy Families Program," Working Paper 8749 (Cambridge, Mass.: National Bureau of Economic Research, February 2002).

25. This example is taken from Jon Barry Forman, Adam Carasso, and Mohammed Adeel Saleem, "Designing a Work-Friendly Tax System: Options and Trade-Offs," Discussion Paper 20 (Washington: Urban-Brookings Tax Policy Center, June 2005).

26. This is calculated before tax credits are applied.

27. Economists believe, though, that it is the marginal tax rate—the rate applying to an individual's next dollar of earnings—that affects most that individual's incentives to work or marry. See Forman, Carasso, and Saleem, "Designing a Work-Friendly Tax System" (see note 25).

28. Note that this is a simple example. We have not included the phase-in of the child tax credit that would lower her effective marginal tax rate (because this credit is still phasing in at her salary level) or her Social Security payroll taxes, which would raise it again.

29. While SCHIP is not an entitlement program, except where it is run as a Medicaid expansion (twelve states only), families who meet the eligibility requirements are rarely turned away. While the economic downturn that began in 2001 has hurt state budgets and challenged states' financing of current benefits, few states have responded with significant—and permanent—retrenchments in either benefit levels or eligibility. Pennsylvania's SCHIP program is run separately from its Medicaid program but has shown consistent enrollment numbers over the past several years, and the state has not resorted to wait lists or enrollment caps. See Vernon K. Smith, David M. Rousseau, and Molly O'Malley, "SCHIP Program Enrollment: December 2003 Update" (Menlo Park, Calif.: Kaiser Commission on Medicaid and the Uninsured, July 2004).

30. Child support is sometimes required from biological noncustodial parents. That money—except for $50 a month (in Pennsylvania)—effectively goes to the state's TANF agency as recompense for welfare benefits. See Primus and Beeson, "Safety Net Programs" (see note 6). In that case, the main effect is the same as taking away some of the TANF benefit, and thereby reducing the marriage penalties that can arise from TANF. See Marcie Carlson and others, "The Effects of Welfare and Child Support Policies in Union Formation," The Fragile Families and Child Wellbeing Study, Working Paper 02-10-FF (Center for Research on Child Wellbeing, Princeton University, June 2004).

31. Although the child and dependent care tax credit is available in theory to anyone filing income tax forms, in practice, filers would need to owe tax to make use of the credit and to have child care expenses they can readily claim. That is why this credit is included in panel 2 rather than panel 1.

32. This example still omits some income-conditioned programs, such as school lunch and a variety of forms of college aid. Participation in multiple programs (say, four or more), although rare for the general low-income population, is not so rare for single-parent households. See Stephen D. Holt, "Making Work *Really* Pay: Income Support and Marginal Effective Tax Rates among Low-Income Working Households" (Holt &

Associates Solutions, presented to the American Tax Policy Institute, March 2005). This monograph uses a data set of 3.2 million household records in Wisconsin in 2000, which matches benefits receipt information with unemployment insurance wage records, and state income tax records. The paper presents comprehensive findings on tax and transfer program participation in Wisconsin for 2000. Holt finds that a quarter of single-parent families with two children earning $18,000 a year or less participated in three tax and transfer programs, while another quarter participated in four programs. Six percent participated in five programs.

33. The maximum amount of benefits received ultimately depends on families' program eligibility and benefit levels (both of which are highly variable by state), marital status, and the number and age of the children. However, most families will encounter a benefit curve that is high at low incomes and falls off as more income is earned.

34. More details at each income level are available from the authors.

35. Holt, "Making Work *Really* Pay" (see note 32), reports comparable findings on the level of effective marginal tax rates affecting single parents in his Wisconsin study of program participation in 2000.

36. Data from the Urban Institute's National Survey of America's Families for 2002 suggest that 45.2 percent of cohabiting couples include one partner who earns three or more times what the other partner earns. The percentage of such cohabiting families is significantly higher when combined earnings are $30,000 or less.

37. When a person receives health insurance benefits from a job, one should technically add those benefits to the measure of total compensation. For instance, if a household getting Medicaid worth $5,000 loses this when the head takes a job offering $15,000 of cash and $5,000 of health insurance, then that household should be treated as if it earned $20,000 (not $15,000) and then effectively loses $5,000 of benefits. Other adjustments would be necessary in the calculation (for example, the EITC would still be based on $15,000 of earnings, not $20,000), but again the story line would not change much from what is presented here.

38. In their study of potential marriage penalties and bonuses, Gregory Acs and Elaine Maag have a similar finding for their sample of cohabiting couples. (As for marriage penalties and bonuses in total, however, they look only at cohabiting couples as defined in the National Survey of America's Families and only at penalties and bonuses within the tax system and TANF, whereas we consider the tax system plus a number of transfer programs and their impact on the much larger, additional groups of married or noncohabiting couples.) See Gregory Acs and Elaine Maag, "Irreconcilable Differences? The Conflict between Marriage Promotion Initiatives for Cohabiting Couples with Children and Marriage Penalties within Tax and Transfer Programs," NSAF Brief, series B, no. B-66 (Washington: Urban Institute, April 2005).

39. As an important aside, asset limits in transfer programs can also cause marriage penalties. These asset limits are often trivial amounts: $1,000 for TANF and $2,000 for food stamps. A single mother who receives these vital program benefits could lose them if she marries someone who has assets in excess of these amounts, *even if* his earnings are very low.

40. The child credit begins phasing out at 5 cents for every dollar earned above $75,000 (or $110,000 if the couple are married). So the child credit is means tested, but only at a relatively high level.

41. See Alm and Melnik, "Taxing the 'Family'" (see note 18), for details and many other examples.